# discover
# LONDON

TOM MASTERS
JOE BINDLOSS, STEVE FALLON, VESNA MARIC

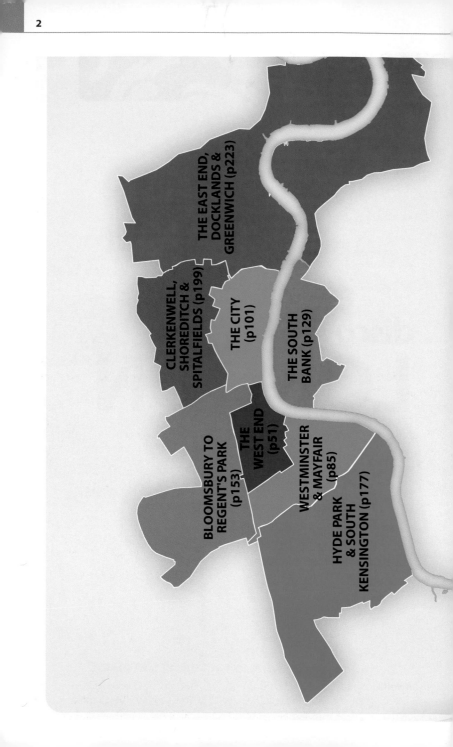

THE EAST END, DOCKLANDS & GREENWICH (p223)

CLERKENWELL, SHOREDITCH & SPITALFIELDS (p199)

THE CITY (p101)

THE SOUTH BANK (p129)

BLOOMSBURY TO REGENT'S PARK (p153)

THE WEST END (p51)

WESTMINSTER & MAYFAIR (p85)

HYDE PARK & SOUTH KENSINGTON (p177)

# DISCOVER LONDON

**The West End (p51)** Shop, drink, eat and dance all night in the city's throbbing heart.

**Westminster & Mayfair (p85)** The home of London's political and aristocratic elite never fails to impress.

**The City (p101)** London's historic walled city now houses one of the world's leading financial centres.

**The South Bank (p129)** London's cultural hub offers an enormous range of art, theatre and music.

**Bloomsbury to Regent's Park (p153)** Academic institutions, grand museums and stately parks make up this teeming area.

**Hyde Park & South Kensington (p177)** The capital's greatest park and biggest museums dominate glamorous West London.

**Clerkenwell, Shoreditch & Spitalfields (p199)** London's engine room of creativity and fashion is where the cool kids hang out.

**The East End, Docklands & Greenwich (p223)** The home of the cockney, Canary Wharf and world time is unmissable.

# ↘ CONTENTS

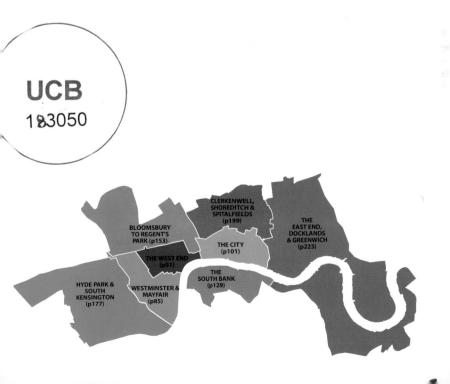

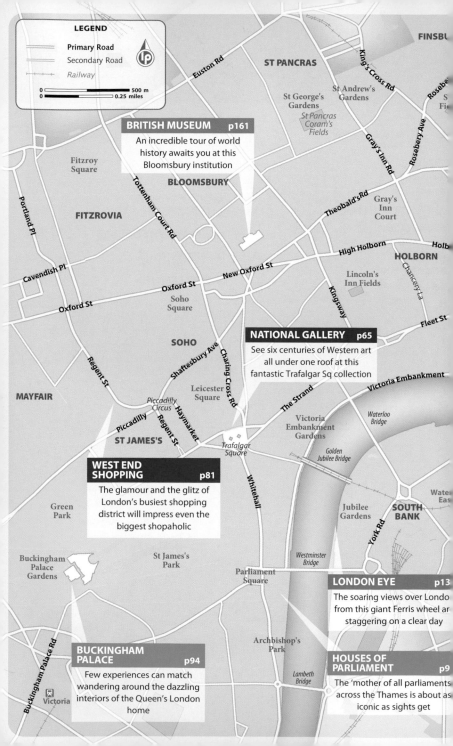

## LEGEND

⎯⎯⎯ Primary Road
⎯⎯⎯ Secondary Road
+++++ Railway

0 _____ 500 m
0 _____ 0.25 miles

### BRITISH MUSEUM  p161

An incredible tour of world history awaits you at this Bloomsbury institution

### NATIONAL GALLERY  p65

See six centuries of Western art all under one roof at this fantastic Trafalgar Sq collection

### WEST END SHOPPING  p81

The glamour and the glitz of London's busiest shopping district will impress even the biggest shopaholic

### BUCKINGHAM PALACE  p94

Few experiences can match wandering around the dazzling interiors of the Queen's London home

### LONDON EYE  p13

The soaring views over London from this giant Ferris wheel are staggering on a clear day

### HOUSES OF PARLIAMENT  p9

The 'mother of all parliaments' across the Thames is about as iconic as sights get

FINSBU

ST PANCRAS

St George's Gardens
St Pancras Coram's Fields
St Andrew's Gardens

King's Cross Rd
Rosebe
S
Fi
Roseberry Ave
Gray's Inn Rd

Euston Rd

Fitzroy Square

BLOOMSBURY

FITZROVIA

Portland Pl

Tottenham Court Rd

Theobald's Rd

Gray's Inn Court

High Holborn

Holb

HOLBORN

Holb

Chancery La

Cavendish Pl

Oxford St

Oxford St

New Oxford St

Soho Square

Lincoln's Inn Fields

Kingsway

Fleet St

SOHO

Regent St

Shaftesbury Ave

Charing Cross Rd

Leicester Square

Victoria Embankment

MAYFAIR

Piccadilly Circus

Haymarket

The Strand

Victoria Embankment Gardens

Waterloo Bridge

Piccadilly

Regent St

ST JAMES'S

Trafalgar Square

Golden Jubilee Bridge

Wate
Eas

Green Park

Whitehall

Jubilee Gardens

York Rd

SOUTH BANK

Buckingham Palace Gardens

St James's Park

Westminster Bridge

Parliament Square

Buckingham Palace Rd

🚇 Victoria

Archbishop's Park

Lambeth Bridge

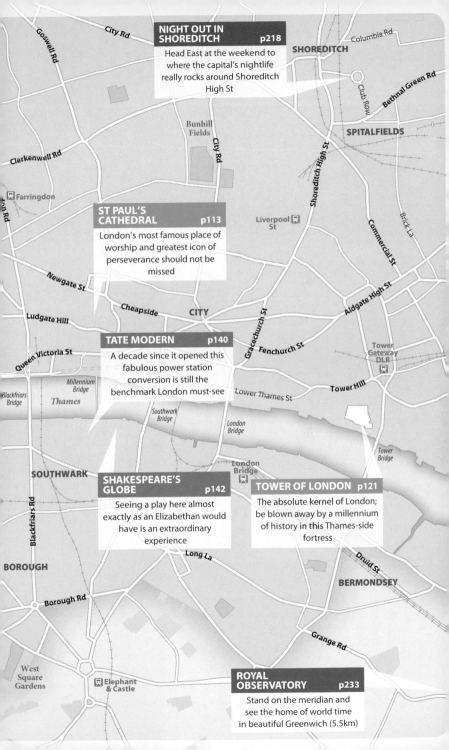

**NIGHT OUT IN SHOREDITCH** p218

Head East at the weekend to where the capital's nightlife really rocks around Shoreditch High St

**ST PAUL'S CATHEDRAL** p113

London's most famous place of worship and greatest icon of perseverance should not be missed

**TATE MODERN** p140

A decade since it opened this fabulous power station conversion is still the benchmark London must-see

**SHAKESPEARE'S GLOBE** p142

Seeing a play here almost exactly as an Elizabethan would have is an extraordinary experience

**TOWER OF LONDON** p121

The absolute kernel of London; be blown away by a millennium of history in this Thames-side fortress

**ROYAL OBSERVATORY** p233

Stand on the meridian and see the home of world time in beautiful Greenwich (5.5km)

# ↘ THIS IS LONDON

**The British capital positively glistens with possibility and variety – its iconic sights never fail to impress, its royal splendour and historic buildings are unmatched anywhere else in the world, and, perhaps most importantly, the city's energy and dynamism can be felt on every street corner.**

London is one of those world capitals that everyone feels they know before they set foot in it. The instantly recognisable icons – the red post boxes, the double-decker buses, the guards at Buckingham Palace in their bearskin hats – are all present and very correct, but the city itself usually surprises first-time visitors by being anything but the stuffy, ordered capital of popular belief. Instead they find a fast-moving and deeply diverse city of art, culture and thriving commerce.

London crowds around the banks of old Father Thames, its sights so closely packed together that it's often hard to know where to start. The Roman-founded square mile known as the City of London is one obvious place, home to the extraordinary Tower

of London, heroic Blitz icon St Paul's Cathedral and innumerable ancient churches, cobbled side streets and hidden treasures.

The West End, London's incontestable present-day heart, will make any serious shopper's heart sing, and provide ample chances for superb meals out, while royal Mayfair and political Westminster next door are the playgrounds of the city's elites and are packed full of impressive stately homes and the world's most famous parliament building.

**'fast-moving and deeply diverse city of art, culture and thriving commerce'**

As well as the unmissable sights, make plenty of time for the little things that truly make London great: a pint and a plate of fish and chips by the river, a day out with friends in one of London's expansive wooded parks or just a rocking night out in Shoreditch or Soho. London is truly one of the great world cities and your only problem coming here is that you're bound to wish you had more time to see it all.

# ↘ LONDON'S TOP 25 EXPERIENCES

**1**

## ↘ TOWER OF LONDON

There's no greater treasure trove of London life than this repository of almost two millennia of British history. The Norman White Tower, the fabulous crown jewels, Traitors' Gate, the famous ravens and the Beefeaters with their stories all await you at the ultimate London sight, the **Tower of London** (p104).

## ↘ TATE MODERN

London's top attraction is this high temple to modern art, a converted power station on the Thames that will thrill any visitor, from art critic to absolute beginner. You can't miss the temporary Turbine Hall installations, and the permanent collection of the **Tate Modern** (p132), from Rodin to Rothko, is sublime.

## ↘ ST PAUL'S CATHEDRAL

Wren's masterpiece and a symbol of London's resilience during the Blitz, this stunning City landmark is as fascinating as it is iconic. Climb the dome of **St Paul's Cathedral** (p106) for a superb view of London from its very heart, and explore the cathedral's incredible interior and crypt.

1 VERONICA GARBUTT; 2 ORIEN HARVEY; 3 PHILIP GAME

1 Tower of London (p104); 2 Tate Modern (p132) at night; 3 St Paul's Cathedral (p106) as seen from Millenium Bridge

## ↘ CRUISE ON THE THAMES

London's tidal river begs your attention. For such a great maritime centre, it's no surprise that many of London's most iconic sights are on the riverbank. A cruise anywhere from **Hampton Court Palace** (p245) to **Tower Bridge** (p124), **Canary Wharf** (p230) and the **O2 Arena** (p234) is unmissable.

## ↘ SHAKESPEARE'S GLOBE

Experience theatre at **Shakespeare's Globe** (p142) just as they did in Elizabethan times by taking a tour (or better still, seeing a play) at this extraordinary reconstruction of the original Globe Theatre, on the site where Shakespeare worked and his plays were performed for their first audiences.

# ↘ LONDON EYE

For a stunning aerial view of the capital, take a 'flight' on this huge Ferris wheel on a clear day. Overlooking the Houses of Parliament, and giving you a clear view in all directions for miles, your glass gondola trip on the **London Eye** (p139) is an unforgettable way to see London.

6

4 DOUG MCKINLAY; 5 NEIL SETCHFIELD ; 6 RICHARD I'ANSON

**4** Cruising on the Thames near the Tower of London (p104); **5** Audience at Shakespeare's Globe Theatre (p142); **6** London Eye (p139)

LONDON'S TOP 25 EXPERIENCES

# ↘ BRITISH MUSEUM

One of the world's great museums, the **British Museum** (p156) boasts the controversial Elgin Marbles, the Rosetta Stone, Lindow Man and the historic Reading Room to name but a tiny number of its vast collection. Come for a tour through world history unmatched anywhere else on earth.

7

**8**

## ⬊ FIND YOUR OWN LOCAL

One of your first jobs in London is to find your 'local'. The best pub nearest to where you're staying may well then become the centre of your trip – a place to meet friends, chat to locals and generally call your own; this is one task that is pure pleasure. For some inspiration, see p40.

## ⬊ BUCKINGHAM PALACE

As experiences go, there's not much more bizarre than paying to snoop around the Queen's London home, **Buckingham Palace** (p94). You pay for the access, but it's well worth it to breach this ultimate symbol of serene imperiousness. Just remember to bow if you run into her in the corridor.

**9**

7 ORIEN HARVEY; 8 NEIL SETCHFIELD; 9 RICHARD I'ANSON

7 The Great Court at the British Museum (p156); 8 Enjoying a London pub (p40); 9 Buckingham Palace (p94)

10

## ⬃ WEST END SHOW

Whether it's world-class drama or smash-hit international musicals, you'll find it all in the theatres of the West End (p79). See Hollywood stars keep it real or sample the newest offerings from the fringe in the world's most famous theatreland.

## ⬃ PICNIC IN HYDE PARK

11

If you're lucky to be in London during one of its better summers, then don't miss having a picnic in this massive and beautiful expanse of parkland. Hyde Park (p190) has it all – a lake, formal gardens, an art gallery, attractive woodland and even a palace.

## ↘ DANCE THE NIGHT AWAY

12

Few cities in the world have the variety of nightlife that London boasts – if you want to dance til dawn to international DJs in superclub **Fabric** (p219), discover the latest cool electroclash DJs or try the truly obscure, it's all here for the taking.

## ↘ FINE DINING IN THE WEST END

With its sheer variety and quality, London remains one of the best places on earth to have a meal, and nowhere more so than the thrilling temples of gastronomy that populate the **West End** (p72). Forget the bad things people may have told you about British food and enjoy.

10 A theatre in the West End (p79); 11 Hyde Park (p190) in bloom; 12 Dancing at a London club (p255); 13 Nobu restaurant (p99)

**14**

## ↘ SEE LIVE MUSIC

The home of modern music, London reverberates with the sounds of the past, present and, of course, the future, and you'll be spoiled for choice nightly during your stay – whether it's an international star playing an intimate venue or a symphony orchestra at the **Barbican** (p128).

## ⬈ BAR HOP IN SHOREDITCH

Head east to find where the cool kids hang out around Shoreditch High St, have drinks at the **George & Dragon** (p216), **Red Lion** (p217) or **Mother Bar** (p217) before clubbing at **333** (p218), **93 Feet East** (p218) or **Bethnal Green Working Men's Club** (p240).

**15**

14 TRAVIS DREVER; 15 AUDE VAUCONSANT

14 Barbican (p119); 15 A drink at the Red Lion (p217) before clubbing

# ↘ PALACE OF WESTMINSTER

There's nothing more iconic or more London than the sublime view of Big Ben and the Houses of Parliament from the River Thames, especially when the sun is shining on the instantly recognisable Gothic facade of the **Houses of Parliament** (p93).

16

**17**

## ◣ FISH & CHIPS

The quintessential London eating experience won't set you back more than a few quid (pounds). Head to any 'chippy' – you'll find them all over the city – and have a battered cod and chips, wrapped in paper, thick with salt and vinegar. Add pint. Relax. Try our favourite central London **chippy** (p174).

## ◣ STAND ON THE MERIDIAN

It's an oddly satisfying feeling, standing on the **Greenwich meridian** (p233) and knowing that everyone on earth is setting their watches in relation to where you are now. Add to that the neighbouring cluster of classical buildings and you have a great day out from central London.

**18**

16 BARBARA VAN ZANTEN; 17 NEIL SETCHFIELD; 18 CHARLOTTE HINDLE

## ↘ HAMPTON COURT PALACE

This is a place to delve headfirst into royal history – London's best-preserved Tudor **palace** (p245) somehow magically manages to feel as if Henry VIII has just left to go hunting, leaving you with a working palace to snoop around. Incomparable.

**19**

**20**

# ⬊ SHOP IN KNIGHTSBRIDGE

Whether its trashily traditional at **Harrods** (p198) or Ab Fab at **Harvey Nichols** (p198) or just names, names, names on Sloane St, Knightsbridge has something for every fashionista. Just don't forget those diamond-encrusted credit cards.

19 GUY MOBERLY; 20 VERONICA GARBUTT

19 Formal gardens at Hampton Court Palace (p245); 20 Harrods (p198) department store

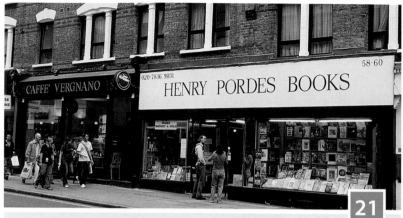

## ↘ CHARING CROSS BOOK SHOPPING

Little known to visitors, the best book shopping in London is to be found on this street running between Soho and Covent Garden. Browse myriad independent book sellers and make time to visit **Foyle's** (p81), perhaps London's very best big bookshop.

## ↘ WEST END SHOPPING

The West End offers one of the most intense, concentrated and – we won't lie – crowded **shopping** (p81) experiences in the world. Come early or stay late, you'll find a vast array of glorious items stocked by some of the very best designers in the world.

## ⬐ HIGH TEA IN STYLE

**23**

Say what you will about the English, but they know how to have tea. High tea is an extravagant selection of jams, scones, de-crusted sandwiches and other sweet delights. Enter any grand **Mayfair hotel** (p98; ensure you are dressed for a wedding) to see how well this English afternoon tea tradition endures.

**24**

## ⬐ ROYAL OPERA HOUSE

Opera and ballet buffs will not want to miss the chance to see a performance or take a tour of the **Royal Opera House** (p81), whose millennial refit has catapulted it back to being one of the world's great opera houses. Start booking tickets now!

LONDON'S TOP 25 EXPERIENCES

21 Bookshop in Charing Cross Road (p81); 22 High-class shopping in the West End (p81); 23 High tea at Brown's hotel (p98); 24 Royal Opera House (p81)

# ↘ PORTOBELLO MARKET

If you want to experience one market in London, the West London institution that is **Portobello Market** (p211) is our pick of the lot – an eclectic and sprawling collection of stalls that sells everything from antiques to funky new designer wear, all spread out along one of West London's most charming streets.

**25**

25 ELLIOT DANIEL

25 Portobello Market (p211) on a sunny day

# WHIRLWIND TOUR OF LONDON

## TWO DAYS Tower Hill to Westminster

This two-day itinerary allows you to see the absolutely unmiss-able highlights of the British capital in half or even a quarter o the time most people spend getting to know London. It takes you from the City's ancient heart to the cultural South Bank, via the West End to Westminster.

### ❶ TOWER OF LONDON

Start at London's kernel, the Tower of London (p121) and spend half of your first day exploring the millennium of history contained within, including the Crown Jewels, Traitors Gate and the White Tower. Take a peek at iconic Tower Bridge (p124) afterwards, and then wander through the narrow streets of the City of London to wards St Paul's.

### ❷ ST PAUL'S CATHEDRAL

Pick up lunch before you enter St Paul's Cathedral (p113) as you won' want to hurry your visit. Don't miss climbing the Dome for its amazing London views, but save plenty of time for exploring the cathedral itsel and the fascinating crypt.

### ❸ TATE MODERN

From St Paul's, head south across the Millennium Bridge (p141) to the Tate Modern (p140) and end the afternoon by seeing London's best collection of modern art in one of its most impressive buildings. From

Palace of Westminster and Big Ben (p93) at dusk

RICHARD I'ANSON

ere, wander along the sublime South Bank to end your day's walk at
the **Southbank Centre** (p139), where there are plenty of eating and
drinking options. Spend the evening seeing a play at the **National
Theatre** (p140) or the **Old Vic** (p152).

## ❹ WEST END

Begin the second day in Bloomsbury for a whistle-stop tour of the
**British Museum** (p161) and then head through the West End to the
excellent **National Gallery** (p65) on Trafalgar Sq. From here, wander
down the Mall towards fabulous **Buckingham Palace** (p94) and peer
through the gates. Wander across stately **St James's Park** (p96) on
the way to Westminster.

## ❺ WESTMINSTER

In Westminster make a beeline for incredible **Westminster Abbey**
(p91) to see even more British history all around you. Across the
square is, of course, the **Palace of Westminster** (p93), and the ultimate London sight, Big Ben. Cross Lambeth Bridge for the best view of
the building and end the day with a flight on the **London Eye** (p139).

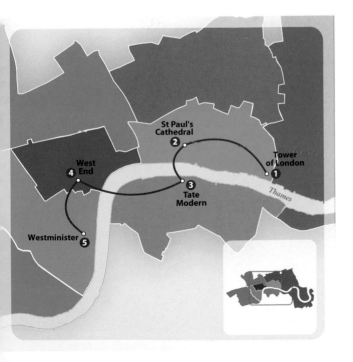

# FOUR DAYS IN LONDON

## FOUR DAYS West London to Greenwich

This four-day itinerary will take you across much of the capital and introduce you to many of its best-known sights and neighbourhoods. The days can be done in any order, and you can walk between most sights.

### ❶ SOUTH KENSINGTON

Start your first day in South Kensington, home to many of the best museums in the city – take your pick between the **Victoria & Albert Museum** (p185), the **Natural History Museum** (p187) and the **Science Museum** (p187). Follow that with a walk in **Hyde Park** (p190) and a spell of shopping at **Harrods** (p198), then have a look around **Kensington Palace** (p189) and **Harvey Nichols** (p198) in Knightsbridge.

### ❷ WESTMINSTER & MAYFAIR

On day two, visit **Buckingham Palace** (p94) during the summer months; outside summer, make do with impressive **Apsley House** (p188) and watch the Changing of the Guard (p96) all the same. Enjoy a walk in St James's Park (p96) to Westminster and see **Westminster Abbey** (p91), the **Palace of Westminster** (p93), walk past **Number 10 Downing St** (p98) and end that day at fascinating **Cabinet War Rooms** (p96).

### ❸ WEST END

Head into the West End on the third day. Check out funky **Soho** (p61), shopping mecca Oxford St and **Covent Garden** (p68), and take time

Buckingham Palace (p94) and the Queen Victoria Monument

RICHARD I'ANSON

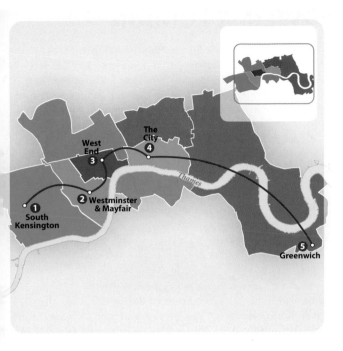

to visit the **National Gallery** (p65) and the **National Portrait Gallery** (p69) on Trafalgar Sq. Have a meal out in one of the many top-notch **West End restaurants** (p72) before seeing a play or musical on or around Shaftsbury Ave.

## ❹ THE CITY
Begin your last day with a walk through the futuristic **Barbican** (p119) and magnificent **St Paul's Cathedral** (p113), then wander past the **Gherkin** (p118) before heading to the **Tower of London** (p121). From here, take the Docklands Light Railway to DLR Cutty Sark, passing right next to **Canary Wharf** (p230) on the way.

## ❺ GREENWICH
From DLR Cutty Sark wander down to **Greenwich Park** (p234), visit the **National Maritime Museum** (p230), the **Queen's House** (p234) and the **Royal Observatory** (p233) before ending the day with a pint in one of Greenwich's pubs.

# A WEEK IN LONDON

## SEVEN DAYS West End to Hampton Court

A week is the perfect amount of time to spend in London – you can see the big sights and museums without hurrying, as well as having time to do some quirkier and lesser known sights and even get out of the city for the day.

### ❶ WEST END & ROYAL LONDON

Begin in Trafalgar Sq where you can see the excellent **National Gallery** (p65) and the next-door **National Portrait Gallery** (p69). From here wander down the Mall towards fabulous **Buckingham Palace** (p94) and peer through the gates, before wandering back into the West End for lunch. Make time while shopping on Oxford St to see the **Photographers' Gallery** (p61) before wandering to the **British Museum** (p161). Spend the evening at a West End show.

### ❷ THE CITY

Spend all of day two immersed in the historic City of London. Start with a wander through the futuristic **Barbican** (p119), stop by the **Museum of London** (p115) before walking on to magnificent **St Paul's Cathedral** (p113). After lunch wander past the **Gherkin** (p118) and on to the **Tower of London** (p121) and **Tower Bridge** (p124).

### ❸ THE SOUTH BANK & WESTMINSTER

Start at the iconic **Tate Modern** (p140) for a morning of art, and walk the South Bank, popping in to see **Shakespeare's Globe** (p142) and checking out the **Southbank Centre** (p139), which makes a good

Overlooking the River Thames with Tower Bridge (p124) in the background

RICHARD I'ANSON

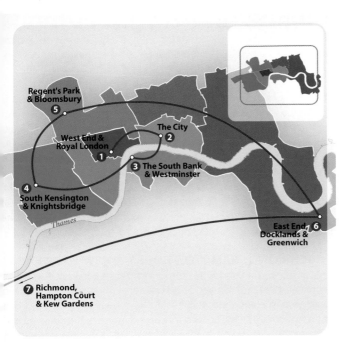

place for lunch. After lunch take a spin on the **London Eye** (p139), walk across Lambeth Bridge to the **Palace of Westminster** (p93), and the ultimate London sight, Big Ben. From here, head to the amazing **Westminster Abbey** (p91) and round off the day at the excellent **Tate Britain** (p95).

## ❹ SOUTH KENSINGTON & KNIGHTSBRIDGE

Today head to South Kensington, home to many of the best museums in the city – take your pick between the **Victoria & Albert Museum** (p185), the **Natural History Museum** (p187) and the **Science Museum** (p187). Follow that with a walk in **Hyde Park** (p190), and don't miss a chance to sniff around Princess Diana's former home of **Kensington Palace** (p189). End the day with a spell of luxury shopping at **Harrods** (p198) and **Harvey Nichols** (p198) in Knightsbridge.

## ❺ REGENT'S PARK & BLOOMSBURY

Begin the day with a wander through beautiful **Regent's Park** (p167), visit **London Zoo** (p170), the world's oldest, and wander down the canal towards Marylebone, where you should take the chance to visit the charming **Wallace Collection** (p164). Head on into Bloomsbury, and visit two of the quirkiest of London's museums, **Sir John Soane's House** (p166) and the **Hunterian Museum** (p166). Continue to wander through Clerkenwell and Shoreditch for some interesting shopping, eating and drinking possibilities.

## ➏ EAST END, DOCKLANDS & GREENWICH

Head to London's East End and get a taste of its multiculturalism on **Brick Lane** (p213) and **Whitechapel High St** (p229), where you should definitely stop in at the excellent **Whitechapel Gallery** (p229). Pick up the Docklands Light Railway at Shadwell and head into the modern world of the rejuvenated Docklands passing right next to **Canary Wharf** (p230) on the way. Get off at Cutty Sark and wander down to **Greenwich Park** (p234), visit the **National Maritime Museum** (p230), the **Queen's House** (p234) and the **Royal Observatory** (p233) before ending the day with a pint in one of Greenwich's pubs.

## ➐ RICHMOND, HAMPTON COURT & KEW GARDENS

Get out of central London for the day and take a train to **Hampton Court Palace** (p245), where you can explore London's best preserved Tudor property (and get lost in the hedge maze in the gardens). Then go on to magical **Kew Gardens** (p248) and grab an afternoon tea and some leisurely shopping in nearby **Richmond** (p245) before heading back to London by train.

DOUG MCKINLAY

Palm House, Kew Gardens (p248)

# ↘ PLANNING YOUR TRIP

# ➲ LONDON'S BEST...

## ↘ TRADITIONAL PUBS

- **Lamb** (p175) One of the most charming original interiors of any pubs in London.
- **George Inn** (p150) London's last surviving coaching inn, this gem is itself a piece of history.
- **Jerusalem Tavern** (p215) This quaint pub serves up artisan brews in a magical setting.
- **Salisbury** (p78) Yes it's a bit of a tourist magnet, but we love this West End favourite nonetheless.

## ↘ PARKS

- **Regent's Park** (p167) Flower beds, the canal and London Zoo – this royal park offers more than any other.
- **Hyde Park** (p190) This enormous central London expanse includes the beautiful Serpentine lake and is a perennial favourite.

- **Richmond Park** (245) See wild deer in London's largest expanse of park and forest.
- **St James's Park** (p96) Feed the geese and take great snaps of Buckingham Palace from this former royal garden.

## ↘ MUSEUMS

- **British Museum** (p161) This treasure trove of world history cannot be missed.
- **Tate Modern** (p140) The biggest art star of them all continues to draw huge numbers.
- **National Gallery** (p65) One of the world's great Western art collections overlooks Trafalgar Sq.
- **National Portrait Gallery** (p69) Spot royalty, popstars and other familiar faces at this excellent gallery.

DOUG MCKINLAY

Taking in the sun on deck chairs, Hyde Park (p190)

## STATELY HOMES

- **Buckingham Palace** (p94) The mother of all palaces can be visited in the summer months during the Queen's summer holidays.
- **Hampton Court Palace** (p245) This extraordinary former home of Henry VIII is amazingly well preserved.
- **Clarence House** (p97) Prince Charles' London home is also open in the summer months.
- **Kensington Palace** (p189) Princess Diana's former home is a fascinating place to look around.

## CITY VIEWS

- **St Paul's** (p113) The classic view of London from the dome of St Paul's is never anything but breathtaking.
- **Tate Modern** (p140) Have a meal on the top-floor restaurant for a panorama of the City skyline across the river.
- **London Eye** (p139) Take a 'flight' in this enormous Ferris wheel for an eye-popping view over the whole city.
- **Monument** (p119) Despite its modest height, the Monument commands great views over the City.

## SHOPPING

- **Selfridges** (p175) This temple of fashion is the undisputed king of Oxford St's department stores.
- **Borough Market** (p145) The South Bank's organic market is something of a holy temple to London foodies.
- **Harrod's** (p198) Check out the fabulous food hall and buy something just for the little green bag.
- **Fortnum & Mason** (p82) Drop in to the royal family's grocery store for a time-warp shopping experience.

## PLACES FOR LOCAL FOOD

- **St John** (p213) Don't miss the famous roast bone-marrow salad at the originator of the British cuisine revolution.
- **Rules** (p75) London's oldest restaurant is great for traditional game.
- **Golden Hind** (p174) Fantastic fish and chips.
- **Sweeting's** (p126) Excellent traditional grub in the heart of the city.

## BEST NIGHTS OUT

- **Fabric** (p219) Party at London's ultimate superclub.
- **Royal Opera House** (p81) See a performance at one of the world's great opera and ballet venues.
- **Old Vic** (p152) See big names perform big drama.
- **333** (p218) Dance the night away at Shoreditch's trashiest disco.

## VITAL STATISTICS

- **Telephone code** ☎ 020
- **Population** 7.56 million
- **Area** 609 sq miles

# THINGS YOU NEED TO KNOW

## AT A GLANCE

- **ATMs** Can be found everywhere in London
- **Bargaining** Unusual except at markets
- **Credit Cards** Visa and MasterCard are accepted almost everywhere
- **Currency** British Pound (GBP or £)
- **Tipping** 12.5% is standard in restaurants and is usually added to the bill
- **Visas** Not required for US, Canadian, Australian or New Zealand passport holders

## ACCOMMODATION

- **B&Bs** Can be found throughout the city and offer a cheaper, usually more intimate experience to staying in hotels.
- **Hostels** Hostel quality varies enormously in London, but some of the best are included in this book.
- **Hotels** Staying in a hotel is an expensive option in London, but with some of the best hotels in the world to choose from, it's also a great pleasure.
- **Halls of Residence** One cheap option during summer holidays is to stay in university halls of residence.

## ADVANCE PLANNING

- **Three months before** Sort your hotel room and theatre tickets.
- **One week before** Make restaurant reservations.
- **One day before** Check www.tfl.gov.uk for transport updates.

## COSTS

- **A one-way Zone 1 journey on the tube** £4
- **A good meal for two with wine** approximately £80
- **Theatre ticket** average £40

LEFT: DOUG MCKINLAY; RIGHT: NEIL SETCHFIELD

Left: Greenwich Park (p234) in winter; Right: Interior of Canary Wharf (p230)

- **Heathrow Express one-way journey to Paddington £18**

## EMERGENCY NUMBERS

- **All emergencies** Call 999 (free from any phone)

## GETTING AROUND

- **Tube** The London Underground is the quickest way to get about town.
- **Bus** Can be a lot slower, but is far more scenic and covers parts of London not served by the tube.
- **Walk** As much as you can – most neighbourhoods lend themselves very well to exploration on foot.
- **Boat** If you get the chance, jump on one of the many pleasure boats or boat services on the Thames to see London from its glorious river.

## GETTING THERE & AWAY

- **Fly** London is served by five airports: Heathrow (p280), Gatwick (p281), Stanstead (p282), Luton (p282) and London City (p282). It is connected to almost everywhere in the world.
- **Train** The zippy Eurostar (p284) connects London St Pancras with Paris and Brussels, and from there with the rest of the European train network.

## TECH STUFF

- **Electricity** In the UK the unique three-pronged socket is used. You can buy adaptors for US and European sockets at many high street stores.
- **Mobile Phones** SIM cards for unlocked GSM phones can be purchased easily in any mobile phone shop.
- **Time** London is on GMT+0 during the winter and GMT+1 during the summer.

## TRAVEL SEASONS

- **Spring** Cold and wet at first, spring ends up usually warm and pleasant and a great time to visit.
- **Summer** The best time to visit, London is great in the summer, though of course you'll be competing for space with thousands of other visitors.
- **Autumn** Can be surprisingly warm and a good time to avoid the crowds.
- **Winter** It rarely snows in London, but it can still be freezing. That said, visitor numbers are down, so the cold can often be very worthwhile.

## WHAT TO BRING

- **Rain jacket** The rumours about the weather aren't exaggerated.
- **Comfortable shoes** Hard to enjoy the endless strolls without them.
- **Small day-pack** For carrying that rain jacket when the sun does shine.

PLANNING YOUR TRIP

GET INSPIRED

# GET INSPIRED

## ↘ BOOKS

- **London: The Biography – Peter Ackroyd** A now classic history of London that deals with London thematically rather than chronologically.
- **Oliver Twist – Charles Dickens** Dickens' classic tale of poverty in Victorian London is melodramatic but fascinating for social detail.
- **The Buddha of Suburbia – Hanif Kureishi** This hilarious account of Asian life in the suburbs of London in the 1970s is a firm London favourite.
- **London Fields – Martin Amis** A grippingly dark tale of London lowlife in the 80s, one of the first great postmodernist novels.
- **London Observed – Doris Lessing** Eighteen brilliant sketches of London life by the Iranian-born, Rhodesian-raised Lessing, herself new to London.

## ↘ FILMS

- **28 Days Later** This horror film set in London has amazing shots of the empty capital that are amazing to watch.
- **Bridget Jones' Diary** Everyone's favourite chick flick is set in and around London's South Bank.
- **Passport to Pimlico** This classic Ealing comedy portrays '50s London in black and white.
- **Shakespeare in Love** The Globe Theatre features heavily in this Oscar-winning love story.

DOUG MCKINLAY

Book shopping at Spitalfields Market (p212)

## ☑ MUSIC

- **Abbey Road – The Beatles** The ultimate London album.
- **London Calling – The Clash** The 1979 album that changed music.
- **Girl VIII – Saint Etienne** The greatest London name check of all time.
- **Alright, Still – Lily Allen** This upbeat album of London life has become an instant classic.
- **London – The Smiths** Stupendous rock anthem to the capital by the Manchester band.

## ☑ WEBSITES

- **Evening Standard** (www.thisislondon.co.uk) All the latest London news, gossip and listings can be found here.
- **Streetmap** (www.streetmap.co.uk) Find any street in London with this excellent website.
- **Transport for London** (www.tfl.gov.uk) Check the best routes, time journeys and keep up to date with the frequent engineering works.
- **Visit London** (www.visitlondon.com) London's official tourism website is packed with useful information.

# CALENDAR

| JAN | FEB | MAR | APR |

SIMON GREENWOO

Oxford & Cambridge Boat Race

## JANUARY

### LONDON ART FAIR
Over 100 major galleries participate in this contemporary art fair (www.londonartfair.co.uk), which is now one of the largest in Europe, with thematic exhibitions, special events and emerging artists.

### CHINESE NEW YEAR
Chinatown fizzes, crackles and pops in this colourful street festival, which includes a Golden Dragon parade, and eating and partying aplenty.

## FEBRUARY

### PANCAKE RACES
On Shrove Tuesday, you can catch pancake races and associated silliness at Spitalfields Market, Covent Garden and Lincoln's Inn Fields and various other venues around town.

## MARCH

### HEAD OF THE RIVER RACE
Some 400 crews participate in this colourful annual boat race (www.horr.co.uk) held over a 7km course between Mortlake and Putney.

## APRIL

### LONDON MARATHON
Approximately 35,000 masochists cross London in the world's biggest road race (www.virginlondonmarathon.com). The route starts in Greenwich Park and ends with a triumphal sprint down the Mall.

### OXFORD & CAMBRIDGE BOAT RACE
Big crowds line the banks of the Thames from Putney to Mortlake for this annual event, where the country's two most famous universities go oar-to-oar. Dates vary each year due to the universities'

| MAY | JUN | JUL | AUG | SEP | OCT | NOV | DEC |

Easter breaks, so check the website (www.theboatrace.org).

## MAY

### CHELSEA FLOWER SHOW
The world's most renowned horticultural show (www.rhs.org.uk), held at the Royal Hospital Chelsea, attracts the cream of London society and is never far from controversy – the ban on garden gnomes was, shock horror, broken by exhibitor Jekka McVicar in 2009, making national headlines. Only in Britain…

Spectacular blooms at Chelsea Flower Show

## JUNE

### ROYAL ACADEMY SUMMER EXHIBITION
Beginning in June and running through August, this is an annual showcase of

Trooping the Colour

works submitted by individuals from all over Britain, distilled to a thousand or so pieces and displayed in the grand surrounds of the Royal Academy of Arts (www.royalacademy.org.uk).

### TROOPING THE COLOUR
The Queen's official birthday (she was born in April but the weather's better in June) is celebrated with much flag waving, parades, pageantry and noisy flyovers (www.trooping-the-colour.co.uk) at Horse Guards Parade in Whitehall.

### WIMBLEDON LAWN TENNIS CHAMPIONSHIPS
For two weeks the quiet south London village of Wimbledon is the centre of the sporting universe as the best players on earth gather to fight for the championship (www.wimbledon.com). While it's as much about strawberries, cream and

# ➘ CALENDAR

JAN    FEB    MAR    APR

tradition as smashing balls for those in attendance, the rest of the capital is riveted by the women and men's finals that take place on the final weekend of the tournament.

## ➘ JULY

### PRIDE LONDON
The gay community in all its many fabulous guises paints the town pink in this annual extravaganza, featuring a morning parade and a huge afternoon event on Trafalgar Sq (although the location changes frequently).

### THE PROMS
Two months of outstanding classical 'promenade concerts' (www.bbc.co.uk/proms) at various prestigious venues, centred on the Royal Albert Hall (p190) in Kensington.

## ➘ AUGUST

### NOTTING HILL CARNIVAL
Europe's biggest – and London's most vibrant – outdoor carnival (www.thecarnival.tv) is a celebration of Caribbean London, featuring music, dancing and costumes over the summer bank holiday weekend.

## ➘ SEPTEMBER

### LONDON OPEN HOUSE
One of London's biggest treats, for a weekend in late September the public is invited in to see over 700 heritage buildings throughout the capital that are normally off-limits. A unique chance that has Londoners and visitors alike heading to their favourite places in droves; see www.londonopenhouse.org.

JULIET COOMB

Colour and spectacle at Notting Hill Carnival

## ↘ OCTOBER

### LONDON FILM FESTIVAL

The city's premier film event (www.lff. org.uk) attracts big overseas names and is an opportunity to see over 100 British and international films before their cinema release. There are master-classes given by world-famous directors and Q&A sessions with the cream of Hollywood and independent movie-makers too.

## ↘ NOVEMBER

### GUY FAWKES NIGHT
### (BONFIRE NIGHT)    5 NOVEMBER

One of Britain's best-loved and noisi-est traditions, Bonfire Night commem-orates Guy Fawkes' foiled attempt to blow up Parliament in 1605. Bonfires and fireworks light up the night on 5 November and effigies of Fawkes are burned, while young kids run around asking for 'a penny for the guy'. Primrose Hill, Highbury Fields, Alexander Palace, Clapham Common and Crystal Palace Park are the places to aim for in order to see the best fire-work displays.

### LORD MAYOR'S SHOW

In accordance with the Magna Carta of 1215, the newly elected Lord Mayor of the City of London travels in a state coach from Mansion House to the Royal Courts of Justice to seek their approval. The floats, bands and fireworks that ac-

NEIL SETCHFIELD

Anything goes at Pride London

company him (www.lordmayorsshow. org) were added later.

## ↘ DECEMBER

### LIGHTING OF THE CHRISTMAS TREE & LIGHTS

A *Heat*-magazine favoured celebrity is normally carted in to switch on all the festive lights that line Oxford, Regent and Bond Streets, and a huge Norwegian spruce is set up in Trafalgar Sq.

### NEW YEAR'S
### CELEBRATIONS    31 DECEMBER

On 31 December there's the famous countdown to midnight on Trafalgar Sq – London's biggest bash, but one worth avoiding unless you love crowds.

THE WEST END

# THE WEST END

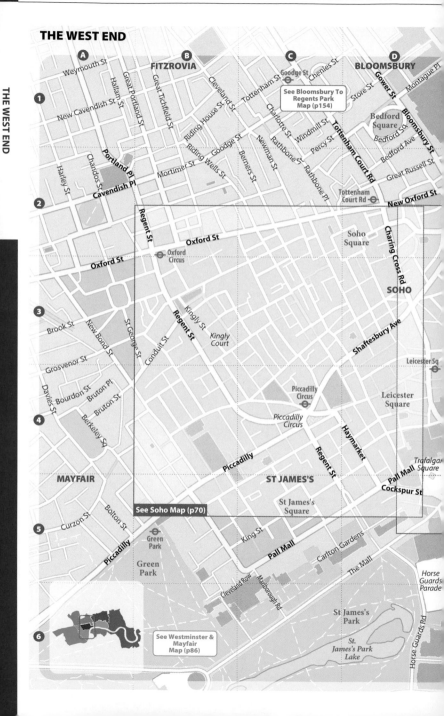

**FITZROVIA**

**BLOOMSBURY**

See Bloomsbury To
Regents Park
Map (p154)

Bedford
Square

Tottenham
Court Rd

New Oxford St

Soho
Square

Oxford
Circus

**SOHO**

Kingly
Court

Leicester Sq

Piccadilly
Circus

Leicester
Square

Piccadilly
Circus

**MAYFAIR**

Piccadilly

**ST JAMES'S**

Trafalgar
Square

Pall Mall

Cockspur St

See Soho Map (p70)

St James's
Square

Green
Park

Green
Park

Pall Mall

Carlton Gardens

The Mall

Horse
Guards
Parade

See Westminster &
Mayfair
Map (p86)

St James's
Park

St.
James's Park
Lake

Weymouth St, Hallam St, Great Portland St, Great Titchfield St, Cleveland St, Tottenham St, Goodge St, Chenies St, Store St, Gower St, Montague Pl, New Cavendish St, Riding House St, Charlotte St, Windmill St, Bedford Sq, Bedford Ave, Bloomsbury St, Harley St, Chandos St, Mortimer St, Riding House St, Goodge St, Berners St, Newman St, Rathbone St, Rathbone Pl, Percy St, Great Russell St, Portland Pl, Cavendish Pl, Regent St, Oxford St, Charing Cross Rd, Brook St, New Bond St, St George St, Conduit St, Regent St, Shaftesbury Ave, Grosvenor St, Davies St, Bourdon St, Bruton Pl, Bruton St, Berkeley Sq, Curzon St, Bolton St, Piccadilly, King St, Cleveland Row, Marlborough Rd, Horse Guards Rd

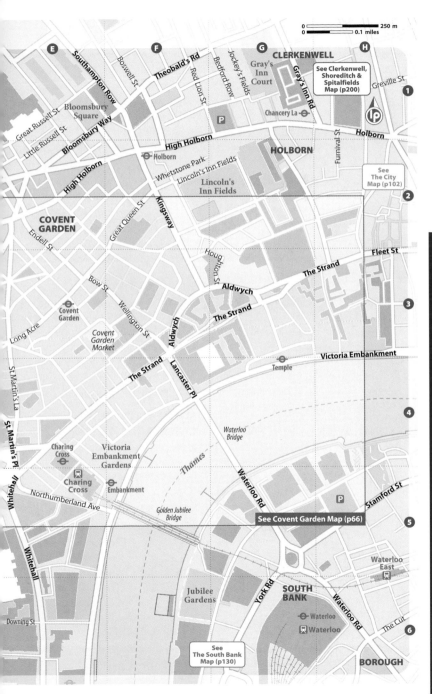

0          250 m
0          0.1 miles

**E**   Southampton Row
Boswell St
**F**   Theobald's Rd
Red Lion St
Jockey's Fields
Bedford Row
**G**   Gray's Inn Court
**CLERKENWELL**
Gray's Inn Rd
Greville St
See Clerkenwell, Shoreditch & Spitalfields Map (p200)
**H**
**1**

Great Russell St
Little Russell St
Bloomsbury Square
Bloomsbury Way
High Holborn
Chancery La
Furnival St
Holborn

High Holborn
Holborn
Whetstone Park
Lincoln's Inn Fields
**HOLBORN**

See The City Map (p102)

Lincoln's Inn Fields
**2**

**COVENT GARDEN**
Endell St
Great Queen St
Kingsway
Houghton St
Aldwych
Fleet St
The Strand

Bow St
Wellington St
Aldwych
The Strand
**3**

Covent Garden
Long Acre
Covent Garden Market
The Strand
Lancaster Pl
Temple
Victoria Embankment

St Martin's La
Waterloo Bridge
Thames
**4**

St Martin's Pl
Charing Cross
Victoria Embankment Gardens
Charing Cross
Embankment
Northumberland Ave
Golden Jubilee Bridge
Waterloo Rd
See Covent Garden Map (p66)
Stamford St
**5**

Whitehall
Downing St
Jubilee Gardens
York Rd
**SOUTH BANK**
Waterloo Rd
Waterloo East
The Cut
**6**

Whitehall
See The South Bank Map (p130)
Waterloo
Waterloo
**BOROUGH**

# THE WEST END HIGHLIGHTS

## 1 | NATIONAL GALLERY

If you're only going to see one art museum in London make it this perennial Trafalgar Sq favourite. Nowhere else in the city gives you such an extensive and fascinating overview of Western art from the 13th to 19th centuries. The collection is enormous though – some 2300 paintings are permanently on display, with regularly changing temporary exhibits enhancing the number. Here are some of our absolute favourites.

### ↘ OUR DON'T MISS LIST

#### ❶ BATHERS AT ASNIÈRES – SEURAT (1884)

This timeless scene of weekend bathers is an icon of modern painting and the most famous of Georges Seurat's large-scale compositions, despite it not actually being an exercise in pointillism, the technique that made his name.

#### ❷ SUNFLOWERS – VINCENT VAN GOGH (1888)

Executed at the 'Yellow House' at Arles in the summer of 1888, this 'symphony in yellow' was one of four paintings of sunflowers that Van Gogh completed out of a total of twelve. This beautiful rendering of dying sunflowers is made particularly convincing by the artist's use of *impasto*, the building up of the brushstrokes to create the texture of the sunflower petals.

#### ❸ THE HAY – WAIN CONSTABLE (1821)

Perhaps the most famous of all British paintings, this bucolic scene depicts a horse-drawn cart (or hay wain) crossing

Clockwise from top: National Gallery (p65); Statue of King James II outside the gallery; Fountain in Trafalgar Sq (p64); 'Sunflowers' by Vincent Van Gogh; Soaking up the sunshine outside the National Gallery

CLOCKWISE FROM TOP: ORIEN HARVEY; CHARLOTTE HINDLE; CHRISTOPHER GROENHOUT; JAVIER LARREA/PHOTOLIBRARY; ORIEN HARVEY

the shallow river Stour in Suffolk. Despite its iconic status in the UK today, the painting failed even to find a buyer when it was exhibited at the Royal Academy in 1821.

## ❹ THE SUPPER AT EMMAUS – CARAVAGGIO (1601)

This little known gospel story of the disciples Luke and Cleophas meeting the resurrected Jesus after his crucifixion and failing to recognise him is given a dramatic, perspective-changing aspect by the gesture of Luke on finally knowing Jesus when he blesses their bread.

## ❺ THE FIGHTING – TEMERAIRE TURNER (1839)

This beautiful late afternoon scene depicts the famous gun ship *Temeraire* being towed from Sheerness to

Rotherhithe to be broken up. Believed to be an allegory of Britain's fading naval power, the picture is undoubtedly melancholic and the sunset aptly suggests decline.

## ↘ THINGS YOU NEED TO KNOW

**Pit stop** Enjoy a good British lunch at the excellent National Dining Rooms **Free tour** The daily 10-minute talk focuses on one painting in detail. It's free to join and happens Mon-Fri at 4pm **Got an hour?** A free introductory tour of the museum happens daily at 11.30am and 2.30pm **See p65 for more information**

# THE WEST END HIGHLIGHTS

## ↘ SHOP TIL YOU DROP

There's simply nowhere like London's **West End** (p81) when it comes to sheer variety, quality and quantity of shopping. Oxford St, the West End's main thoroughfare, is packed with shoppers from dawn til dusk, and while it has a few great department stores, you'll find the best stuff in the backstreets.

## ↘ NATIONAL PORTRAIT GALLERY

Often overlooked in favour of its almost-namesake next door, the small but perfectly formed **National Portrait Gallery** (p69) does just what it says on the tin – displays portraits of famous Brits from the Middle Ages on. See the famous Chandos portrait of William Shakespeare and generations of royalty in paint, before enjoying the more celluloid delights of present-day stars from Damon Albarn to Lily Allen.

THE WEST END

THE WEST END HIGHLIGHTS

**4**

## ⬊ TAKE IN TRAFALGAR SQUARE

Having improved immeasurably in the past decade London's most central plaza can again be enjoyed. With two great galleries on its northern side, the 'fourth plinth' (see p63) and the magnificent Nelson's Column in the centre, **Trafalgar Square** (p64) is a great place to take in London.

**5**

## ⬊ SOHO NIGHTLIFE

The West End's heart is the bohemian quarter of **Soho** (p76), which has an almost villagelike atmosphere by day but becomes a rampant theatre of debauchery by night. You'll find everything from dive bars to cocktail bars here and once you've sampled the many drinking opportunities, head for one of the area's nightclubs.

**6**

## ⬊ ROYAL ACADEMY OF ARTS

The **Royal Academy of Arts** (p63) is home to the British art establishment and is worth visiting for its excellent temporary art exhibits, and particularly its annual Summer Exhibition, in which artworks submitted by members of the British public are put on display – it's a fascinating insight into the state of the nation.

2 Selfridges (p175); 3 Inside of the National Portrait Gallery (p69); 4 Trafalgar Sq (p64); 5 Drinking in a Soho pub (p76); 6 Royal Academy of Arts (p63)

# THE WEST END WALK

This short walk starts from tourist-mecca Covent Garden, snakes through colourful Chinatown and bohemian Soho and ends up on glorious Trafalgar Sq, showing you the many faces of the West End. There are plenty of places to stop for a drink on the way and soak up the very heart of London.

## ❶ COVENT GARDEN PIAZZA

Yes it's touristy, but it's worth seeing this Inigo Jones **Piazza** (p68) and some of the street performers who make a living in front of St Paul's Church. These are the modern day descendents of the street performers who put on the first ever Punch and Judy show here in 1662.

## ❷ CHINATOWN

Avoid Leicester Sq and walk down Lisle St and Gerrard St under the ersatz Oriental gates of **Chinatown** (p68). Breathe in the aromatic spices and stop for some delicious Chinese food at one of the many restaurants.

## ❸ SOHO

Wander across Shaftesbury Ave, the main street of 'theatreland' and home to some of the West End's most prestigious theatres. Continue up Wardour St, turning right onto Old Compton St, London's gayest thoroughfare and the main street of **Soho** (p77).

## ❹ SOHO SQUARE

Take Frith St, past Mozart's former home at number 20, and emerge into the open space of **Soho Square** (p61), the perfectly formed park at the heart of the West End and the heart of much of the UK film industry.

## ❺ OXFORD STREET

Head into the avenue of human traffic that is **Oxford St** (p81), past many of London's premier shops. At Oxford Circus, turn left into Regent St, the centrepiece of Nash's design for Regency London.

## ❻ REGENT STREET

Wander down this regal shopping avenue and look out for world famous toyshop **Hamleys** (p84) and one of London's smartest department stores, **Liberty** (p82), both on the left hand side as you go down.

## ❼ PICCADILLY CIRCUS

Hectic and traffic-choked, but still lovely, **Piccadilly Circus** (p62) is like London's Times Sq, full of flashing ads, tons of shops and tourists. Don't miss the famous statue known incorrectly as **Eros** (p62).

# THE WEST END WALK

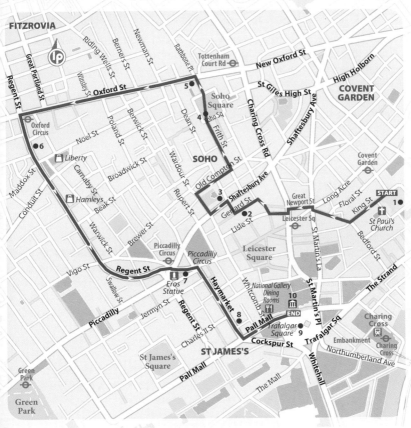

## ❼ HAYMARKET

Escape the chaos of Trafalgar Sq by heading down grand Haymarket, on the way noticing terribly chic **Jermyn St**, noted for its gentlemen's clothing and accessories shops. From Haymarket turn left onto Pall Mall.

## ❽ TRAFALGAR SQUARE

Another tourist magnet, but worth it all the way, **Trafalgar Square** (p64) is a magnificent beauty of a square. Check out the views of Big Ben from its southern side, and don't miss the so-called **fourth plinth** (p63).

## ❾ NATIONAL GALLERY

Take a few hours to admire the artwork at the **National Gallery** (p65). Sit down for a well-deserved lunch or dinner in the new and stylish National Dining Rooms, where you can enjoy British cuisine in its finest form.

# THE WEST END'S BEST...

## ⬊ PLACES TO RELAX

- **Soho Square** (p61) Find your own space to chill out in Soho's tiny green lung.
- **Hamleys** (p84) Let the kids run wild in London's best toy shop.
- **Soho Cafes** (p75) Take your pick of some great coffee houses.
- **Ronnie Scott's** (p80) Unwind at London's most famous jazz venue.

## ⬊ GLAMOROUS HANGOUTS

- **Yauatcha** (p73) The chicest cakes in town await at this uber-fashionable Chinese tea house.
- **Royal Opera House** (p81) Meet friends at the champagne bar.
- **St Martin's Lane** (p71) *The* London hotel for A-listers and their entourages.
- **Liberty** (p82) This is the West End's truly glam department store.

## ⬊ QUIRKY SHOPPING

- **Agent Provocateur** (p83) Bonkers underwear and other classy erotica await.
- **Paul Smith** (p82) Choose from the exquisite yet playful range of clothing.
- **Neal's Yard Dairy** (p83) Grab a smelly, ripe English cheese to take home with you.
- **Fortnum & Mason** (p82) What isn't quirky inside this historic slice of traditional Britain?

## ⬊ FREE THINGS

- **Photographers' Gallery** (p61) This excellent spot is all free.
- **Chinatown** (p61) Travel from England to China for free along Gerrard St.
- **National Gallery** (p65) One of the world's great art collections costs nothing to enter – incredible!
- **National Portrait Gallery** (p69) See this quirky gem without spending a cent.

LEFT: DOUG MCKINLAY; RIGHT: NEIL SETCHFIELD

Left: Royal Opera House (p81); Right: Liberty (p82)

# DISCOVER THE WEST END

London's shopping, eating and entertainment epicentre is the fabulous West End, made up of Soho, Chinatown and Covent Garden and stretched out in a rough rectangle between Oxford Circus, Piccadilly Circus, Aldwych and Holborn. You'll find few real sights here but you will find glitz, glamour and crowds of shoppers any day of the year, and this is the best place for an introduction to fast-paced London life.

Historically a low-class, poor area of the city (Eliza Doolittle sold flowers at Covent Garden market before becoming the plaything of two eccentric gentlemen in Shaw's *Pygmalion*), the West End's centrality between the political village of Westminster and the financial City of London means that today retail space here is astronomically expensive. The world-famous West End theatres dominate the main avenues, while in the back streets cocktail bars, sublime fashion stores and cutting-edge restaurants can be found almost anywhere you go. This exciting and chaotic place is where your London adventure should start.

# SIGHTS
## SOHO & CHINATOWN
### SOHO SQUARE & AROUND
Map p70

At Soho's northern end, leafy Soho Sq is the area's back garden. This is where people come to laze in the sun on spring and summer days, and where office workers have their lunch or gather for a picnic. It was laid out in 1681, and originally named King's Sq, which is why the statue of Charles II stands in its northern half. In the centre is a tiny mock-Tudor-style house – the gardener's shed – whose lift was a passage to underground shelters during WWII.

Heading south of Soho Sq, down **Dean Street**, you'll come upon No 28, the home of Karl Marx and his family from 1851 to 1856. Seducer and heart-breaker Casanova and opium-addicted writer Thomas de Quincey lived on **Greek Street**, whereas the parallel **Frith Street** (No 20) housed Wolfgang Amadeus Mozart for a year from 1764.

### CHINATOWN Map p70
North of Leicester Sq – but a world away in atmosphere – are Lisle and Gerrard Sts, the focal point for London's Chinese community. Although not as big as Chinatowns elsewhere – it's just two streets really – this is a lively quarter with fake oriental gates, Chinese street signs, red lanterns, many, many restaurants and great Asian supermarkets. London's original Chinatown was further east, near Limehouse, but moved here after heavy bombardments in WWII. To see it at its effervescent best, time your visit for Chinese New Year in late January/early February (see p46).

### PHOTOGRAPHERS' GALLERY
Map p70

☎ 0845 262 1618; www.photonet.org.uk; 16-18 Ramillies St W1; admission free; ⏱ 11am-6pm Tue, Wed & Sat, 11am-8pm Thu & Fri, noon-6pm Sun; ⊖ Oxford Circus; ⚿

Moved from its two-part gallery space off Leicester Sq in December 2008, this fantastic institution has massively benefited from the new premises. Designed by O'Donnell + Tuomey Architects, the gallery now consists of two floors of exhibition space, a lovely cafe and well-stocked bookshop, plus a top-floor shop where you can buy original prints. The prestigious Deutsche Börse Photography Competition (annually 9 February to 8 April) is of major importance for contemporary photographers; past winners include Richard Billingham, Luc Delahaye, Andreas Gursky, Boris Mikhailov and Juergen Teller. The gallery always exhibits excellent and thought-provoking work.

## PICCADILLY CIRCUS
Map p70
⊖ Piccadilly Circus

Together with Big Ben and Trafalgar Sq, this is postcard London. And despite the stifling crowds and racing midday traffic, the flashing ads and buzzing liveliness of Piccadilly Circus always make it exciting to be in London. The circus looks its best at night, when the flashing advertisement panels really shine against the dark sky.

Designed by John Nash in the 1820s the hub was named after the street Piccadilly, which earned its name in the 17th century from the stiff collars (piccadils) that were the sartorial staple of the time (and were the making of a nearby tailor's fortune). At the centre of the circus is the famous lead statue, the Angel of Christian Charity, dedicated to the philanthropist and child-labour abolitionist Lord Shaftesbury, and derided when unveiled in 1893, sending the sculptor into early retirement. Down the years the angel has been mistaken for **Eros** the God of Love, and the misnomer has stuck (you'll even see signs for 'Eros' from the Underground). It's a handy meeting place for tourists, though if you don't like the crowds, meet at the charging **Horses of Helios** statue at the edge of Piccadilly and Haymarket – apparently a much cooler place to convene.

Shaftesbury Memorial Fountain, Piccadilly Circus

CHRISTOPHER GROENHOUT

## THE FOURTH PLINTH

Three of the four plinths located at Trafalgar Sq's corners are occupied by notables, King George IV on horseback, and military men General Sir Charles Napier and Major General Sir Henry Havelock. One, originally intended for a statue of William IV, has largely remained vacant for the past 150 years. The Royal Society of Arts conceived the unimaginatively titled **Fourth Plinth Project** (www.london. gov.uk/fourthplinth) in 1999, deciding to use the empty space for works by contemporary artists. The stunning *Ecce Homo* by Mark Wallinger (1999) was the first one, a life-size statue of Jesus which appeared tiny in contrast to the enormous plinth, commenting on the human illusions of grandeur; it was followed by Bill Woodrow's *Regardless of History* (2000) and Rachel Whiteread's *Monument* (2001), a resin copy of the plinth, turned upside down.

Possibly the most interesting so far has been Anthony Gormley's *One & Other* (2009) which featured no inanimate object but simply a space for individuals to occupy – each person spent an hour on the plinth, addressing the crowds on any chosen subject, performing or simply sitting quietly. The project ran 24 hours a day, every day for 100 days and the rules specified that the participants spent their hour on the plinth alone, could do what they wanted as long as it wasn't illegal and were allowed to take with them anything they could carry.

## REGENT STREET Map p70

Regent St is the border separating the hoi polloi of Soho and the high-society residents of Mayfair. Designed by John Nash as a ceremonial route, it was meant to link the Prince Regent's long-demolished city dwelling with the 'wilds' of Regent's Park, and was conceived by the architect as a grand thoroughfare that would be the centrepiece of a new grid for this part of town. Alas, it was never to be – too many toes were being stepped on and Nash had to downscale his plan. There are some elegant shop fronts that look older than their 1920s origins (when the street was remodelled) but, as in the rest of London, the chain stores have almost completely taken over. Two distinguished retail outlets are **Hamleys** (p84), London's premier toy and game store, and the upmarket department store **Liberty** (p82).

## ROYAL ACADEMY OF ARTS

Map p70

☎ 7300 8000; www.royalacademy.org.uk; Burlington House, Piccadilly W1; admission varies; ⏰ 10am-6pm, to 10pm Fri; ⊖ Green Park; ⚹

Britain's first art school was founded in 1768, though it only moved here in the following century. It's a great place to come for some free art, thanks to the John Madejski's Fine Rooms, where drawings ranging from Constable, Reynolds, Gainsborough and Turner to Hockney are displayed. The Academy's galleries have sprung back to life in recent years with mega successful exhibitions such as the great Byzantium and Kuniyoshi shows. The famous Summer Exhibition (early June to mid-August), which has showcased art submitted by the general public for nearly 250 years, is the Academy's biggest event.

NEIL SETCHFIELD

Leicester Sq

## WHITE CUBE GALLERY Map p70

☎ 7930 5373; www.whitecube.com; 25-26 Mason's Yard SW1; admission free; ☼ 10am-6pm Tue-Sat; ⊖ Piccadilly Circus

This central sister to the Hoxton original (p210) hosted Tracey Emin's first exhibition in five years, 'Those who suffer Love', in 2009, thus, together with the massively publicised Damien Hirst 'For the Love of God' exhibition two years before, bringing back some of the publicity for the (now not-so-young) Young British Artists (YBAs). Housed in Mason's Yard, a traditional courtyard with brick houses and an old pub, the White Cube looks like an ice block – white, straight-lined and angular. The two contrasting styles work well together and the courtyard often serves as a garden for the gallery on popular opening nights.

## LEICESTER SQUARE Map p70
⊖ Leicester Sq

Enormous cinemas and nightclubs dominate this 'aesthetically challenged' square which could really do with a makeover. It heaves with crowds on weekends and becomes the playground of the inebriated at night. There was a serious pickpocketing problem here some years ago, until a heavy police presence improved matters, but still keep an eye on your bag wallet, especially when the square is very crowded. Britain's glitzy film premieres take place here, as well as the majority of London Film Festival screenings.

# COVENT GARDEN & LEICESTER SQUARE
## TRAFALGAR SQUARE Map p66
⊖ Charing Cross

In many ways this is the centre of London where rallies and marches take place, tens of thousands of revellers usher in the New Year and locals congregate for anything from communal open-air cinema to various political protests. The great square was neglected over many years, ringed with gnarling traffic and given over to flocks of pigeons that would dive-bomb anyone with a morsel of food on their person. But things changed in 2000 when Ken Livingstone became London Mayor and embarked on a bold and imaginative scheme to transform it into the kind of space John Nash had intended when he designed it in the early 19th century. Traffic was banished from the northern flank in front of the National Gallery, and a new pedestrian plaza built. The front of the National Gallery itself was dolled up with a new facade and entrance hall, and feeding pigeons was banned.

The pedestrianisation has made it easier to appreciate not only the square but also the splendid buildings around it:

ne National Gallery, the National Portrait Gallery and the newly renovated church of t Martin-in-the-Fields. The ceremonial **Pall Mall** runs southwest from the top of the quare. To the southwest stands **Admiralty Arch**, with The Mall leading to Buckingham Palace beyond it. To the west is **Canada House** (1827), designed by Robert Smirke. tanding in the centre of the square since 843, the 52m-high **Nelson's Column** upon which the admiral surveys his fleet of ships to the southwest) commemorates Nelson's victory over Napoleon off Cape Trafalgar in Spain in 1805.

**NATIONAL GALLERY** Map p66
☎ 7747 2885; www.nationalgallery.org.uk; Trafalgar Sq WC2; admission free, prices vary for emporary exhibitions; ⏱ 10am-6pm Thu-Tue, to 9pm Wed; ⊖ Charing Cross; ⓖ

With more than 2000 Western European paintings on display, this is one of the largest galleries in the world. But it's the quality of the works, and not the quantity, that impresses most. Almost five million people visit each year, keen to see seminal paintings from every important epoch in the history of art, including works by Giotto, Leonardo da Vinci, Michelangelo, Titian, Velázquez, Van Gogh and Renoir, just to name a few. Although it can get ridiculously busy in here, the galleries are spacious, sometimes even sedate, and it's never so bad that you can't appreciate the works. That said, weekday mornings and Wednesday evenings (after 6pm) are the best times to visit, as the crowds are small. If you have the time to make multiple visits, focus on one section at a time to fully appreciate the astonishing collection.

## SEX & DRUGS & ROCK'N'ROLL – THE HISTORY OF SOHO

Soho's character was formed by the many waves of immigration, and residential development started in the 17th century, after the Great Fire had levelled much of the city. An influx of Greek and Huguenot refugees and, later, the 18th-century influx of Italian, Chinese and other artisans and radicals into Soho replaced the bourgeois residents, who moved out of the area and into Mayfair. During the following century Soho was no more than a slum, with cholera frequently attacking the impoverished residents. But despite its difficulties, the cosmopolitan vibe attracted writers and artists, and the overcrowded area became a centre for entertainment, with restaurants, taverns and coffee houses springing up.

The 20th century was even more raucous, when a fresh wave of European immigrants settled in, making Soho a bona fide bohemian enclave for two decades after WWII. Ronnie Scott's famous club, originally on Gerrard St, provided Soho's jazz soundtrack from the 1950s, while the likes of Jimi Hendrix, the Rolling Stones and Pink Floyd did their early gigs at the legendary Marquee club, which used to be on Wardour St. Soho had long been known for its seediness but when the hundreds of prostitutes who served the Square Mile were forced off the streets and into shop windows, it became the city's red-light district and a centre for porn, strip joints and bawdy drinking clubs. Gay liberation soon followed, and by the 1980s Soho was the hub of London's gay scene, as it remains today. The neighbourhood has a real sense of community, best absorbed on a weekend morning when Soho is at its most villagelike.

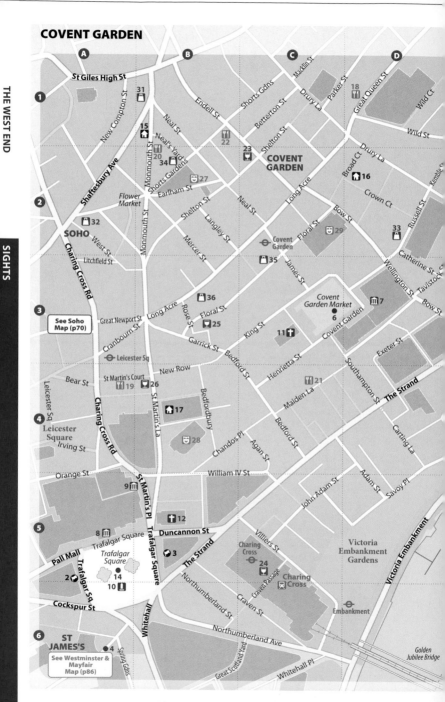

# COVENT GARDEN

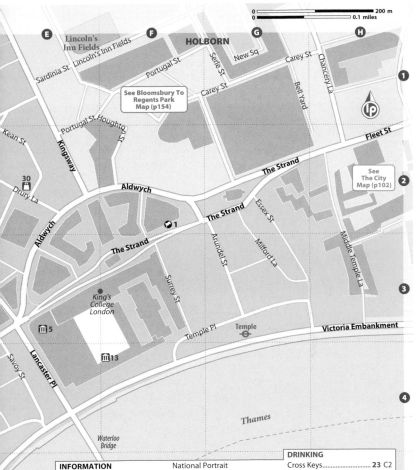

**INFORMATION**

Australian High
  Commission .......................**1** F2
Canadian
  Embassy.............................**2** A5
South African
  High
  Commission .......................**3** B5

**SIGHTS**

Admiralty Arch....................**4** A6
Canada House....................(see 2)
Courtauld
  Institute of Art .................**5** E3
Covent Garden
  Piazza..............................**6** C3
London
  Transport
  Museum...........................**7** D3
National Gallery..................**8** A5

National Portrait
  Gallery...............................**9** A5
Nelson's Column................**10** A6
St Paul's Church ................**11** C3
St Martin-in-the-Fields......**12** B5
Somerset House.................**13** F4
Trafalgar Square................**14** A5

**SLEEPING**

Covent Garden Hotel ........**15** B1
Fielding Hotel ....................**16** D2
St Martin's Lane................**17** B4

**EATING**

Great Queen Street...........**18** D1
J Sheekey...........................**19** A4
Monmouth Coffee
  Company ..........................**20** B2
Rules..................................**21** C4
Scoop.................................**22** B1

**DRINKING**

Cross Keys..........................**23** C2
Heaven ...............................**24** C5
Lamb & Flag ......................**25** B3
Salisbury.............................**26** B4

**ENTERTAINMENT &
ACTIVITIES**

Donmar Warehouse...........**27** B2
London Coliseum...............**28** B4
Royal Opera House............**29** C2

**SHOPPING**

Aram...................................**30** E2
Forbidden Planet
  Megastore .........................**31** B1
Magma ...............................**32** A2
Molton Brown ...................**33** D2
Neal's Yard Dairy ..............**34** B2
Paul Smith .........................**35** C3
Stanford's..........................**36** B3

The size and layout can be confusing, so make sure you pick up a free gallery plan at the entrance. To see the art in chronological order, start with the Sainsbury Wing on the gallery's western side, which houses paintings from 1260 to 1510. In these 16 rooms you can explore the Renaissance through paintings by Giotto, Leonardo da Vinci, Botticelli, Raphael and Titian, among others.

The High Renaissance (1510–1600) is covered in the West Wing, where Michelangelo, Titian, Correggio, El Greco and Bronzino hold court, while Rubens, Rembrandt and Caravaggio can be found in the North Wing (1600–1700). The most crowded part of the gallery – and for good reason – is likely to be the East Wing (1700–1900) and particularly the many works of the impressionists and postimpressionists, including Van Gogh, Gauguin, Cézanne, Monet, Degas and Renoir. Although it hardly stands out in such exalted company, the impressive display featuring 18th-century British landscape artists Gainsborough, Constable and Turner is also well worth checking out.

The highlights listed on p54 include some of the most important works, but if you want to immerse yourself in this pool of riches rather than just skim across the surface, borrow a themed or comprehensive audioguide (£3.50 donation recommended) from the Central Hall. Free one-hour introductory **guided tours** leave from the information desk in the Sainsbury Wing daily at 11.30am and 2.30pm, with an extra tour at 6.30pm on Wednesday. There are also special trails and activity sheets for children.

## ST MARTIN-IN-THE-FIELDS Map p66

☎ general info/box office 7766 1100, for brass-rubbing 7766 1122; www.stmartin-in-the-fields.org; Trafalgar Sq WC2; admission free, brass-rubbing from £4.50; ☼ 8am-6.30pm, brass-rubbing

centre 10am-7pm Mon-Wed, 10am-9pm Thu-Sa 11.30am-6pm Sun, evening concerts 7.30pm; ⊖ Charing Cross

The 'royal parish church' is a delightful fu sion of classical and baroque styles tha was completed by James Gibbs in 1726 A £36-million refurbishment project, com pleted at the end of 2007, provided a nev entrance pavilion and foyer, and severa new areas at the rear of the church, incluc ing spaces offering social care to London' Chinese community and the many home less people who rely on the church's help

Refurbishment excavations unearthe a 1.5-tonne limestone Roman sarcopha gus containing a human skeleton i the churchyard; the yard also holds th graves of 18th-century artists Reynold and Hogarth.

## COVENT GARDEN PIAZZA
Map p66
⊖ Covent Garden

London's first planned square is now th exclusive reserve of tourists who floc here to shop in the quaint old arcades, b entertained by buskers, pay through th nose for refreshments at outdoor cafe and bars, and watch men and women pretend to be statues.

On its western flank is **St Paul's Church** ( ☎ 7836 5221; www.actorschurch.org; Bedford S WC2; admission free; ☼ 8.30am-5.30pm Mon-Fri 9am-1pm Sun). The Earl of Bedford, the mar who had commissioned Inigo Jones to design the piazza, asked for the simples possible church, basically no more than a barn. The architect responded by pro ducing 'the handsomest barn in England' It has long been regarded as the actors church for its associations with the thea tre, and contains memorials to the likes of Charlie Chaplin and Vivien Leigh. The first Punch and Judy show took place in front of it in 1662.

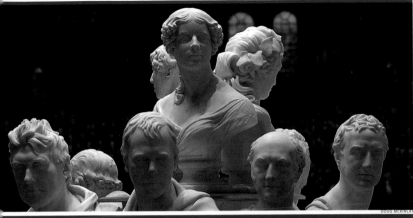

THE WEST END

SIGHTS

Ghostly faces from the past at the National Portrait Gallery

DOUG MCKINLAY

## ⬛ NATIONAL PORTRAIT GALLERY

Excellent for putting faces to names over the last five centuries of British history, the gallery houses a primary collection of some 10,000 works, which are regularly rotated, among them the museum's first acquisition, the famous Chandos portrait of Shakespeare. Despite the recent discovery that the Royal Shakespeare Company's Flower portrait of the Bard was a 19th-century forgery, the National Portrait Gallery still believes this one to have been painted during Shakespeare's lifetime.

To follow the paintings chronologically you should take the huge escalator to the top floor and work your way down. The 1st floor is dedicated to the Royal Family, but the most fun is seeing one of the two portraits of the Queen made by Andy Warhol. The ground floor is most interesting with portraits of contemporary figures using a variety of media, including sculpture and photography.

Audioguides (a £3.50 donation is suggested) highlight some 200 portraits and allow you to hear the voices of some of the people portrayed. The Portrait Café and bookshop are in the basement and the Portrait restaurant is on the top floor, offering some superb views towards Westminster.

**Things you need to know:** Map p66; ☎ 7306 0055; www.npg.org.uk; St Martin's Pl WC2; admission free, prices vary for temporary exhibitions; ⏲ 10am-6pm, to 9pm Thu & Fri; ⊖ Charing Cross or Leicester Sq; ♿

## LONDON TRANSPORT MUSEUM

Map p66

☎ 7379 6344; www.ltmuseum.co.uk; Covent Garden Piazza WC2; adult/senior/student/concession/under 16s £10/8/6/5/free; ⏲ 10am-6pm Sat-Thu, 11am-6pm Fri; ⊖ Covent Garden; ♿

The museum reopened in late 2007, after a £22-million refurbishment and redesign. You can now see the revitalised existing collection (consisting of buses from the horse age until today, plus taxis, trains and all other modes of transport) and new collections that feature other major cities' transport systems, as well as tons of great original poster art and a 120-seat lecture theatre for educational purposes. Check out the poster collection (ranging from £10) for original and interesting souvenirs.

# SLEEPING
## SOHO & CHINATOWN

**SOHO HOTEL** Map p70      Hotel £££
☎ 7559 3000; www.sohohotel.com; 4 Richmond Mews W1; d £280-350, ste from £385-3000; ⊖ Tottenham Court Rd; ⊠

One of London's hippest hotels, the Soh is in a reconverted car park just off Dea St. All the hallmarks of the eclectically ch hoteliers and designers Tim and Kit Kem have been writ large over 91 individuall designed rooms, the colours lean toward the raspberries and puces, and there's stunning black cat Botero sculpture at th entrance.

**HAZLITT'S** Map p70      Hotel ££
☎ 7434 1771; www.hazlittshotel.com; 6 Frith S W1; s £175, d & tw £210-265, ste £400; ⊖ Tottenham Court Rd; ⊠

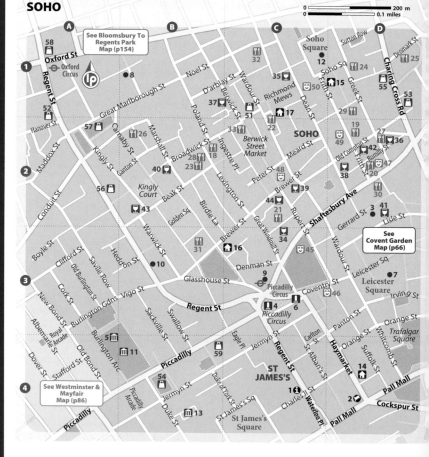

SOHO

Built in 1718 and comprising three original Georgian houses, this is the one-time home of essayist William Hazlitt (1778–1830), and all 23 rooms are named after former residents or visitors to the house. Bedrooms boast a wealth of seductive details, including mahogany four-poster beds, Victorian claw-foot tubs, sumptuous fabrics and genuine antiques. It's a listed building, so there is no lift.

## HAYMARKET
Map p70     Boutique Hotel £££
☎ 7470 4000; www.haymarkethotel.com; 1 Suffolk Pl SW1; r from £260-340, ste from £410; ⊖ Piccadilly Circus; 🏠 📶

Named by *Condé Nast Traveller* as one of the world's finest hotels *before* it opened, the 50-room Haymarket in a John Nash building next to the Theatre Royal is further proof that London is becoming the epicentre of stylish boutique hotels. It's the progeny of Tim and Kit Kemp and it shows – from the hand-painted Gournay wallpaper to the 18m pool with funky drawing room.

## PICCADILLY BACKPACKERS
Map p70     Hostel £
☎ 7434 9009; www.piccadillyhotel.net; 12 Sherwood St W1; dm £12-19, s/d £40/60; ⊖ Piccadilly Circus

The most centrally located budget accommodation in London, Piccadilly Backpackers has more than 700 beds spread over five floors, with dormitory rooms containing anything from four to 10 beds. Rooms are bright and clean, and we especially like the pod dorms with wooden bunk beds in their own little compartments.

# COVENT GARDEN & LEICESTER SQUARE
**ST MARTIN'S LANE** Map p66   Hotel £££
☎ 7300 5500; www.stmartinslane.com; 45 St Martin's Lane; standard s & d £220-270, garden r £310, ste from £600; ⊖ Covent Garden or Leicester Sq; 🏠 ♿

A slice of New York urban chic just a stone's throw from Covent Garden, this Philippe Starck-designed hotel is so cool you'd hardly notice it was there.

THE WEST END

EATING

Saatchi Gallery

TRAVIS DREVER

## ↘ IF YOU LIKE...

If you liked the **National Gallery** (p65) and the **National Portrait Gallery** (p69), then we think you'll like these other London gems:

- **Courtauld Institute of Art** (Map p66) Housed in fabulous Somerset House, this gallery contains paintings by the likes of Rubens, Botticelli, Cézanne, Monet and Van Gogh to name but a few.
- **Saatchi Gallery** (Map p178) This remarkable hoard of contemporary art collected by the reclusive advertising mogul Charles Saatchi is on display for free next to Sloane Sq. The collection, which was recently donated to the nation, includes such modern giants as Tracey Emin and Damien Hirst.
- **Haunch of Venison** (Map p70) Behind the Royal Academy of Arts, this fabulous private gallery is where you'll find some big international name artists on display. Drop by to see what's hot in the London art world.

Its 204 rooms have floor-to-ceiling windows with sweeping West End views, the public rooms are bustling meeting points and everything (and everyone) is beautiful.

### COVENT GARDEN HOTEL Map p66
Boutique Hotel ££

☎ 7806 1000; www.coventgardenhotel.co.uk; 10 Monmouth St WC2; s/d from £230/310, ste from £410; ⊖ Covent Garden or Tottenham Court Rd; ⊠

As fresh as the morning but in a stylishly reserved British sort of way, this 58-room boutique hotel housed in an old French hospital and dispensary uses antiques (don't miss the marquetry desk in the drawing room), gorgeous fabrics and quirky bric-a-brac to stake out its individuality.

### FIELDING HOTEL Map p66
Hotel ££

☎ 7836 8305; www.the-fielding-hotel.co.uk; 4 Broad Ct, Bow St WC2; s/d £90/115; ⊖ Covent Garden

You can almost feel the pulse of the West End – and the odd high C from the Royal Opera House a block away – at this 24-room hotel, in a pedestrianised court in the heart of Covent Garden. It's named after the novelist Henry Fielding (1707–54), who lived on the street. Space is at a premium, but you can't beat the location at this price.

# EATING
## SOHO & CHINATOWN

### LA TROUVAILLE Map p70
French £££

☎ 7287 8488; www.latrouvaille.co.uk; 12a Newburgh St W1; 2-/3-course set lunch £17/20, dinner £30/35; ☖ closed Sun; ⊖ Oxford Circus

Just what its name suggests it is, the 'Find' is perfect for a romantic dinner. You'll find a gorgeous, warm space perfect for candlelit canoodling and an excellent menu of rich French cuisine on a quiet backstreet.

### BAR SHU Map p70
Chinese ££

7287 8822; www.bar-shu.co.uk; 28 Frith St W1; mains £8-28; ⊖ Leicester Sq

The story goes that a visiting businessman from Sichuan Province in China found London's Chinese food offerings so inauhentic that he decided to open up his own restaurant with five chefs from home. Well, it's authentic all right, with dishes redolent of smoked chillies and the all-important Sichuan peppercorn. We love the spicy *gung bao* chicken with peanuts and the *mapo doufu* (bean curd braised with minced pork and chilli).

### BOCCA DI LUPO Map p70 Italian ££
☎ 7734 2223; www.boccadilupo.com; 12 Archer St W1; mains £8.50-17.50; ⊖ Piccadilly Circus
Bocca di Lupo hides on a dark Soho back-street and radiates elegant sophistication. The menu has dishes such as the *cacciucco* (fish and shellfish stew with spicy tomato), grilled lemony langoustines or pasta with chicken liver ragout, or you can go for the more straightforward grilled swordfish or parmigiana.

### GIACONDA DINING ROOM
Map p70 Modern European ££
☎ 7240 3334; www.giacondadining.com; 9 Denmark St; mains £9-13; ⊖ Tottenham Court Rd
A tiny room off Charing Cross Rd hides some of the best food around, with simple dishes such as half-a-chicken and chips, good fresh fish of the day or great steak tartare. The wine list is decent and you're greeted with a carafe of delicious sparkling water and friendly staff.

### GAY HUSSAR Map p70 Hungarian ££
☎ 7437 0973; www.gayhussar.co.uk; 2 Greek St W1; mains £10-17; ☼ closed Sun; ⊖ Tottenham Court Rd
This is the Soho of the 1950s, when dining was still done in the grand style in wood-panelled rooms with brocade and sepia prints on the walls. Try the roast duck leg with all the trimmings or the 'Gypsy quick dish' of pork medallions, onions and green peppers.

### ANDREW EDMUNDS
Map p70 Modern European ££
☎ 7437 5708; 46 Lexington St W1; mains £9-18; ⊖ Piccadilly
This cosy little place is exactly the sort of restaurant you wish you could find everywhere in Soho. Two floors of wood-panelled bohemia with a mouth-watering menu of European country cooking – it's a real find and reservations are essential.

### YAUATCHA Map p70 Dim Sum ££
☎ 7494 8888; 15 Broadwick St W1; dim sum £3.80-15.90; ⊖ Oxford Circus
This most glamorous of dim sum restaurants is divided into two parts. The upstairs tearoom offers an exquisite blue-bathed oasis of calm from the chaos of Berwick St Market as well as some of the

**Busker at Covent Garden (p68)**

THE WEST END

EATING

Chinatown restaurants (p72)

most arrestingly beautiful cakes we've ever seen. The downstairs dining room has a smarter, more atmospheric feel with an original offering of the three main categories of dim sum all day.

### MILDRED'S Map p70      Vegetarian £
☎ 7494 1634; www.mildreds.co.uk; 45 Lexington St W1; mains £7-9; ⊙ closed Sun; ⊖ Oxford Circus
Central London's most inventive veggie restaurant, Mildred's heaves at lunchtime so don't be shy about sharing a table in the sky-lit dining room. Expect the likes of roasted fennel and chickpea terrine and puy lentil casserole as well as more standard (and hugely portioned) salads and stir-fries.

### FERNANDEZ & WELLS
Map p70      European, Spanish £
☎ 7734 1546; www.fernandezandwells.com; 43 Lexington St W1; mains £4-14; ⊖ Oxford Circus
A wonderful Soho mini-chain, this is one of the three branches of Fernandez & Wells, each located within 200m of each other in small, friendly and elegant spaces. This branch offers simple lunche and dinners of Spanish *jamón* (ham) and cured meats and cheese platters accom panied by quality wine. Grilled chorizo sandwiches are perfect for quick lunch time bites and there are ample breakfasts too (until 11am).

### NEW WORLD Map p70      Chinese
☎ 7734 0677; 1 Gerrard Pl W1; mains £6.50-9.90; ⊖ Leicester Sq
If you hanker after dim sum, the three storey New World can oblige. All the old favourites – from *ha gau* (prawn dump ling) to *pai gwat* (steamed pork spare rib) – are available from steaming carts wheeled around the dining room daily 11am to 6pm.

### MILK BAR Map p70      Cafe
☎ 7287 4796; 3 Bateman St W1; mains £4-6; ⊖ Tottenham Court Rd
This place has some of the best breakfasts in central London, with great big ome lettes, homemade beans on toast, por ridge, pancakes with fruit and honey, and

o on, none of which exceed the £5 mark – ust what you need on a weekend morning.

## NORDIC BAKERY
Map p70                                           Scandinavian £

☎ 3230 1077; www.nordicbakery.com; 14a Golden Sq W1; mains £3-4;  ⊖ Oxford Circus
The perfect place to escape the chaos that s Soho and relax in the dark-wood pan- elled space. Lunch on some Scandinavian smoked fish sandwiches or have an after- noon break with coffee and cake.

## COVENT GARDEN & LEICESTER SQUARE

### J SHEEKEY Map p66                          Seafood £££
☎ 7240 2565; www.j-sheeky.co.uk; 28-32 St Martin's Ct WC2; mains £11.75-37.50;  ⊖ Leicester Sq

A jewel of the local scene, this incred- ibly smart restaurant, whose pedigree stretches back to 1896, has four elegant, discreet and spacious wood-panelled rooms in which to savour the riches of the sea, cooked simply and exquisitely. The fish pie (£11.75) is justifiably legen- dary, though the Cornish fish stew is just as good. Three-course weekday lunch is £24.75.

### RULES Map p66                     Traditional British ££
☎ 7836 5314; www.rules.co.uk; 35 Maiden Lane WC2; mains £16.95-21;  ⊖ Covent Garden
Established in 1798, this very posh and very British establishment is London's oldest restaurant. The menu is inevita- bly meat-oriented – Rules specialises in classic game cookery, serving up tens of

---

## SOHO CAFES

Soho presents the nearest thing London has to a sophisticated cafe culture to match that of its Continental neighbours. The area has been synonymous with sipping and schmoozing since Victorian times, but its heyday came with the mod hangouts of the '60s.

**Bar Italia** (Map p70; ☎ 7437 4520; 22 Frith St W1; sandwiches £4-7;  ⊗ 24hr;  ⊖ Leicester Sq or Tottenham Court Rd) Pop into this Soho favourite at any time of day or night and you'll see slumming celebrities lapping up reviving juices and chunky sandwiches amid retro '50s decor.

**Maison Bertaux** (Map p70; ☎ 7437 6007; 28 Greek St W1; cakes £3-3.50;  ⊗ 8.30am- 10.30pm Mon-Sat, to 8pm Sun;  ⊖ Tottenham Court Rd) Bertaux has exquisite confections, unhurried service, a French bohemian vibe and 130 years of history on this spot. Seating is limited to a half-dozen tables.

**Monmouth Coffee Company** (Map p66; ☎ 7836 5272, 7379 3516; www.monmouthco ffee.co.uk; 27 Monmouth St WC2; cakes from £2.50;  ⊗ 8am-6.30pm Mon-Sat;  ⊖ Tottenham Court Rd or Leicester Sq) Essentially a shop selling beans from just about every coffee- growing country in the world, Monmouth has a few wooden alcoves at the back where you can squeeze in and savour blends from around the world.

**Star Café** (Map p70; ☎ 7437 8778; www.thestarcafe.co.uk; 22 Great Chapel St W1; mains £6-9;  ⊗ 7am-4pm Mon-Fri;  ⊖ Tottenham Court Rd) So Soho, this wonderfully atmospheric cafe has vintage advertising and Continental decor that makes it feel like not much has changed since it opened in 1933. It's best known for its breakfast, particularly the curiously named Tim Mellor Special of smoked salmon and scrambled eggs.

THE WEST END

EATING

THE WEST END

thousands of birds between mid-August and January from its own estate – but fish dishes are also available. Puddings are traditional: trifles, treacles and lashings of custard.

### GREAT QUEEN STREET

Map p66                                        British ££

☎ 7242 0622; 32 Great Queen St WC2; mains £9-18; ⊖ Covent Garden or Holborn

One of Covent Garden's best places to eat, Great Queen St is sister to the **Anchor & Hope** (p148) in Waterloo. The menu is seasonal (and changes daily), with an emphasis on quality, hearty dishes and good ingredients – there are always delicious stews, roasts and simple fish dishes.

Bar Italia (p75), Soho

CHARLOTTE HINDLE

### SCOOP Map p66                                 Cafe

☎ 7240 7086; www.scoopgelato.com; 40 Shorts Gardens WC2; ice creams £2.50-5; ⊕ 8am-11pm ⊖ Covent Garden

This is central London's only true *gelateria* and, boy, does it set a precedent. Storms of ice cream swell in the fridge, all the ingredients are natural and the servings are huge. Try the pistachio, coconut, mango, pure chocolate or any of the incredible flavours.

# DRINKING
## SOHO & CHINATOWN

### COACH & HORSES Map p70             Pub

☎ 7437 5920; 29 Greek St W1; ⊖ Leicester Sq

Famous as the place where *Spectator* columnist Jeffrey Bernard drank himself to death, this small, busy and thankfully unreconstructed boozer retains an old Soho bohemian atmosphere with a regular clientele of soaks, writers, hacks, tourists and those too pissed (drunk) to lift their heads off the counter. Pretension will be prosecuted.

### ENDURANCE Map p70                      Bar

☎ 7437 2944; 90 Berwick St W1; ⊖ Oxford Circus or Piccadilly Circus

A Soho favourite, especially for music lovers who comb the vinyl shops on this street before surrendering to the pull of the pint. The Endurance has a retro jukebox that's full of indie hits, there's good wine and draught ales to be savoured, and there's decent food, too.

### FRENCH HOUSE Map p70                   Bar

☎ 7437 2799; 49 Dean St W1; ⊖ Leicester Sq

French House is Soho's legendary boho boozer (with a good restaurant downstairs) with a history to match: this was the meeting place of the Free French Forces during WWII, and De Gaulle is said

DRINKING

## ⬂ GAY SOHO

Soho is the centre of the London gay scene and many of the scene's best venues can be found on and around Old Compton St, London's gayest street. The following are some of the better gay bars and clubs in the neighbourhood. For full listings pick up a copy of free gay scene magazine Boyz (www.boyz.co.uk), available at any gay bar.

**Barcode** (Map p70; ☎ 7734 3342; www.bar-code.co.uk; 3-4 Archer St W1; ⏲ 4pm-1am Mon-Sat, to 11pm Sun; ⊖ Piccadilly Circus) This cruisy, fun spot is full of a diverse range of people enjoying a pint or two and the music from the in-house DJs.

**Candy Bar** (Map p70; ☎ 7494 4041; 4 Carlise St W1; ⏲ to midnight Sun-Thu, to 2am Fri & Sat; ⊖ Tottenham Court Rd) Busy most nights of the week, this is very much a girls space (one male guest per two women are allowed though) and this should definitely be your first port of call on the London lesbian scene.

**Friendly Society** (Map p70; ☎ 7434 3805; 79 Wardour St W1; ⏲ 6-11pm Mon-Thu, to midnight Fri & Sat, to 10.30pm Sun; ⊖ Piccadilly Circus) is one of Soho's friendliest and more relaxed gay bars, and thankfully one of the few fashionable queer drinking establishments that hasn't initiated a dubious door policy or membership scheme to ensure that only the rich and beautiful arrive.

**Heaven** (Map p66; ☎ 7930 2020; www.heavennightclub-london.com; Villiers St WC2; ⏲ 10.30pm-3am Mon, 10pm-3am Thu & Fri, 10pm-5am Sat; ⊖ Embankment or Charing Cross) One of London's oldest and most famous gay clubs, Heaven hosts G-A-Y on Saturday nights, London's busiest gay night.

**Ku Bar** (Map p70; ☎ 7437 4303; www.ku-bar.co.uk; 30 Lisle St WC2; ⏲ 5pm-midnight Sun-Thu, to 3am Fri & Sat; ⊖ Leicester Sq) Both venues of this Soho bar are very popular – the former pub on Lisle St is always rammed with teens warming up for the evening while the newer **Ku Bar Frith St** (Map p70; 25 Frith St; ⏲ until midnight Fri & Sat; ⊖ Leicester Sq) is popular with a slightly older, smarter crowd.

**Yard** (Map p70; ☎ 7437 2652; www.yardbar.co.uk; 57 Rupert St W1; ⏲ 1-11pm Mon-Sat, 1-10.30pm Sun; ⊖ Piccadilly Circus) This relaxed, mixed crowd pub is the perfect pre-club drinks venue. There are DJs upstairs in the Loft most nights as well as a friendly crowd in the eponymous courtyard downstairs.

to have drunk here often, while Dylan Thomas, Peter O'Toole and Francis Bacon all frequently ended up on the wooden floors. Come here to sip on Ricard, French wine or Kronenbourg and check out the quirky locals.

**JOHN SNOW** Map p70      Pub
☎ 7437 1344; 39 Broadwick St W1; ⊖ Oxford Circus or Piccadilly Circus

This is one of Soho's most popular pubs, as attested by the crowds inside, in winter, and outside, in spring and summer, on almost any day of the week. The interior is simple and quietly stylish, there's no music, just plenty of chat and good ale, lager, bitter and stout from independent British brewery Sam Smith's. You can also get organic beer and cider, plus, for the sweet-tooths, cherry beer.

**TWO FLOORS** Map p70         Bar

☎ 7439 1007; 3 Kingly St W1; ⌚ to midnight Fri & Sat, closed Sun; ⊖ Oxford Circus or Piccadilly Circus

It's amazing that Two Floors has kept its relaxed atmosphere when so many bars in Soho have been mobbed by drunken weekenders, but it might be to do with the fact that it's hard to notice from the outside, and this low profile has helped maintain its cool personality. The punters are young and bohemian, the bar staff equally so, and the music is usually uber-now.

## COVENT GARDEN & LEICESTER SQUARE

**CROSS KEYS** Map p66         Pub

☎ 7836 5185; 31 Endell St WC2; ⊖ Covent Garden

Covered in ivy and frequented by loyal locals who come here for pints of Young's and spicy fry-ups, the Cross Keys is Covent Garden's tourist-free local pub. Eccentric landlord Brian shows off his pop purchases as bar decorations (such as his £500 Elvis Presley napkin); brass pots, kettles and diving gear hang off the ceiling; and the punters range from bar props and fruit-machine (poker machine) devotees to Covent Garden professionals, all of whom spill onto the pavement and outside tables on summer days.

**LAMB & FLAG** Map p66         Pub

☎ 7497 9504; 33 Rose St WC2; ⊖ Covent Garden or Leicester Sq

Good pubs can be hard to come by in over-touristy Covent Garden, but the Lamb & Flag makes up for any character or soul the area has lost – the interior is more than 350 years old, with creaky wooden floors and winding stairs, there's live jazz on Sunday afternoons and, come sunshine or summer evenings, it's a miracle if you can approach the bar for all the people crowding outside.

**SALISBURY** Map p66         Pub

☎ 7836 5863; 90 St Martin's Lane WC2; ⌚ to midnight Fri & Sat; ⊖ Leicester Sq

Facing off the superchic St Martin's Lane Hotel, the Salisbury offers everything

Relaxing in Soho Sq (p61)

KARL BLACKWELL

:s opposite number doesn't: warmth, enturies of history, and a glorious, raditionally British pub interior. The alisbury is packed in the evenings by re- and post-theatre drinkers and, while : can be a little touristy, it's still a true ondon gem.

# ENTERTAINMENT & ACTIVITIES

## BAR RUMBA

Map p70  Clubbing
☎ 7287 2715; www.barrumba.co.uk; 36 Shaft-sbury Ave W1; ⏰ 10.30pm-3am Mon & Wed, 0.30pm-3am Tue, Thu & Fri, 9pm-5am Sat, 8pm-.30am Sun; ⊖ Piccadilly Circus
A small club just off Piccadilly with a loyal ollowing and fab DJs, specialising in hip nop, Latin, and drum and bass. It was elaunched in 2008, and has once again reasserted its appeal with drum and bass and hip-hop lovers. Movement is all about ungle, every other Thursday, while salsa and Latin urban dance parties are on at Barrio Latino on Tuesday.

## MADAME JO JO'S Map p70  Clubbing
☎ 7734 2473; www.madamejojos.com; 8 Brewer St W1; ⏰ 10.30pm-3am Wed-Fri, from 0.30pm Thu, cabaret 7-10pm & club 10pm-3am sat; ⊖ Leicester Sq or Piccadilly Circus
The renowned subterranean crimson cabaret bar and all its sleazy fun kitsch comes into its own with London Burlesque Social Club on the first Thursday of the month, and there's Kitsch Cabaret on Saturday.

## COMEDY STORE Map p70  Comedy
☎ 7344 4444; www.thecomedystore.co.uk; Hay-market House, 1a Oxendon St SW1; admission from £13-18; ⏰ Tue-Sun; ⊖ Piccadilly Circus
This was one of the first (and is still one of the best) comedy clubs in London. It

An array of theatre options in the West End (p80)

was established down the road in Soho in 1979. Wednesday and Sunday night's Comedy Store Players is the most famous improv outfit in town with the wonderful Josie Lawrence; while Thursday's, Friday's and Saturday's brilliant The Best in Stand Up features the best on London's comedy circuit.

## CURZON SOHO Map p70  Film
☎ info 7734 2255, bookings 0870 756 4620; www.curzoncinemas.com; 99 Shaftesbury Ave W1; ⊖ Leicester Sq or Piccadilly Circus
Curzon Soho is London's best cinema. It has fantastic programming with the best of British, European, world and American indie films; regular Q&As with directors; shorts and minifestivals; a Konditor & Cook

THE WEST END

ENTERTAINMENT & ACTIVITIES

RICHARD I'ANSC

All the world's a stage, especially here in Leicester Sq (p64)

cafe upstairs with tea and cakes to die for, and an ultracomfortable bar.

### RONNIE SCOTT'S Map p70            Jazz Clubs
☎ 7439 0747; www.ronniescotts.co.uk; 47 Frith St W1;  ⊖ Leicester Sq

Ronnie Scott originally opened his jazz club on Gerrard St in 1959 under a Chinese gambling den. The club moved to its current location six years later and became widely known as Britain's best jazz club. It was the only place the British public could listen to modern jazz – luminaries such as Miles Davis, Charlie Parker, Thelonious Monk, plus Ella Fitzgerald, Count Basie and Sarah Vaughan. The atmosphere is great, but talking during music is a big no-no. Door staff can be terribly rude and the service slow, but that's how it's always been. Gigs are nightly and usually last until 2am.

### DONMAR WAREHOUSE Map p66
Off-West End & Fringe
☎ 0870 060 6624; www.donmarwarehouse. com; 41 Earlham St WC2;  ⊖ Covent Garden

The small Donmar Warehouse, the 'thinking man's theatre' in London, stage interesting and inventive production such as Ibsen's *A Doll's House* with Gillian Anderson and *Hamlet* with the blue-eyed Jude Law.

### SOHO THEATRE
Map p70                            Off-West End & Fringe
☎ information 7478 0100, bookings 0870 429 6883; www.sohotheatre.com; 21 Dean St W1;  ⊖ Tottenham Court Rd

The Soho Theatre Company dedicates itself to the noble task of finding new writing talent, having put on hundreds of new plays since it started operating from its smart Dean St premises in 2000. This is the place to see where London drama is heading.

### LONDON COLISEUM
Map p66                                        Opera
☎ info 7632 8300, bookings 0870 145 0200; www.eno.org; Coliseum, St Martin's Lane WC2; admission £10-85;  ⊖ Leicester Sq or Charing Cross

he Coliseum is home to the English ational Opera (ENO), celebrated for making opera modern and relevant; all operas ere are sung in English. The building, uilt in 1904 and lovingly restored 100 ears later, is very impressive. Five hundred £10-and-under tickets are available or all weekday performances.

**ROYAL OPERA HOUSE** Map p66    Opera
☎ 7304 4000; www.royaloperahouse.org; Bow ▸ WC2; admission £7-195;  ⊖ Covent Garden
he Royal Opera House has been doing ts best to ward off the stuffy, exclusive mage it was accused of having some ears ago, and is attracting a younger, vealthy audience. Its £210 million redevelopment for the millennium gave the lassic a fantastic setting, and coming ere for a night is a sumptuous prospect.

# SHOPPING

Ve're not sure the West End's shopping needs introducing. This is the very area vhere you can spend your monthly salary on a pair of shoes or a handbag. Oxford it is heaven or hell, depending on your shopping stamina: it is *the* quintessential high street and brimming with an ocean of people most of the day. It can be a nightmare to tackle, so if you want to shop here, focus on what you want – you night find that strolling is more stressful han is warranted. Covent Garden is better thanks to its smaller-size High-Street outlets and little side-street boutiques. It throbs with shoppers on weekends, but s less hectic than Oxford St. Carnaby St and Newburgh Sts, and the independent boutique-laden Kingly Ct, are excellent for fashion – vintage and designer. Soho s superb for music stores, and Charing Cross Rd for books. You'll find excellent

electronics and computer shops along Tottenham Court Rd.

**BLACKWELL'S**
Map p70                                    Books
☎ 7292 5100; www.bookshop.blackwell.co.uk; 100 Charing Cross Rd WC2;  ⊖ Tottenham Court Rd
Once a specialist in academic titles, this shop has now branched out into travel and other general-interest books. It is still, however, the favourite haunt for those hunting for academic textbooks and is perfect for anyone starting a new course.

**FORBIDDEN PLANET MEGASTORE**
Map p66                                    Books
☎ 7836 4179; www.forbiddenplanet.com; 179 Shaftesbury Ave WC1;  ⊖ Covent Gardens or Tottenham Court Rd
A massive trove of comics, sci-fi, horror and fantasy literature, this is an absolute dream for anyone into manga comics or off-beat genre titles.

**FOYLE'S** Map p70                        Books
☎ 7437 5660; www.foyles.co.uk; 113-119 Charing Cross Rd WC2;  ⊖ Tottenham Court Rd
This is London's best and most legendary bookshop, where you can bet on finding even the most obscure of titles. The lovely, now extended cafe is on the 1st floor, and Ray's Jazz Shop is up on the 5th floor.

**STANFORD'S** Map p66                     Books
☎ 7836 1321; www.stanfords.co.uk; 12-14 Long Acre WC2;  ⊖ Leicester Sq or Covent Garden
As a 150-year-old seller of maps, guides and literature, the grand daddy of travel bookshops is a destination in its own right. Ernest Shackleton, David Livingstone, Michael Palin and even Brad Pitt have all popped in here.

**WATERSTONE'S** Map p70     Books
☎ 7851 2400; www.waterstones.co.uk; 203-206 Piccadilly W1; ⊖ Piccadilly Circus
The chain's megastore is the largest bookshop in Europe, boasting knowledgeable staff and regular author readings. This is London's biggest Waterstone's, with four floors of titles, a cafe in the basement and a nice rooftop bar.

**APPLE STORE** Map p70     Computers
☎ 7153 9000; www.apple.com/uk/retail/regent street; 235 Regent St W1; ⏱ 10am-9pm Mon-Sat, noon-6pm Sun; ⊖ Oxford Circus
Mac geeks of the world unite! Here's your temple, your winter fireplace, so come and warm your faces on the soft glow emanating from MacBooks and iPods,

Friday night crowd in Leicester Sq (p64)

laptops and desktops, inside this whit and airy two-storey emporium.

**MOLTON BROWN** Map p66     Cosmeti
☎ 7240 8383; www.moltonbrown.co.uk; 18 Russell St WC2; ⏱ 10am-7pm Mon-Fri, to 6pm Sat, noon-6pm Sun; ⊖ Covent Garden
A fabulously fragrant British natura beauty range, Molton Brown is *the* choic for boutique hotel and posh restaurar bathrooms. Its skin-care products offe plenty of pampering for men and womer

**FORTNUM & MASON**
Map p70     Department Stor
☎ 7734 8040; www.fortnumandmason.co.uk; 181 Piccadilly W1; ⏱ 10am-6.30pm Mon-Sat, noon-6pm Sun; ⊖ Piccadilly Circus
London's oldest department store ce ebrated its 300th birthday in 2007 by nc yielding to modern times (its staff are sti dressed in old-fashioned tailcoats) an keeping its glam food hall supplied wit its famed food hampers, cut marmalade speciality teas and so on.

**LIBERTY** Map p70     Department Stor
☎ 7734 1234; www.liberty.co.uk; 210-220 Regent St W1; ⏱ 10am-7pm Mon-Sat, to 8pm Thu, noon-6pm Sun; ⊖ Oxford Circus
An irresistible blend of contemporar styles in an old-fashioned mock-Tudor at mosphere, Liberty has a huge cosmetic department and an accessories floor, alon with a breathtaking lingerie section. A clas sic London souvenir is a Liberty fabric print

**PAUL SMITH**
Map p66     Fashion & Designe
☎ 7379 7133; www.paulsmith.co.uk; 40-44 Floral St WC2; ⏱ 10am-6.30pm Mon-Sat, to 7pm Thu, noon-5pm Sun; ⊖ Covent Garden
Paul Smith represents the best of Britist classic with innovative twists. Super stylish menswear, suits and tailored shirt are all laid out on open shelves in thi

RICHARD I'ANSON

**Street art in Covent Garden (p68)**

walk-in closet of a shop. Smith also does womenswear.

## TOPSHOP & TOPMAN

Map p70        Fashion & Designer
☎ 7636 7700; www.topshop.co.uk; 36-38 Great
Castle St W1; ☺ 9am-8pm Mon-Sat, to 9pm Thu,
noon-6pm Sun; ⊖ Oxford Circus
Topshop is the it-store when it comes
to high-street shopping. Encapsulating
London's supreme skill at bringing catwalk fashion to the youth market afford-
ably and quickly, it constantly innovates
by working with young designers and
celebrities.

## NEAL'S YARD DAIRY

Map p66        Food & Drink
☎ 7240 5700; 17 Shorts Gardens WC2; ☺ 9am-
7pm Mon-Sat; ⊖ Covent Garden
A fabulous, smelly cheese house that
would fit in rural England, this place is
proof that the British can do just as well
as the French when it comes to big rolls of
ripe cheese. There are more than 70 varieties that the shopkeepers will let you taste,
including independent farmhouse brands.

## ARAM

Map p66        Homewares
☎ 7557 7557; www.aram.co.uk; 110 Drury
Lane WC2; ☺ 10am-6pm Mon-Sat, to 7pm Thu;
⊖ Covent Garden or Holborn
Despite the fact that most of the furniture stocked by Aram is unaffordable to
ordinary mortals, admiring the designer
pieces in this fantastic shop is an experience to be cherished. Among the many
accomplished designers, Aram stocks
pieces by Alvar Aalto, Eileen Grey, Eames,
Le Corbusier and Arne Jacobsen.

## AGENT PROVOCATEUR

Map p70        Lingerie
☎ 7439 0229; www.agentprovocateur.com; 6
Broadwick St W1; ☺ 11am-7pm Mon-Sat, to
8pm Thu, noon-5pm Sun; ⊖ Oxford Circus
For women's lingerie that is to be worn
and seen, and certainly *not* hidden, pull
up to Joseph (son of Vivienne Westwood)
Corre's wonderful Agent Provocateur. Its
sexy and saucy corsets, bras and nighties

THE WEST END

for all shapes and sizes exude confident and positive sexuality.

**HAMLEYS** Map p70                    Toys
☎ 0870 333 2455, 7494 2000; www.hamleys.
com; 188-196 Regent St W1; ☒ 10am-8pm Mon-
Sat, noon-6pm Sun; ⊖ Oxford Circus
Reportedly the largest toy store in the world and certainly the most famous,

Hamleys is a layer cake of plaything Computer games are in the basemen the latest playground trends at groun level. Science kits are on the 1st floo preschool toys on the 2nd, girls' play things on the 3rd and model cars o the 4th, while the whole confection topped off with Lego world and its ca on the 5th.

SHOPPING

# WESTMINSTER & MAYFAIR

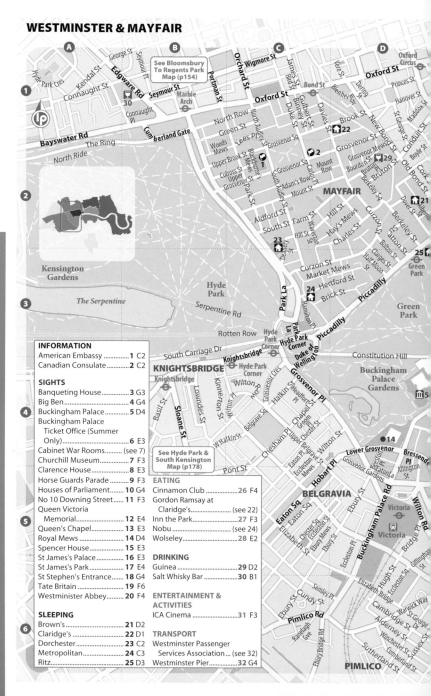

See Bloomsbury To Regents Park Map (p154)

See Hyde Park & South Kensington Map (p178)

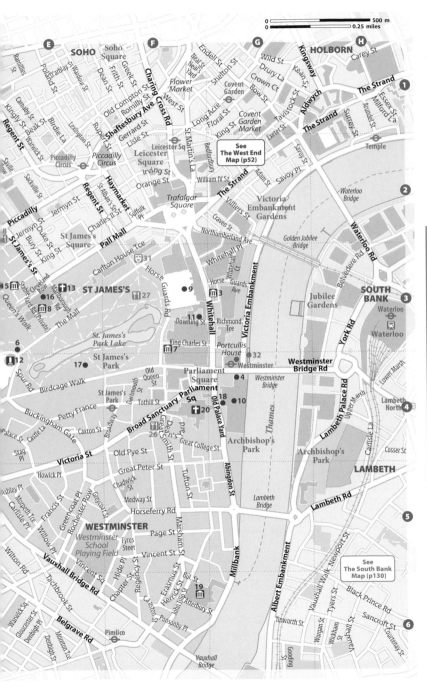

0     500 m
0     0.25 miles

**E**    **F**    **G**    **H**

SOHO
Soho Square
HOLBORN

See The West End Map (p52)

Trafalgar Square

Victoria Embankment Gardens

Golden Jubilee Bridge

Waterloo Bridge

SOUTH BANK

Waterloo

Jubilee Gardens

St James's Park Lake

St James's Park

Parliament Square

Westminster

Westminster Bridge Rd

Westminster Bridge

Thames

Archbishop's Park

Archbishop's Park

LAMBETH

Lambeth Bridge

WESTMINSTER
Westminster School Playing Field

See The South Bank Map (p130)

Pimlico

Vauxhall Bridge

PICCADILLY

ST JAMES'S

St James's Square

Pall Mall

Leicester Square

Piccadilly Circus

Regent St

Haymarket

Buckingham Gate

Victoria St

Belgrave Rd

**1**   **2**   **3**   **4**   **5**   **6**   **8**

# HIGHLIGHTS

1

## ↘ PALACE OF WESTMINSTER

Despite the fact that very few visitors to London actually go inside (though it's perfectly possible to do so if you apply in advance to a British Embassy for tickets), seeing the sublime **Houses of Parliament** (p93) overlooking the Thames in their Gothic splendour with impressive Big Ben towering above is one of the most unforgettable sights in London, if not the world.

2

## ↘ WESTMINSTER ABBEY

The surprisingly small **Westminster Abbey** (p91) has been witness to more historical events than most major cities. Indeed, this was where William the Conqueror was crowned in 1066 after the Battle of Hastings, and has been the place of coronation of almost every other monarch since, as well as their final resting place and that of such luminaries as Chaucer, Dickens, Hardy and Lawrence Olivier.

WESTMINSTER & MAYFAIR

HIGHLIGHTS

## ⬆ TATE BRITAIN

Do not pass over this superb museum simply because you're going to the Tate Modern. The Tate Britain (p95) is a totally different experience, and one to be savoured at that. Here you'll find a treasure trove of British art from the past four centuries, including Hogarth, Turner, Gainsborough and Constable. Savour this place!

## ⬆ BUCKINGHAM PALACE

Even if you don't go inside (and we freely admit that it's very pricey and only accessible during the summer months when the Queen is on her summer holidays in Scotland – but still worth it), you can't miss checking out Buckingham Palace (p94), the London residence of the monarch and the nexus of the royal family.

## ⬆ CHANGING OF THE GUARD

The ultimate free spectacle for anyone curious about the bizarre ceremony and pomp of British royalty, the Changing of the Guard (p96) happens most mornings in the forecourt of Buckingham Palace. Come early to get a good view – the crowds can be huge, though most people agree that it's well worth it for such arcane ritual.

1 DAVID TOMLINSON; 2 DOUG MCKINLAY; 3 CHRISTINE OSBORNE; 4 ADINA TOVY AMSEL; 5 MANFRED GOTTSCHALK

1 Houses of Parliament (p93); 2 Westminster Abbey (p91); 3 Tate Britain (p95); 4 Buckingham Palace (p94); 5 Changing of the Guard (p96)

# BEST...

## ⬎ THINGS FOR FREE

- **House of Commons** (p94) Apply for tickets in advance or queue to watch a debate here.
- **Changing of the Guard** (p96) See this unrivalled display of ceremony outside Buckingham Palace.
- **Tate Britain** (p95) Entrance to the permanent collection is always free.
- **Feed the ducks in St James's Park** (p96) You may need to buy your own bread, though.

## ⬎ ROYALTY SPOTTING

- **Buckingham Palace** (p94) Stand here long enough and you may even see the Queen herself.
- **Ritz** (p98) The royal family's supposed home away from home.
- **St James's Palace** (p96) London home to Princess Anne.
- **Clarence House** (p97) London home to Prince Charles, Camilla, Prince William and Prince Harry.

## ⬎ GLAMOROUS HANGOUTS

- **Claridges** (p99) The bar at London's top hotel is *the* place for divas to hold court.
- **Buckingham Palace** (p94) Unlikely you'll get an invite, but it's hard to beat this address if you do.
- **Nobu** (p99) This Japanese restaurant and notorious celebrity haunt is the place to dine in style.
- **Metropolitan** (p98) After Nobu, head to the Met Bar for a cocktail with the glitterati.

## ⬎ POLITICAL SIGHTS

- **Number 10 Downing St** (p98) The ultimate political sight in London.
- **Palace of Westminster** (p93) Home to the Houses of Commons and Lords.
- **Cinnamon Club** (p99) The unofficial 'canteen' for the House of Commons, you may well spot cabinet ministers having a curry here.

LEFT: DOUG MCKINLAY; RIGHT: LEE FOSTER

Left: St James's Palace (p96); Right: St James's Park (p96)

# DISCOVER WESTMINSTER & MAYFAIR

This is stately, aristocratic and political London at its finest – the home to powerbrokers, royalty and an elite international crowd, and an ideal place to discover the London of postcards – palaces, parks, uniformed guards, grand avenues and genteel squares are the name of the game here.

Westminster is south of Trafalgar Sq and is the nerve centre of British politics, housing the Palace of Westminster, the mother of all parliaments, and the surprisingly modest prime ministerial residence of Number 10 Downing St. Mayfair is west of Regent St and is where high society congregates in mammoth private clubs, dines out at world-famous restaurants and resides quietly in astonishingly large mansions. Between the two are magnificent St James's Park and Green Park, surrounding Buckingham Palace, the London home of the British monarch, and a must-see for any London visitor, even if you choose not to pay the entry fee during the summer months and just watch the free spectacle of the changing of the guard instead.

# SIGHTS

## WESTMINSTER

### WESTMINSTER ABBEY

☎ 7222 5152; www.westminster-abbey.org; Dean's Yard SW1; adult/under 11yr/11-17yr/ concession £15/free/6/12; ⏲ 9.30am-3.45pm Mon-Fri, to 6pm Wed, to 1.45pm Sat, last entry 1hr before closing; ⊖ Westminster; ♿

Westminster Abbey is such an important commemoration site for both the British royalty and the nation's political and artistic idols, it's difficult to overstress its symbolic value or imagine its equivalent anywhere else in the world. With the exception of Edward V and Edward VIII, every English sovereign has been crowned here since William the Conqueror in 1066, and most of the monarchs from Henry III (died 1272) to George II (died 1760) were also buried here.

The abbey is a magnificent sight. Though a mixture of architectural styles, it is considered the finest example of Early English Gothic (1180–1280). The original church was built in the 11th century by King (later St) Edward the Confessor, who is buried in the chapel behind the main altar. Henry III (r 1216–72) began work on the new building but didn't complete it; the French Gothic nave was finished in 1388. Henry VII's huge and magnificent chapel was added in 1519. Unlike St Paul's, Westminster Abbey has never been a cathedral – it is what is called a 'royal peculiar' and is administered directly by the Crown.

Immediately past the barrier through the north door is what's known as Statesmen's Aisle, where politicians and eminent public figures are commemorated mostly by staggeringly large marble statues. The Whig and Tory prime ministers who dominated late Victorian politics, Gladstone (who is buried here) and Disraeli (who is not), have their monuments uncomfortably close to one another.

At the eastern end of the sanctuary, opposite the entrance to the Henry VII

Chapel, is the rather ordinary-looking Coronation Chair, upon which almost every monarch since the late 13th century is said to have been crowned. Up the steps in front of you and to your left is the narrow Queen Elizabeth Chapel, where Elizabeth I and her half-sister 'Bloody Mary' share an elaborate tomb.

The Henry VII Chapel, in the easternmost part of the abbey, has spectacular circular vaulting on the ceiling. Behind the chapel's altar is the elaborate sarcophagus of Henry VII and his queen, Elizabeth of York.

Beyond the chapel's altar is the Royal Air Force (RAF) Chapel, with a stained-glass window commemorating the force's finest hour, the Battle of Britain. Next to it, a plaque marks the spot where Oliver Cromwell's body lay for two years until the Restoration, when it was disinterred, hanged and beheaded. The bodies believed to be those of the two child princes (allegedly) murdered in the Tower of London in 1483 are also buried here. The chapel's southern aisle contains the tomb of Mary Queen of Scots, beheaded on the orders of her cousin Elizabeth and with the acquiescence of her son, the future James I.

The Chapel of St Edward the Confessor, the most sacred spot in the abbey, lies just east of the sanctuary and behind the high altar; access may be restricted to protect the 13th-century floor. St Edward was the founder of the abbey and the original building was consecrated a few weeks before his death. His tomb was slightly altered after the original was destroyed during the Reformation.

The south transept contains Poets' Corner, where many of England's finest writers are buried and/or commemorated; a memorial here is the highest honour the Queen can bestow. Just north is the Lantern, the heart of the abbey, where coronations take place. If you face eastwards while standing in the centre, the sanctuary is in front of you. George Gilbert Scott designed the ornate high altar in 1897. Behind you, Edward Blore's

Westminster Abbey (p91)

WILL ROBB

chancel, dating from the mid-19th century, is a breathtaking structure of gold, blue and red Victorian Gothic. Where monks once worshipped, boys from the Choir School and lay vicars now sing the daily services.

The entrance to the **Cloister** is 13th century, while the cloister itself dates from the 14th. Eastwards down a passageway off the Cloister are three museums run by English Heritage. The octagonal **Chapter House** (🕙 9.30am-5pm Apr-Sep, 10am-5pm Oct, 10am-4pm Nov-Mar) has one of Europe's best-preserved medieval tile floors and retains traces of religious murals. It was used as a meeting place by the House of Commons in the second half of the 14th century. To the right of the entrance to Chapel House is what is claimed to be the oldest door in the UK – it's been there 950 years. The adjacent **Pyx Chamber** (🕙 10am-4.30pm) is one of the few remaining relics of the original abbey and contains the abbey's treasures and liturgical objects. The **Abbey Museum** (🕙 10.30am-4pm) exhibits the death masks of generations of royalty, wax effigies representing Charles II and William III (who is on a stool to make him as tall as his wife Mary), as well as armour and stained glass.

On the western side of the cloister is **Scientists' Corner**, where you will find **Sir Isaac Newton's tomb**; a nearby section of the northern aisle of the nave is known as **Musicians' Aisle**.

The two towers above the west door are the ones through which you exit. These were designed by Nicholas Hawksmoor and completed in 1745. Just above the door, perched in 15th-century niches, are the latest sacred additions to the abbey: 10 stone statues of international 20th-century martyrs. These were unveiled in 1998 and they include the likes of Martin Luther King and the Polish priest St Maximilian Kolbe, who was murdered by the Nazis at Auschwitz.

The 90-minute **guided tours** (☎ 7222 7110; tours £3) leave several times during the day (Monday to Saturday). One of the best ways to visit the abbey is to attend a service, particularly evensong (5pm weekdays, 3pm at weekends). Sunday Eucharist is at 11am.

## HOUSES OF PARLIAMENT
☎ 7219 4272; www.parliament.uk; St Stephen's Entrance, St Margaret St SW1; admission free; 🕙 during Parliamentary sessions 2.30-10.30pm Mon, 11.30am-7pm Tue & Wed, 11.30am-6.30pm Thu, 9.30am-3pm Fri; 🚇 Westminster; ♿

The House of Commons and House of Lords are housed here in the sumptuous **Palace of Westminster**. Charles Barry, assisted by interior designer Augustus Pugin, built it between 1840 and 1860, when the extravagant neo-Gothic style was all the rage. The most famous feature outside the palace is the Clock Tower, commonly known as **Big Ben**. Ben is the bell hanging inside and is named after Benjamin Hall, the commissioner of works when the tower was completed in 1858. If you're very keen (and a UK resident) you can apply in writing for a free tour of the Clock Tower (see the website). Thirteen-tonne Ben has rung in the New Year since 1924, and the clock gets its hands and face washed by abseiling cleaners once every five years. The best view of the whole complex is from the eastern side of Lambeth Bridge. At the opposite end of the building is **Victoria Tower**, completed in 1860.

The House of Commons is where Members of Parliament (MPs) meet to propose and discuss new legislation, and to grill the prime minister and other ministers. The best time to watch a debate is during Prime Minister's Question Time, for which you will have to book advance tickets through your MP or local British embassy.

The layout of the Commons Chamber is based on that of St Stephen's Chapel in the original Palace of Westminster. The current chamber, designed by Giles Gilbert Scott, replaced the earlier one destroyed by a 1941 bomb. Although the Commons is a national assembly of 646 MPs, the chamber has seating for only 437. Government members sit to the right of the Speaker and Opposition members to the left.

When Parliament is in session, visitors are admitted to the **House of Commons Visitors' Gallery** via **St Stephen's Entrance**. Expect to queue for an hour or two if you haven't already organised a ticket. Parliamentary recesses last for three months over the summer and a couple of weeks over Easter and Christmas, so it's best to ring in advance. To find out what's being debated on a particular day, check the notice board beside the entrance, or look in the *Daily Telegraph* or the freebie *Metro* newspaper under 'Today in Parliament', though it has to be said that the debates leave a lot to be desired both in terms of attendance and enthusiasm. Bags and cameras must be checked at a cloakroom before you enter the gallery and no large suitcases or backpacks are allowed through the airport-style security gate.

When Parliament is in recess, there are 75-minute **guided summer tours** ( ☎ 0870 906 3773; St Stephen's Entrance, St Margaret St; adult/child/concession £12/5/8) of both chambers and other historic buildings. Times change, so telephone or check www.parliament.uk for latest details.

# ST JAMES'S
## BUCKINGHAM PALACE
☎ 7766 7300, for disabled access 7766 7324; www.royalcollection.org.uk; Buckingham Palace Rd SW1; adult/child/concession/family £15.50/8.75/14/39.75; ⏲ 9.30am-4.30pm 28 Jul-25 Sep, timed ticket with admission every 15min; ⊖ St James's Park, Victoria or Green Park; ♿

Built in 1705 as Buckingham House for the duke of the same name, this palace has been the royal family's London lodgings since 1837, when St James' Palace was judged too old-fashioned and insufficiently impressive. It is dominated by the 25m-high **Queen Victoria Memorial** at the end of The Mall. Tickets for the palace are on sale from the **Ticket Office** ( ⏲ 9.15am to 5pm, summer only) at the Visitor Entrance, Buckingham Palace Rd.

After a series of crises and embarrassing revelations in the early 1990s, it was decided to swing open the doors of Buck House to the public for the first time. Well, to 19 of the 661 rooms, at least. And only during August and September, when HRH is holidaying in Scotland.

The 'working rooms' are stripped down each summer for the arrival of the commoners, and the usual carpet is replaced with industrial-strength rugs, so the rooms don't look all that lavish. The tour starts in the Guard Room (too small for the Ceremonial Guard, who actually use adjoining quarters); allows a peek inside the State Dining Room (all red damask and Regency furnishings); then moves on to the Blue Drawing Room, with a gorgeous fluted ceiling by John Nash; to the White Drawing Room, where foreign ambassadors are received; and to the Ballroom, where official receptions and state banquets are held. The Throne Room is pretty hilarious with kitschy his-and-hers pink

CHRISTINE OSBORNE

Tate Britain

## ↘ TATE BRITAIN

You'd think that Tate Britain might have suffered since its lavish, sexy sibling, **Tate Modern** (p140), took half its collection and all of the limelight upriver when it opened in 2000, but on the contrary, things have worked out perfectly for both galleries. The venerable Tate Britain, built in 1897, stretched out splendidly to fill the increased space with its definitive collection of British art from the 16th to the late 20th centuries, while the Modern sister devoted its space to, well, modern art.

The permanent galleries are broadly chronological in order, and you can expect to see some of the most important works by artists such as Constable and Gainsborough – who have entire galleries devoted to them – and Hogarth, Reynolds, Stubbs, Blake and Henry Moore, among others. Adjoining the main building is the Clore Gallery, which houses the superb JMW Turner, including the two recovered classics *Shade and Darkness* and *Light and Colour*, which were nicked in 1994 and found nine years later.

There are several free one-hour **thematic tours** each day, mostly on the hour (last tour at 3pm), along with free 15-minute talks on paintings, painters and styles at 1.15pm Tuesday to Thursday in the Rotunda. **Audio-guide tours** (adult/ concession £3.50/3) for the collection are available. A good time to visit the gallery is Late at Tate night, on the first Friday of every month, when the gallery stays open until 10pm. The best way to see both Tates and have a fabulous art day is to catch the boat that connects the two galleries; see p141.

**Things you need to know:** ☎ 7887 8000, 7887 8888; www.tate.org.uk; Millbank SW1; admission free, prices vary for temporary exhibitions; ⏰ 10am-5.50pm; ⊖ Pimlico; ♿

chairs initialled 'ER' and 'P', sitting smugly under what looks like a theatre arch.

The most interesting part of the tour is the 76.5m-long Picture Gallery, featur-

ing splendid works by artists such as Van Dyck, Rembrandt, Canaletto, Poussin, Canova and Vermeer, although the likes of these and much more are yours for free at the National Gallery. Wandering the gardens is another highlight here – it's bound to give you a real royal feeling.

## CHANGING OF THE GUARD

☎ 7766 7300; Buckingham Palace, Buckingham Palace Rd SW1; ⏰ 11.30am daily Apr-Jul & alternate days, weather permitting Aug-Mar; ⊖ St James's Park or Victoria

This is a London 'must see' – if you actually get to see anything from among the crowds. The old guard (Foot Guards of the Household Regiment) comes off duty to be replaced by the new guard on the forecourt of Buckingham Palace, and tourists gape – sometimes from behind as many as 10 people – at the bright red uniforms and bearskin hats of shouting and marching soldiers for just over half an hour.

## ST JAMES'S PARK

☎ 7930 1793; The Mall SW1; ⏰ 5am-dusk; ⊖ St James's Park

This is one of the smallest but most gorgeous of London's parks. It has brilliant views of the London Eye, Westminster, St James's Palace, Carlton Terrace and Horse Guards Parade, and the view of Buckingham Palace from the footbridge spanning St James's Park Lake is the best you'll find (get those cameras out). The central lake is full of different types of ducks, geese, swans and general fowl, and its southern side's rocks serve as a rest stop for pelicans (fed at 3pm daily). Some of the technicolour flowerbeds were modelled on John Nash's original 'floriferous' beds of mixed shrubs, flowers and trees, and old-aged squirrel-feeders congregate under the trees daily, with bags of nuts and bread. Spring and summer days see Londoners and tourists alike sunbathing, picnicking and generally enjoying the sunshine, though sometimes in annoyingly large numbers.

## ST JAMES'S PALACE

Cleveland Row SW1; closed to the public; ⊖ Green Park

The striking Tudor gatehouse of St James' Palace, the only surviving part of a build ing initiated by the palace-mad Henr VIII in 1530, is best approached from S James's St to the north of the park. Thi was the official residence of kings an queens for more than three centurie: Foreign ambassadors are still formall accredited to the Court of St James, a though the tea and biscuits are actuall served at Buckingham Palace. Princes Diana, who hated this place, lived her until her divorce from Charles in 199∈ when she moved to Kensington Palace.

# WHITEHALL

## CHURCHILL MUSEUM & CABINET WAR ROOMS

☎ 7930 6961; www.iwm.org.uk; Clive Steps, King Charles St SW1; adult/under 16yr/senior & student £13/free/10.40; ⏰ 9.30am-6pm, last admission 5pm; ⊖ Charing Cross or Westminster; ♿

Down in the bunker where Prime Ministe Winston Churchill, his cabinet and gener als met during WWII, £6 million has beer spent on a huge exhibition devoted t 'the greatest Briton'. This whizz-bang multimedia Churchill Museum joins th highly evocative Cabinet War Rooms where chiefs of staff slept, ate and plotted Hitler's downfall, blissfully believing they were protected from Luftwaffe bombs by the 3m slab of concrete overhead. (Turn: out it would have crumpled like paper hac the area taken a hit.) Together, these two sections make you forget the Churchill who was a maverick and lousy peacetime politician, and drive home how much the cigar-chewing, wartime PM was a case o right man, right time.

DOUG MCKINLAY

**Spencer House**

## ↘ IF YOU LIKE...

If you liked Buckingham Palace (p94) then we think you'll like these other grand aristocratic mansions and royal sights:

- **Clarence House** Famous as the long-time residence of the late Queen Mother, Clarence House is now London home to Prince Charles and the Duchess of Cornwall. It's open to visitors in the summer months.
- **Spencer House** Ancestral home to Princess Diana, this grand Mayfair house is now owned by the Rothschild family who have restored it to its original glory.
- **Royal Mews** Come and see the royal stables, as well as the incredibly opulent royal vehicles. As garages go, this has to be one of the world's most luxurious.
- **Queen's Chapel** This 17th century church is where royals lie in state before their burial. Most famously this is where thousands came to pay their last respects to Princess Diana.
- **Banqueting House** The site of Charles I's execution after the Civil War, this is the only surviving part of the former Whitehall Palace that burned down in 1698. It's well worth going inside to see the stunning ceiling panels, painted by Rubens and depicting the 'divine right' of kings.

The Churchill Museum contains all sorts of posters, trivia and personal effects, from the man's cigars to a 'British bulldog' vase in his image, and from his formal Privy Council uniform to his shockingly tasteless red velvet 'romper' outfit.

In stark contrast, the old Cabinet War Rooms have been left much as they were when the lights were turned off on VJ Day in August 1945 and everyone headed off for a well-earned drink. The room where the Cabinet held more than 100 meetings, the Telegraph Room with a hotline to Roosevelt, the cramped typing pool, the converted broom cupboard that was Churchill's office and scores of bedrooms have all been preserved.

The free audioguide is very informative and entertaining and features plenty of anecdotes, including some from people who worked here in the nerve centre of Britain's war effort – and weren't even allowed by their irritable boss to relieve the tension by whistling.

### NO 10 DOWNING STREET

www.number10.gov.uk; 10 Downing St SW1; ⊖ Westminster or Charing Cross

This has been the official office of British leaders since 1732, when George II presented No 10 to Robert Walpole, and since refurbishment in 1902 it's also been the PM's official London residence. As Margaret Thatcher, a grocer's daughter, famously put it, the PM 'lives above the shop' here.

For such a famous address, however, No 10 is a small-looking building on a plain-looking street, hardly warranting comparison to the White House, for example. A stoic bobby stands guard outside, but you can't get too close; the street was cordoned off with a rather large iron gate during Margaret Thatcher's times.

# SLEEPING
## MAYFAIR
### RITZ
Hotel £££

☎ 7493 8181; www.theritzlondon.com; 150 Piccadilly W1; s/d from £400/500, ste from £730; ⊖ Green Park; ❀

What can you say about a hotel that has lent its name to the English lexicon? Arguably London's most celebrated hotel, this 136-room caravanserai has a spectacular position overlooking Green Park and is supposedly the royal family's 'home away from home'. The Long Gallery and Palm Court restaurant have Louis XVI themes; book weeks ahead if you want to

sample afternoon tea (£37). A planned extension on Arlington St just east will add 45 rooms.

### METROPOLITAN
Hotel ££

☎ 7647 1000; www.metropolitan.co.uk; 19 Old Park Lane W1; r £375-475, ste £650-3200; ⊖ Hyde Park Corner; ❀ ♿

The 155-room Metropolitan is another minimalist hotel – 'stripped of nonessentials' (as they say) and decorated in shades of cream and burlwood. It attracts a super trendy, well-heeled crowd (more rock star than royal, really). The hotel's Japanese restaurant, **Nobu** (p99), is outstanding.

### BROWN'S
Hotel ££

☎ 7493 6020; www.brownshotel.com; 30 Albemarle St W1; s & d from £340, ste from £800; ⊖ Green Park; ❀ ♿

A stunner of a five-star number, this 117-room hotel was created in 1837 from 11 houses joined together. Some traditional features retained from an earlier refurbishment of the public areas include stained glass windows, Edwardian oak panelling, working fireplaces and gilt mirrors. The 117 updated rooms have soft colours and works by young English artists.

### DORCHESTER
Hotel ££

☎ 7629 8888; www.dorchesterhotel.com; Park Lane W1; s/d from £400/570, ste from £710, breakfast £25; ⊖ Hyde Park Corner; ❀ ♿

This opulent *tour de force* has been the hotel of choice for movie stars, fashionistas and those with a wallop of cash to spend and an image to cultivate since it opened for business in 1931. The lobby is possibly the most lavish in London and the enormous ballroom with its sparkling mirrored walls remains one of the most grand today. In the 250 guestrooms a mixture of antique and individual furniture, four-poster beds, chaise lounges nd roaring fireplaces evoke an English country-house feel.

### CLARIDGE'S Hotel £££

☎ 7629 8860; www.claridges.co.uk; 55 Brook St W1; r from £500, ste from £740, breakfast £21-8; ⊖ Bond St; ⊠

Claridge's, with 203 rooms, is one of the greatest of London's five-star hotels, a cherished reminder of a bygone era. Many of the art deco features of the public areas and suites were designed in the late 1920s, and some of the 1930s-vintage furniture once graced the staterooms of the decommissioned SS *Normandie*. Celebrity chef Gordon Ramsay reigns over the kitchen (see p100).

# EATING

## WESTMINSTER

### CINNAMON CLUB Indian £££

☎ 7222 2555; www.cinnamonclub.com; Old Westminster Library, 30 Great Smith St SW1; mains £11-32; ⊗ closed lunch Sat & all day Sun; ⊖ St James's Park

Domed skylights, high ceilings, parquet flooring and a book-lined mezzanine – this just had to be a library in a former life – and the hushed, efficient staff only add to the illusion. The atmosphere is colonial club and the food modern – or perhaps palace – Indian.

## MAYFAIR

### NOBU Japanese £££

☎ 7447 4747; www.noburestaurants.com; 1st fl, Metropolitan Hotel, 19 Old Park Lane W1; mains £7-33, set lunches/dinners from £50/70; ⊖ Hyde Park Corner

You'll have to book a month in advance to eat here, but you'll get to chew and view the greatest celebrity restaurant magnet in town. It's minimalist in decor, anonymously efficient in service, and out of this

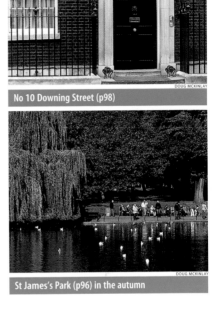

No 10 Downing Street (p98)

DOUG MCKINLAY

St James's Park (p96) in the autumn

DOUG MCKINLAY

world when it comes to exquisitely prepared and presented sushi and sashimi. Both the black cod with miso and salmon kelp roll are divine.

### INN THE PARK British ££

☎ 7451 9999; www.innthepark.com; St James's Park SW1; mains £10-18; ⊗ 8am-11pm Sun-Thu, 9am-11pm Fri & Sat; ⊖ Trafalgar Sq

This stunning wooden cafe and restaurant in **St James's Park** (p96) is run by the Irish wonder that is Oliver Peyton and offers cakes and tea as well as substantial and quality British food. The recent addition of extra seating under the trees for the cafe part and the new roof terrace are perfect, but if you're up for a special dining experience, come here for dinner, when the park is quiet and slightly illuminated.

### GORDON RAMSAY AT CLARIDGE'S
Modern British £££

☎ 7499 0099, 7592 1373; www.gordonramsay.com; 55 Brook St W1; 3-course set lunch/dinner £30/70; ⊖ Bond St

This match made in heaven – London's most celebrated chef in arguably its grandest hotel – will make you weak at the knees. A meal in the gorgeous art deco dining room is a special occasion indeed; consider the six-course tasting menu (£80).

### WOLSELEY          Modern European £££
☎ 7499 6996; www.thewolseley.com; 160 Piccadilly W1; mains £10-36; ☽ 7am-midnight Mon-Fri, 8am-midnight Sat, 8am-11pm Sun; ⊖ Green Park

This erstwhile Bentley car showroom has been transformed into an opulent Viennese-style brasserie, with golden chandeliers and stunning black-and-white tiled floors, and it remains a great place for spotting celebrities. Daily specials are £15.75.

# DRINKING
## MAYFAIR
### GUINEA          Pub
☎ 7409 1728; 30 Bruton Pl W1; ⊖ Green Park or Bond St

Top-quality Young's beers, famous autographs on the toilet walls and the whiff of money define this quiet and out-of-the-way pub in London's most exclusive neighbourhood, Mayfair. There are very few places to sit, though, and it sometimes feels little more than a waiting room for the rear restaurant (renowned for its pies).

### SALT WHISKY BAR          Ba
☎ 7402 1155; www.saltbar.com; 82 Seymour St W1; ☽ to 1am Mon-Sat, to 12.30am Sun; ⊖ Marble Arch

Two hundred whiskies and bourbon and a sleek, dark-wood interior make this friendly bar and comfortable lounge a fab place for drinking. Staff are knowledgeable and keen to share their tips with customers.

# ENTERTAINMENT & ACTIVITIES
### ICA CINEMA          Film
☎ information 7930 6393, bookings 7930 3647; www.ica.org.uk; Nash House, The Mall SW1; ⊖ Charing Cross or Piccadilly Circus

The Institute of Contemporary Arts (ICA) is a treasure for all lovers of indie cinema – its program always has material no-one else is showing, such as the latest American independents, odd seasons, all-night screenings and rare documentaries. The two screens are quite small, but the seats are comfortable enough.

# THE CITY

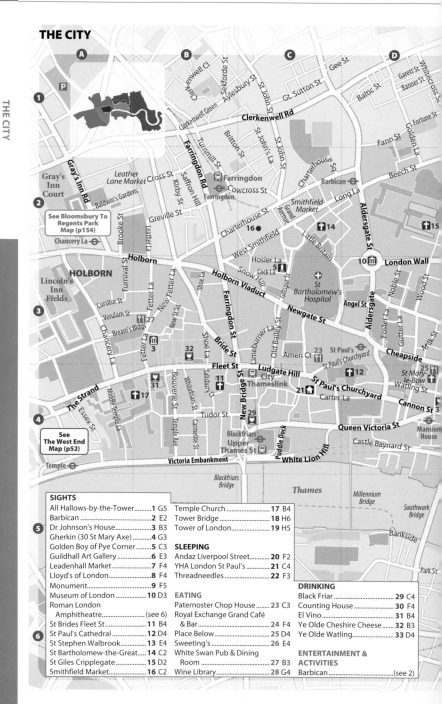

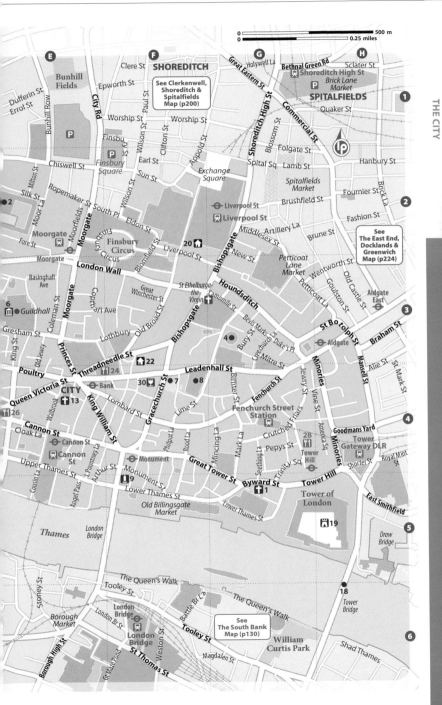

# THE CITY HIGHLIGHTS

## 1 THE TOWER OF LONDON

### BY JOHN KEOHANE, CHIEF YEOMAN WARDER AT THE TOWER OF LONDON

The Yeomen Warders (or Beefeaters as we're often known) have been a part of the Tower's history since 1485. Our official role is to guard the Tower and the Crown Jewels. To qualify you must have served at least 22 years in the Armed Forces and have earned a Long Service and Good Conduct Medal.

## ↘ JOHN KEOHANE'S DON'T MISS LIST

### ❶ A TOWER TOUR

To understand the Tower and its history, a guided tour with one of the Yeomen Warders is essential. Few people appreciate that the Tower is actually our home as well as our place of work; all the Warders live inside the outer walls. The Tower is rather like a miniature village – visitors are often rather surprised to see our washing hanging out beside the castle walls!

### ❷ CROWN JEWELS

Visitors often think the Crown Jewels are the Queen's personal jewellery collection. They're not, of course; the Crown Jewels are actually the ceremonial regalia used during the Coronation. The highlights are the Sceptre and the Imperial State Crown, which contains the celebrated diamond known as the Star of Africa. People are often surprised to hear that the Crown Jewels aren't insured (as they could never be replaced).

Clockwise from top: Tower of London at dusk; Guard on alert; The Tower from the River Thames; Sightseers, Tower of London; Chapel inside the Tower

THE CITY

THE CITY HIGHLIGHTS

### ❸ WHITE TOWER

The White Tower is the original royal palace of the Tower of London, but it hasn't been used as a royal residence since 1603. It's the most iconic building in the complex – inside you can see exhibits from the Royal Armouries, including a suit of armour belonging to Henry VIII.

### ❹ RAVENS

A Tower legend states that if its resident ravens ever left, the monarchy would topple – a royal decree states that we must keep a minimum of six ravens at any time. We currently have nine ravens, looked after by the Ravenmaster and his two assistants.

### ❺ CEREMONY OF THE KEYS

We hold three daily ceremonies: the 9am Official Opening, the Ceremony of the Word (when the day's password is issued), and the 10pm Ceremony of the Keys, when the gates are locked after the castle has closed; visitors are welcome to attend the latter, but must apply directly to the Tower in writing.

## ↘ THINGS YOU NEED TO KNOW

**Top tip** Booking online will allow you to dodge the queues **Photo op** Standing on the battlements overlooking the Thames **Did You Know?** The Yeoman Guards' famous red-and-gold ceremonial outfits cost around £7000 **For full details on the Tower of London, see p121**

# THE CITY HIGHLIGHTS

## 2 ST PAUL'S CATHEDRAL

It's hard to overstate the significance of London's most famous cathedral: the masterpiece of Christopher Wren, London's greatest architect, and an icon of the city's forbearance during the Blitz when its vast dome went amazingly unscathed by the bombs. But even before Wren's masterpiece went up, Ludgate Hill had been a site of worship for well over a millennium. St Paul's is therefore a history of London in one building. Here are our tips for its lesser-known gems.

### ⬂ OUR DON'T MISS LIST

**❶ EFFIGY OF JOHN DONNE**
One of the very few items to have been saved from the Old St Paul's Cathedral, which was destroyed by fire in 1666, this often overlooked statue of one of England's great poets (and a Dean of St Paul's) only survived as it fell down into the crypt during the fire.

**❷ WREN'S WORKING MODEL**
Next to Wren's tomb in the crypt, look out for the working model for rebuilding the cathedral in a niche nearby. You'll also see his various different,

highly controversial plans for St Paul's all of which were rejected before the final design was eventually accepted.

**❸ AMERICAN MEMORIAL CHAPEL**
This moving chapel in the apse of the cathedral was paid for entirely by donations from British individuals and commemorates the 28,000 US soldiers based in Britain who died in WWII; all their names are recorded in a roll of honour.

Clockwise from top: Dome of St Paul's Cathedral; Basilica of St Paul's at dawn; The Choir and apse; Bird's-eye view of the cathedral

CLOCKWISE FROM TOP: DAVID TOMLINSON; RYAN FOX; NEIL SETCHFIELD; MANFRED GOTTSCHAL

## ❹ WREN'S EPITAPH

Just beneath the dome are a compass and an epitaph written for Wren by his son: *Lector, si monumentum requiris, circumspice* (Reader, if you seek his monument, look around you). What better monument to posterity could there possibly be?

## ❺ PHOENIX FROM THE ASHES

In the south transept just below the dome you can see an often-overlooked carved stone phoenix. Beneath it is the inscription 'resurgam' ('I shall rise again') – this represents the Cathedral after the fire. One story runs that after the great fire, a stone with the same inscription visible was found in the wreckage, inspiring the cathedral's rebuilding.

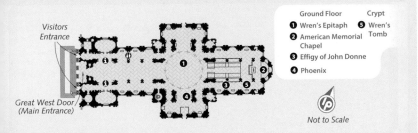

Visitors Entrance

Great West Door / (Main Entrance)

| Ground Floor | Crypt |
|---|---|
| ❶ Wren's Epitaph | ❺ Wren's Tomb |
| ❷ American Memorial Chapel | |
| ❸ Effigy of John Donne | |
| ❹ Phoenix | |

Not to Scale

## ↘ THINGS YOU NEED TO KNOW

**Transport** Cross over the Millennium Bridge from the Tate Modern **Top tip** Call ahead to check opening times – the cathedral can close unexpectedly **Photo op** Snap the cathedral itself from Fleet St, with the dome looming over Ludgate Hill **For full details on St Paul's Cathedral, see p113**

# THE CITY HIGHLIGHTS

**3**

## ◥ WATCH TOWER BRIDGE RISE

This London icon is a masterpiece of Victorian engineering and a sight you're unlikely to miss if you spend anytime around the City of London. Some of the best views of **Tower Bridge** (p124) can be had from the embankment in front of the Tower of London. However, the best way to see the bridge is when it rises dramatically to allow large boats through. You can find rising times at www.towerbridge.org.uk.

**4**

## ◥ SEE A BARBICAN SHOW

You may have walked through its bizarrely futuristic public spaces, gaped at the carp and marvelled at the juxtaposition of old and new within its grounds, but until you see a performance at the marvellous **Barbican** (p128), you're barely scraping the surface. Take your pick of world-class cinema, dance, live music and theatre any night of the week.

## ↘ CLIMB THE MONUMENT

The Great Fire of London in 1666 was an event nothing short of apocalyptic at the time, and the Monument (p119) is Wren's 1677 memorial to the event and would have towered above the city. Climb the 311-step spiral staircase to get a unique city view over the heart of London's oldest quarter.

## ↘ WANDER AROUND LEADENHALL MARKET

You quite simply won't see an old market as atmospheric and charmingly preserved as this beautiful complex of cobbled streets nestled between the skyscrapers of the City. It's no wonder that Leadenhall Market (p120) was used for the set of Diagon Alley in the Harry Potter films.

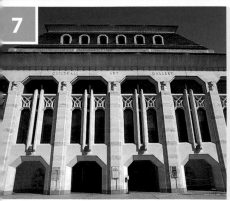

## ↘ RELIVE LONDON'S ROMAN PAST

There are few obvious indicators of London's Roman past, but if you descend the stairs from the excellent Guildhall Art Gallery (p120) you can see the remains of Londinium's coliseum, discovered in 1988. The remnants are fleshed out by clever lighting and audio effects designed to bring you back to the days of the gladiators.

THE CITY

THE CITY HIGHLIGHTS

3 RICHARD I'ANSON; 4 TRAVIS DREVER; 5 TRAVIS DREVER; 6 RICHARD I'ANSON; 7 DOUG MCKINLAY

3 Tower Bridge (p124); 4 Barbican (p128); 5 Monument (p119); 6 A drink at Leadenhall Market (p120); 7 Guildhall Art Gallery (p120)

# THE CITY WALK

**Beginning at Chancery Lane tube station, this lovely saunter through the ancient heart of the city can be done in just an hour or two, or equally stretched out to fill and entire day depending on how long you spend at each sight. You'll end up at iconic Tower Bridge.**

### ❶ DR JOHNSON'S HOUSE

Find your way to this miraculously well-preserved **early 18th-century mansion** (p116) in the heart of the City and explore the story of Dr Johnson's amazing life and wit within, perhaps even dropping by to his local, **Ye Olde Cheshire Cheese** (p127) on Fleet St.

### ❷ ST PAUL'S CATHEDRAL

Wren's masterpiece, this **cathedral** (p113) is an unlikely survivor of the Blitz and one of the London skyline's best-loved features. Join the crowds to see the dazzling interior, the fascinating crypt, the whispering gallery and the breathtaking views over the capital from the cupola.

### ❸ MUSEUM OF LONDON

This wonderful **museum** (p115) may not look like much from the outside, but it's one of the city's best, totally devoted to documenting the multifaceted history of the capital through its many stages of development from Saxon village to three-time Olympic city.

### ❹ BARBICAN

Built on the site of an old Roman watchtower (whence its name), the modern **Barbican** (p128) is the City's fabulous arts centre and an architectural wonder all of its own – check out the **greenhouse** the **lakes** and Shakespeare's parish Church, **St Giles' Cripplegate**.

### ❺ GUILDHALL

Once the very heart of the City, seat of power and influence, the **Guildhall** is today still the home to the Corporation of London. Here see the excellent **Guildhall Art Gallery** (p120) and go back in time two millennia to see the remains of London's **Roman Amphitheatre** (p120).

### ❻ MONUMENT

This **column** (p119) commemorates the Great Fire of London, and – while not for the vertiginous – is a superb way to see the City up close. Despite the number of high-rises all around, the Monument

# THE CITY WALK

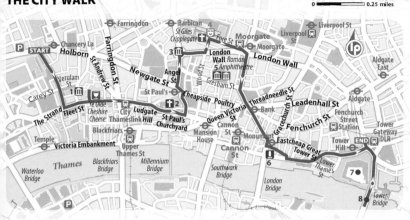

till feels extremely high, giving you an idea of how massive it would have looked in the 17th century.

## ❼ TOWER OF LONDON

The sheer amount of history within the massive stone walls of the Tower of London (p121) is hard to fathom. The **White Tower**, the **Crown Jewels**, the **Yeoman Warders** and **Traitor's Gate** are all fascinating and the Tower of London deserves at least a half-day's visit at the end of the walk.

## ❽ TOWER BRIDGE

A symbol of London since the day it was built, **Tower Bridge** (p124) is a must-see. A walk across it (and a visit to the interesting exhibition, from which the views are spectacular) is a must to appreciate old Father Thames at its widest and most spectacular.

THE CITY

THE CITY'S BEST...

# THE CITY'S BEST...

## ⤵ PLACES WITH A VIEW

- **St Paul's Cathedral** (p113) The view from the dome is simply unbeatable.
- **Monument** (p119) Have an intimate look at the City of London.
- **Tower of London** (p121) For the best views of Tower Bridge, wander along the walls of the Tower.
- **Tower Bridge** (p124) Look back at the Tower from Tower Bridge.

## ⤵ THINGS FOR FREE

- **Wander around the Barbican** (p128) Take in this fantastic yet divisive piece of London architecture.
- **Museum of London** (p115) A fantastic account of London's exciting history.
- **Temple Church** (p117) Beware of albino Monks at this Da Vinci code favourite.
- **Guildhall Art Gallery** (p120) Free all day every Friday.

## ⤵ QUIRKY SIGHTS

- **Golden Boy of Pye Corner** (p117) A rather puritan memorial to the 'gluttony' that caused the Great Fire of London.
- **Margaret Thatcher Sculpture** (p120) This statue was decapitated by an angry citizen when it first appeared. It's now behind glass.
- **Roman Amphitheatre** (p120) Don't miss this unusual archaeological discovery.
- **St Giles Cripplegate** (p119) This ancient parish church looks truly out of place amid the modernity of the Barbican complex.

## ⤵ TRADITIONAL PLACES

- **Leadenhall Market** (p120) This charming market in the middle of the financial district is a must-see.
- **Ye Olde Cheshire Cheese** (p127) One of London's least changed pubs.
- **Sweeting's** (p126) Serving up its famous fish pie since 1830.

Museum of London (p115)

DOUG MCKINLA

# DISCOVER THE CITY

he ancient, hallowed streets of the City are some of London's most ascinating. The Square Mile occupies pretty much exactly the same patch of land around which the Romans first constructed a defensive vall almost two millennia ago and probably contains more history vithin it than the rest of the city put together.

The tiny backstreets and ancient churches are today juxtaposed vith skyscrapers and office blocks as this is the home of London's tock exchange, the Bank of England and countless other financial nstitutions. Very few people now live in the City (which was badly oombed during the Blitz) and so, while it's very animated Monday o Friday, you can hear a pin drop at the weekend and even on a veeknight after 9pm once the commuters are all safely on their way ome.

Don't miss the city's standout sights, such as London skyline icons t Paul's Cathedral, the Gherkin and the Monument, or the ultimate ondon sight – the Tower of London.

# SIGHTS

## T PAUL'S CATHEDRAL

☎ 7236 4128; www.stpauls.co.uk; St Paul's hurchyard EC4; adult/7-16yr/senior/student 11/3.50/10/8.50; ☻ 8.30am-4pm (last entry) lon-Sat; ⊖ St Paul's; ♿

)ccupying a superb position atop Ludgate 1ill, one of London's most recognisable uildings is Sir Christopher Wren's master-vork, completed in 1710 after the previ-us building was destroyed in the Great ire of 1666. The proud bearer of the apital's largest church dome, St Paul's Cathedral has seen a lot in its 300-plus ears, although Ludgate Hill has been a lace of worship for almost 1400 years, he current incarnation being the fifth to tand on this site. St Paul's almost didn't nake it off the drawing board, as Wren's nitial designs were rejected. However, ince its first service in 1697, it's held unerals for Lord Nelson, the Duke of Vellington and Winston Churchill, and nas played host to Martin Luther King as vell as the ill-fated wedding of Charles

and Diana. For Londoners the vast dome, which still manages to loom amid the far higher skyscrapers in the Square Mile, is a symbol of resilience and pride – miraculously surviving the Blitz unscathed. Having undergone a huge restoration project to coincide with its 300th anniversary in 2010, the cathedral is today looking better than it has done for decades.

Despite all the fascinating history and its impressive interior, people are usually most interested in climbing the **dome** for one of the best views of London imaginable. Exactly 530 stairs take you to the top, but it's a three-stage journey. The cathedral is built in the shape of a cross, with the dome at its intersection. So first find the circular paved area between the eight massive columns supporting the dome, then head to the door on the western side of the south transept. Some 30m and precisely 259 steps above, you reach the interior walkway around the dome's base. This is the **Whispering Gallery**, so called because if you talk close to the wall

THE CITY

SIGHTS

it really does carry your words around to the opposite side, 32m away.

Climbing even more steps (another 119) you reach the **Stone Gallery**, which is an exterior viewing platform, with 360-degree views of London, all of which are rather obscured by pillars and other suicide-preventing measures.

The further 152 iron steps to the **Golden Gallery** are steeper and narrower than below but are really worth the effort as long as you don't suffer from claustrophobia. From here, 111m above London, the city opens up to you, the view unspoilt by superfluous railings; you'll be hard pushed to see anything better.

Of course, back on the ground floor, St Paul's offers plenty of riches for those who like to keep their feet firmly on its black-and-white tiled floor – and the interior has been stunningly restored in recent years.

In the northern aisle you'll find the **All Souls' Chapel** and the **Chapel of St Dunstan**, dedicated to the 10th-century archbishop of Canterbury, and the grandiose **Duke of Wellington Memorial**

(1875). In the north transept chapel Holman Hunt's celebrated painting **The Light of the World**, which depicts Chri knocking at an overgrown door that, sym bolically, can only be opened from th inside. Beyond, in the cathedral's hear are the particularly spectacular **quire** (chancel) – its ceilings and arches dazzlin with green, blue, red and gold mosaics and the **high altar**. The ornately carve **choir stalls** by Grinling Gibbons on eithe side of the quire are exquisite, as are th ornamental **wrought-iron gates**, sepa rating the aisles from the altar, by Jea Tijou (both men also worked on Hampto Court Palace). Walk around the altar, wit its massive gilded oak canopy, to th **American Memorial Chapel**, a memoria to the 28,000 Americans based in Britai who lost their lives during WWII.

On the eastern side of both the nort and south transepts are stairs leadin down to the **crypt**, treasury and **OB Chapel**, where weddings, funerals an other services are held for members c the Order of the British Empire. The cryp

Display at Museum of London (p115)

DOUG MCKINL

as memorials to some 300 military demi-gods, including Florence Nightingale and Lord Kitchener, while both the **Duke of Wellington** and **Admiral Nelson** are actually buried here, Nelson having been placed in a black sarcophagus that is directly under the centre of the dome. On the surrounding walls are plaques in memory of those from the Commonwealth who died in various conflicts during the 20th century.

**Wren's tomb** is in the crypt, while architect Edwin Lutyens, painter Joshua Reynolds and poet William Blake are also remembered here.

The **treasury** hosts temporary exhibitions and is not always open, but it's worth a look when it is, depending on what's on. Elsewhere in the crypt is the **Crypt Café** ( 9am-5pm Mon-Sat, 10.30am-4pm Sun) and the restaurant **Refectory** ( 9am-5.30pm Mon-Sat, 10.30am-5.30pm Sun), in addition to a **shop** ( 9am-5pm Mon-Sat, 10.30am-5pm Sun).

Just outside the north transept, there's a simple **monument to the people of London**, honouring the 32,000 civilians killed (and another 50,000 seriously injured) in the City during WWII. **Audioguide tours** (adult/senior & student £4/3.50) in multiple languages last 45 minutes; **guided tours** (adult/senior & student/child aged 6-16 years £3/1/2.50) lasting 1½ to two hours leave the tour desk at 10.45am, 11.15am, 1.30pm and 2pm. There are free **organ recitals** at St Paul's at 5pm most Sundays, as well as regular **celebrity recitals**, which are listed on the website. Evensong takes place at 5pm Monday to Saturday and at 3.15pm on Sunday. The cathedral can close unexpectedly for events and services, so call ahead.

There is limited disabled access. Call ahead for further information.

## MUSEUM OF LONDON

☎ 7001 9844; www.museumoflondon.org.uk; London Wall EC2; admission free; 🕙 10am-6pm; ⊖ Barbican or St Paul's; ♿

The Museum of London is one of the capital's best museums but remains largely off the radar for most visitors. That's not surprising when you consider that it's encased in concrete and located above a roundabout in the Barbican. Despite this, once you're inside it's a fascinating walk through the various incarnations of the capital from Anglo-Saxon village to global financial centre. The lower floor of the museum, covering the period 1666 to the present day, was shut recently for a total revamp, but should now be open once more.

The first gallery here, London Before London, outlines the development of the Thames Valley from 450 million years ago. Harnessing computer technology to enliven its exhibits and presenting impressive fossils and stone axe heads in shiny new cases, it does a good job of bringing to life the ancient settlements that pre-dated the capital. Next up is the city's Roman era, a far more interactive experience, full of interesting displays and models of how the city would have looked at the height of Roman influence. The rest of the floor takes you through the Saxon, medieval, Tudor and Stuart periods, culminating in the Great Fire of 1666.

You can pause for a breather in the pleasant garden in the building's central courtyard or head for the adjoining **Museum Café**, which serves light meals from 10am to 5.30pm (from 11.30am on Sunday). Alternatively, on a sunny day, pack some sandwiches and lunch in the next-door **Barber Surgeon's Herb Garden**.

THE CITY

SIGHTS

When arriving, look for the Barbican's gate 7; before leaving, don't forget to have a browse through the well-stocked bookshop and check in on the temporary exhibits also held here.

## DR JOHNSON'S HOUSE

☎ 7353 3745; www.drjohnsonshouse.org; 17 Gough Sq EC4; adult/child/concession/family £4.50/1.50/3.50/10; ⏰ 11am-5.30pm Mon-Sat May-Sep, to 5pm Mon-Sat Oct-Apr; ⊖ Chancery Lane or Blackfriars

This wonderful house, built in 1700, is a rare surviving example of a Georgian city mansion. All around it today huge office blocks loom and tiny Gough Sq can be quite hard to find as a result. The house has been preserved, of course, as it was the home of the great Georgian w Samuel Johnson, the author of the fir serious dictionary of the English languag (transcribed by a team of six clerks in th attic) and the man who proclaimed 'Whe a man is tired of London, he is tired of lif

The museum doesn't exactly crack with Dr Johnson's immortal wit, yet it still an atmospheric and worthy place t visit, with its antique furniture and arte facts from Johnson's life (his brick fro the Great Wall of China must surely b the oddest of these). Across Gough S is a statue of Johnson's cat, Hodge, si ting above the full quote explaining wh when a man is tired of London, he is tire of life: 'For there is in London all that lif can afford.'

## ST BARTHOLOMEW-THE-GREAT

☎ 7606 5171; www.greatstbarts.com; West Smithfield EC1; adult/concession £4/3; ⏰ 8.30am-5pm Mon-Fri, to 4pm mid-Nov–mid-Feb, plus 10.30am-4pm Sat & 8.30am-8pm Sun year-round; ⊖ Farringdon or Barbican

This spectacular Norman church date from 1123, originally a part of the monas tery of Augustinian Canons, but becomin the parish church of Smithfield in 153 when King Henry VIII dissolved the mon asteries. The authentic Norman arches the weathered and blackened stone, the dark wood carvings and the low light ing lend this space an ancient calm especially as you'll often be the only visi tor. There are historical associations with William Hogarth, who was baptised here and with politician Benjamin Franklin who worked on site as an apprentic printer. The church sits on the corner o the grounds of St Bartholomew's Hospital on the side closest to Smithfield Market Another selling point for modern audi ences is that scenes from *Shakespeare in Love* and *Four Weddings and a Funera*

Dr Johnson's House

THE CITY

Temple Church

NEIL SETCHFIELD

SIGHTS

## ⬎ TEMPLE CHURCH

This magnificent church lies within the walls of the Temple, built by the legendary Knights Templar, an order of crusading monks founded in the 12th century to protect pilgrims travelling to and from Jerusalem. The order moved here around 1160, abandoning its older headquarters in Holborn. Today the sprawling oasis of fine buildings and pleasant traffic-free green space is home to two Inns of Court (housing the chambers of lawyers practising in the City), the Middle and the Lesser Temple.

The Temple Church has a distinctive design: the Round (consecrated in 1185 and designed to recall the Church of the Holy Sepulchre in Jerusalem) adjoins the Chancel (built in 1240), which is the heart of the modern church. Both parts were severely damaged by a bomb in 1941 and have been lovingly reconstructed. Its most obvious points of interest are the life-size stone effigies of nine knights that lie on the floor of the Round. These include the Earl of Pembroke, who acted as the go-between for King John and the rebel barons, eventually leading to the signing of the Magna Carta in 1215. In recent years the church has become a must-see for readers of *The Da Vinci Code*, in which a key scene was set here.

Check opening times in advance as they change frequently. During the week, the easiest access to the church is via Inner Temple Lane, off Fleet St. At the weekends, you'll need to enter from the Victoria Embankment.

**Things you need to know:** ☎ 7353 3470; www.templechurch.com; Temple EC4; admission free; ⏱ approx 2-4pm Wed-Sun, call or email to check; ⊖ Temple or Chancery Lane

were filmed here. The location managers for those movies knew what they were doing: St Bartholomew-the-Great is indeed one of the capital's most atmospheric places of worship.

### GOLDEN BOY OF PYE CORNER
Cnr Cock Lane & Giltspur St; ⊖ St Paul's or Farringdon
This small statue of a corpulent boy opposite St Bartholomew's Hospital, at the

TIM GARTSIDE LONDON/ALAMY

**Interior of St Stephen Walbrook**

## ⬇ IF YOU LIKE...

If you liked St Bartholomew-the-Great (p116) then we think you'll like these other ancient parish churches hidden away around the City:

- **St Bride's Fleet Street** Known as the 'journalists' church' due to its location on Fleet St, one-time home to all of Britain's national newspapers, this gorgeous Wren church has a tiered spire that is said to have inspired the first layered wedding cake.
- **St Stephen Walbrook** One of Wren's most acclaimed churches, St Stephen Walbrook is located behind the Mansion House at Bank and boasts an incongruously modern Henry Moore altarpiece.
- **St Giles Cripplegate** Bizarrely located amid the utopian surrounds of the Barbican Centre, this wonderfully named church has counted one William Shakespeare's among its congregation over its long history.

corner of Cock Lane and Giltspur St, has a somewhat odd dedication: 'In memory put up for the fire of London occasioned by the sin of gluttony 1666'. All becomes clear, however, when you realise the Great Fire started in a busy bakery on Pudding Lane and finally burned itself out in what was once called Pye (Pie) Corner, wher the statue now stands. This was interpreted by many as a sign that the fir was an act of God as punishment for th gluttony of Londoners.

### SMITHFIELD MARKET
**West Smithfield EC1;** ⊙ 4am-noon Mon-Fri;
⊖ **Farringdon**
Smithfield is central London's last surviving meat market. Its name derives from being a smooth field where animals coul be grazed, although its history is far from pastoral. Built on the site of the notorious St Bartholomew's fair, where witche were traditionally burned at the stake this is where Scottish Independenc leader William Wallace was executed i 1305 (there's a large plaque on the wa of St Bart's Hospital south of the market as well as the place where the leader o the Peasants' Revolt, Wat Tyler, met hi end in 1381. Described in terms of pur horror by Dickens in *Oliver Twist,* thi was once the armpit of London, wher animal excrement and entrails create a sea of filth. Today it's a very smart a nexe of Clerkenwell and full of bars an restaurants, while the market itself is wonderful building, although one con stantly under threat of destruction an redevelopment into office blocks.

### 30 ST MARY AXE
**Gherkin;** ☎ 7071 5008; www.30stmaryaxe.com
**St Mary Axe EC3;** ⊖ **Aldgate or Bank**
Known to one and all as 'the Gherkin' (fo obvious reasons when you see its incredi ble shape), 30 St Mary Axe – as it is officiall and far more prosaically named – remains London's most distinctive sky scraper, dominating the city despit actually being slightly smaller than th neighbouring NatWest Tower. The pha

c Gherkin's futuristic, sci-fi exterior has become an emblem of modern London nd is as recognisable as Big Ben or the ondon Eye.

## MONUMENT

☎ 7626 2717; www.themonument.info; Monument St EC3; adult/5-15yr/concession £3/1/2; ⏰ 9.30am-5.30pm; ⊖ Monument

ir Christopher Wren's vast 1677 column, known simply as the Monument, s definitely one of the best vantage points over London due to its centrality s much as to its height: with the river, t Paul's and the City surrounding it, you ruly feel at London's bustling heart. The olumn itself is a memorial to the Great ire of London in 1666, whose impact on .ondon's history cannot be overstated. lightly southeast of King William St, near .ondon Bridge, the Monument is exactly i0.6m from the bakery in Pudding Lane vhere the fire started and exactly 60.6m nigh. To reach the viewing platform, just pelow a gilded bronze urn of flames that ome call a big gold pincushion, you will need to climb 311 steps on the impressive circular staircase.

## BARBICAN

☎ information 7638 8891, switchboard 7638 4141; www.barbican.org.uk; Silk St EC2; ⏰ 9am-11pm Mon-Sat, noon-11pm Sun; ⊖ Barbican or Moorgate

Londoners remain fairly divided about the architectural legacy of this vast housing and cultural complex in the heart of the City. While the Barbican is named after a Roman fortification protecting ancient Londinium that may once have stood here, what you see here today is very much a product of the 1960s and '70s. Built on a huge bombsite abandoned since WWII and opened progressively between 1969 and 1982, it's fair to say that its brutalist concrete isn't everyone's cup of tea. Yet, although it topped several recent polls as London's ugliest building, many Londoners see something very beautiful about its cohesion and ambition – incorporating Shakespeare's local church, **St Giles Cripplegate**, into

Relaxing at a bar on the forecourt of 30 St Mary Axe, aka the Gherkin (p118)

RICHARD I'ANSON

THE CITY

SIGHTS

Step back in time inside Leadenhall Market

RICHARD I'ANSO

its brave-new-world design and embellishing its public areas with lakes and ponds. With a £7-million refit bringing the complex a much-needed facelift in 2005, the Barbican is much better loved than London's other modernist colossus, the Southbank Centre. Trendy urban architects have long prized apartments here, and the residences in the three high-rise towers that ring the cultural centre are some of the city's most sought-after living spaces.

## LEADENHALL MARKET

www.leadenhallmarket.co.uk; Whittington Ave EC3; ⊗ public areas 24hr, shop opening times vary; ⊖ Bank

Like stepping into a small slice of Victorian London, a visit to this dimly lit, covered mall off Gracechurch St is a minor time-travelling experience. There's been a market on this site since the Roman era, but the architecture that survives is all cobblestones and late-19th-century ironwork; even modern restaurants and chain stores decorate their facades in period style here.

The market also appears as Diagon Alley in *Harry Potter and the Philosopher's Stone*.

## GUILDHALL ART GALLERY & ROMAN LONDON AMPHITHEATRE

☎ 7332 3700; www.guildhall-art-gallery.org. uk; Guildhall Yard EC2; adult/senior & student £2.50/1, all day Fri & daily after 3.30pm free; ⊗ 10am-5pm Mon-Sat, noon-4pm Sun; ⊖ Bank

The gallery of the City of London provides a fascinating look at the politics of the Square Mile over the past few centuries, with a great collection of paintings of London in the 18th and 19th centuries, as well as the vast frieze entitled *The Defeat of the Floating Batteries* (1791), depicting the British victory at the Siege of Gibraltar in 1782. This huge painting was removed to safety just a month before the gallery was hit by a German bomb in 1941 – it spent 50 years rolled up before a spectacular restoration in 1999.

An even more recent arrival is a sculpture of former prime minister Margaret Thatcher, which has to be housed in a protective glass case as the iron lady was decapitated here by an angry punter with a cricket bat soon after its installation in 2002. Today, following some tricky neck surgery, Maggie has finally rejoined the gallery's collection, but her contentious legacy lives on.

The real highlight of the museum is deep in the darkened basement, where the archaeological remains of Roman London's amphitheatre (coliseum) lie. Discovered only in 1988 when work finally began on a new gallery following the original's destruction in the Blitz, they were immediately declared an Ancient Monument, and the new gallery was built around them. While only a few remnants of the stone walls lining the eastern entrance still stand, they're imaginatively fleshed out with a black-and-fluorescent-green trompe l'oeil of the missing seating, and computer-meshed outlines of spectators and gladiators. The roar of the crowd goes up as you reach the end of the entrance tunnel and hit the central stage, giving a real sense of how Roman London might have felt. Markings on the square outside the Guildhall indicate the original extent of the amphitheatre, allowing people to visualise its scale.

## TOWER OF LONDON

☎ 0844 482 7777; www.hrp.org.uk; Tower Hill EC3; adult/5-15yr/senior & student/family £17/9.50/14.50/47; ☷ 9am-5.30pm Tue-Sat, 10am-5.30pm Sun & Mon Mar-Oct, closes 4.30pm daily Nov-Feb, last admission 30min before closing time; ⊖ Tower Hill; ♿

The absolute kernel of London with a history as bleak and bloody as it is fascinating, the Tower of London should be first on anyone's list of London's sights. Despite ever-growing ticket prices and the hordes of tourists that descend here in the summer months, this is one of those rare pleasures: somewhere worth the hype.

The Tower is in fact a castle, and not towerlike at all (although in the Middle Ages it's easy to imagine how the White Tower would have dwarfed the huts of the peasantry surrounding the castle walls) and has been the property (and sometime London residence) of the monarch since it was begun during the reign of William the Conqueror (1066–87). By far the best preserved medieval castle in London, it will fascinate anyone with any interest in history, the monarchy and warfare.

With more than two million visitors a year, this place is seriously crowded in the high season so it's best to buy a ticket in advance, and to visit later in the day. You can buy Tower tickets online (for a £1 discount), or at any tube station up to a week beforehand, which can save you a lot of time when you arrive. Also, after 3pm the groups have usually left and the place is a lot more pleasant to stroll around. During the winter months it's far less crowded, so there's no need to take either of these precautions.

Your best bet is to start with a free hour-long tour given by the Yeoman Warders, which is a great way to bring the various parts of the tower to life. Known affectionately as 'beefeaters' by the public (due to the large rations of beef given to them in the past), there are 35 Yeoman Warders today. While officially they guard the tower and Crown Jewels at night, their main role today is as tour guides (and to pose for photographs with curious foreigners).

You enter the tower via the **West Gate** and proceed across the walkway over the dry moat between the **Middle Tower** and **Byward Tower**. The original moat was finally drained of centuries of festering sewage in the 19th century, necessitated by persistent cholera outbreaks, and a superbly manicured lawn now takes its

THE CITY

SIGHTS

place. Before you stands the **Bell Tower**, housing the curfew bells and one-time home to Thomas More. The politician and author of *Utopia* was imprisoned here in 1534 before his execution for refusing to recognise King Henry VIII as head of the Church of England in place of the Pope. To your left are the **casements of the former Royal Mint**, which were moved from this site to new buildings northeast of the castle in 1812.

Continuing past the Bell Tower along **Water Lane** between the walls you come to the famous **Traitors' Gate**, the gateway through which prisoners being brought by river entered the tower. Above the gate, rooms inside **St Thomas's Tower** show what the hall and bedchamber of Edward I (1272–1307) might once have looked like. Here also archaeologists have peeled back the layers of newer buildings to find what went before. Opposite St Thomas's Tower is **Wakefield Tower**, built by Henry III between 1220 and 1240. Its upper floor is actually entered via St Thomas's Tower and has been even more

enticingly furnished with a replica throne and huge candelabra to give an impression of how, as an anteroom in a medieval palace, it might have once looked in Edward I's day. During the 15th-century War of the Roses between the Houses of Lancaster and York, Henry VI was almost certainly murdered in this tower.

Below, in the basement of Wakefield Tower, there's a **Torture at the Tower** exhibition. However, torture wasn't practised as much in England as it was on the Continent apparently, and the display is pretty perfunctory, limiting itself to a rack, a pair of manacles and an instrument for keeping prisoners doubled up called a Scavenger's Daughter. Frankly you'd see scarier gear at any London S&M club (or the London Dungeon (p142) across the river near London Bridge). To get to this exhibition and the basement level of Wakefield Tower, enter the tower courtyard through the arch opposite Traitors' Gate.

As you do so, you'll also observe at the centre of the courtyard the Norman

VERONICA GARBUT

**Changing of the Guard at the Tower of London (p121)**

White Tower with a turret on each of its four corners and a golden weather vane pinning atop each. This tower has a couple of remnants of Norman architecture, including a fireplace and garderobe (lavatory). However, most of its interior is given over to a collection of cannons, guns and suits of armour for men and horses, which come from the Royal Armouries in Leeds. Among the most remarkable exhibits are the 2m suit of armour made for John of Gaunt (to see that coming towards you on a battlefield must have been terrifying) and alongside it a tiny child's suit of armour designed for James I's young son, Henry. Another unmissable suit is that of Henry VIII, a virtually cuboid shape to match the monarch's bloated body in his 40s, and featuring what must have been the most impressive posing pouch in the kingdom.

The stretch of green between the Wakefield and White Towers is where the Tower's famous **ravens** are found. According to legend, if these birds leave the Tower it would presage the fall of the kingdom, so their wings are clipped to ensure this will never happen.

Opposite Wakefield Tower and the White Tower is the **Bloody Tower**, with an exhibition on Elizabethan adventurer Sir Walter Raleigh, who was imprisoned here three times by the capricious Elizabeth I, most significantly from 1605 to 1616.

The Bloody Tower acquired its nickname from the story that the 'princes in the tower', Edward V and his younger brother, were murdered here to annul their claims to the throne. The blame is usually laid at the door of their uncle Richard III, although Henry VII might also have been responsible for the crime.

Beside the Bloody Tower sits a collection of black-and-white half-timbered Tudor houses that are home to Tower of

30 St Mary Axe, also known as the Gherkin (p118)
RICHARD I'ANSON

London staff. The **Queen's House**, where Anne Boleyn lived out her final days in 1536, now houses the resident governor and is closed to the public.

North of the Queen's House, across **Tower Green**, is the **scaffold site**, where seven people were executed by beheading in Tudor times: two of Henry VIII's six wives, the alleged adulterers Anne Boleyn and Catherine Howard; the latter's lady-in-waiting, Jane Rochford; Margaret Pole, countess of Salisbury, descended from the House of York; 16-year-old Lady Jane Grey, who fell foul of Henry's daughter Mary I by being her rival for the throne; William, Lord Hastings; and Robert Devereux, Earl of Essex, once a favourite of Elizabeth I. These people were executed within the tower precincts largely to spare the monarch the embarrassment of the usual public execution on Tower Hill, an event that was usually attended by thousands of spectators.

To the east of the chapel and north of the White Tower is the building that visitors most want to see: **Waterloo Barracks**, the home of the **Crown Jewels**. You file past footage of Queen Elizabeth II's coronation backed by stirring patriotic music before you reach the vault itself (check out the doors as you go in – they look like they'd survive a nuclear attack). Once inside you'll be confronted with ornate sceptres, plates, orbs and, naturally, crowns. A very slow-moving travelator takes you past the dozen or so crowns that are the centrepiece, including the £27.5 million Imperial State Crown, set with diamonds (2868 of them to be exact), sapphires, emeralds, rubies and pearls, and the platinum crown of the late Queen Mother, Elizabeth, which is famously set with the 105-carat Koh-i-Noor (Mountain of Light) diamond. Surrounded by myth and legend, the 14th-century diamond has been claimed by both India and Afghanistan. It reputedly confers enormous power on its owner, but male owners are destined to die a tormented death.

Behind the Waterloo Barracks is the **Bowyer Tower**, where George, Duke of Clarence, brother and rival of Edward IV, was imprisoned and, according to a long-standing legend that has never been proved, was drowned in a barrel of malmsey (sweet Madeira wine).

The **Wall Walk** begins with the 13th-century **Salt Tower**, probably used to store saltpetre for gunpowder, and takes in **Broad Arrow Tower**, which houses an exhibit about the gunpowder plotters imprisoned here, many of their original inscriptions having been discovered on the walls. The walk ends at the **Martin Tower**, which houses an exhibition about the original coronation regalia. Here you can see some of the older crowns, whose jewels have been removed.

There is limited disabled access to the tower. Call ahead for more information.

## AROUND THE TOWER OF LONDON

Despite the Tower's World Heritage Site status, the area immediately to the north is fairly disappointing, especially as in recent years much of it has been a construction site. Just outside Tower Hill tube station, a giant bronze **sundial** depicts the history of London from AD 43 to 1982. It stands on a platform offering a view of the neighbouring **Trinity Square Gardens**, once the site of the Tower Hill scaffold and now home to Edwin Lutyens' memorial to the marines and merchant sailors who lost their lives during WWI. A grassy area, off the steps leading to a subway under the main road, lets you inspect a stretch of the **medieval wall** built on Roman foundations, with a modern statue of Emperor Trajan (r AD 98–117) standing in front of it. At the other end of the tunnel is a postern (gate) dating from the 13th century.

## TOWER BRIDGE
### ⊖ Tower Hill

Perhaps second only to Big Ben as London's most recognisable symbol, Tower Bridge doesn't disappoint up close. There's something about its neo-Gothic towers and blue suspension struts that that make it quite enthralling to look at. Built in 1894 as a much-needed crossing point in the east, it was equipped with a then revolutionary bascule (seesaw) mechanism that could clear the way for oncoming ships in three minutes. Although London's days as a thriving port

re long over, the bridge still does its stuff,
fting around 1000 times per year and as
many as 10 times per day in summer.

## ALL HALLOWS-BY-THE-TOWER
☎ 7481 2928; www.ahbtt.org.uk; Byward St
C3; admission free; ⊙ 8am-6pm Mon-Fri,
0am-5pm Sat & Sun; ⊖ Tower Hill

All Hallows is the parish where famous
diarist Samuel Pepys recorded his observations of the nearby Great Fire of London
in 1666. Above ground it's a pleasant
enough church, rebuilt after WWII. There's
a copper spire (added in 1957 to make the
church stand out more), a pulpit from a
Wren church in Cannon St that was destroyed in the WWII, a beautiful 17th-
century font cover by the master wood-
carver Grinling Gibbons, and some interesting modern banners. Free 20-minute
church tours leave at 2pm each day.

However, a church by the name All
Hallows (meaning 'All Saints') has stood
on this site since AD 675, and the best bit
of the building today is undoubtedly its
atmospheric Saxon **undercroft** (crypt).

There you'll find a pavement of reused
Roman tiles and walls of the 7th-century
Saxon church, as well as coins and bits of
local history.

William Penn, founder of Pennsylvania,
was baptised here in 1644 and there's a
memorial to him in the undercroft. John
Quincy Adams, sixth president of the USA,
was also married at All Hallows in 1797.

# SLEEPING
### THREADNEEDLES          Boutique Hotel £££
☎ 7657 8080; www.theetoncollection.com; 5
Threadneedle St EC2; s & d £282-558, ste from
£480; ⊖ Bank; 🔀 🛜

You have to know this place is here. It's
wonderfully anonymous, though once
through the doorway the grand circular
lobby, which is furnished in a vaguely
art deco style and covered with a hand-
painted glass dome, comes into view. The
69 rooms here may not be cutting edge,
but they're very pleasantly done, all with
high ceilings, free wi-fi and dark, sleek
furnishings.

Tower Bridge (p124) with ships in the foreground

RICHARD I'ANSON

TRAVIS DREVER

Inside the Barbican (p128)

## ANDAZ LIVERPOOL STREET

Hotel £££

☎ 7961 1234; www.andaz.com; 40 Liverpool St EC2; r from £115-230, ste from £260; ⊖ Liverpool St; 🍴 ♿ 🛜

There's no reception here, just black-clad staff who check you in on mini laptops. Rooms are cool and spacious, with free nonalcoholic drinks, wi-fi and local calls. This is a solid choice, well located, and a good compromise between business and boutique.

## YHA LONDON ST PAUL'S

Hostel £

☎ 0845 371 9012; www.yha.org.uk; 36 Carter Lane EC4; 11-bed dm £15.95-28.95, s £18.95-35.95, d £38.95-71.95, tr £58.95-107.95; ⊖ St Paul's

This excellent 193-bed hostel stands in the very shadow of St Paul's Cathedral and opposite the Tate Modern. Most room have two, three or four beds, though 1 rooms have five to 11 beds. There's a li censed cafeteria but no kitchen. Chec out the building's gorgeous facade i Carter St while you're here!

# EATING

## SWEETING'S

Seafood £

☎ 7248 3062; 39 Queen Victoria St EC4; mains £12.50-25; 🕐 lunch Mon-Fri; ⊖ Mansion House

Sweeting's is a City institution, hav ing been around since 1830. It hasn' changed much, with its small sit-down restaurant area, mosaic floor and nar row counters, behind which stand wait ers in white aprons. Dishes include wild smoked salmon, oysters (in season from September to April), potted shrimps, eel and Sweeting's famous fish pie (£12.50)

## WHITE SWAN PUB & DINING ROOM

Gastropub £

☎ 7242 9696; www.thewhiteswanlondon.com; 108 New Fetter Lane EC4; pub mains £9.50-14; 🕐 closed Sat & Sun; ⊖ Chancery Lane

Despite looking like any other anonymou City pub from the street, inside the White Swan is anything but typical – a smar downstairs bar that serves excellent pub food (£10 for a main with a glass of wine under the watchful eyes of animal tro phies and an upstairs dining room with a classic, meaty British menu (two-/three course meal £24/29).

## PATERNOSTER CHOP HOUSE

British £

☎ 7029 9400; www.paternosterchophouse. com; Warwick Ct, Paternoster Sq EC4; mains £16.50-20; 🕐 closed all day Sat & dinner Sun; ⊖ St Paul's

Right next to St Paul's Cathedral, thi sprawling upmarket chop house serve delightfully British fare – from the 'beast of the day' (£19) to a huge shellfish and grill selection, and favourites such as bubble and squeak (fried leftover veggies from a roast dinner) and haggis. Sunday brunch (noon to 4pm) features carvery.

### ROYAL EXCHANGE GRAND CAFÉ & BAR
Modern European ££

☎ 7618 2480; www.danddlondon.com; Royal Exchange Bank, Threadneedle St EC3; mains £10-9; ⊗ 8am-11pm Mon-Fri; ⊖ Bank

This cafe sits in the middle of the covered courtyard of the beautiful Royal Exchange Bank building. The food runs the gamut from sandwiches to oysters (from £10.75 a half-dozen), whole roast Dover Sole (£18) and pork belly (from £12). It's the perfect place for an informal business meeting.

### WINE LIBRARY
Modern European ££

☎ 7481 0415; www.winelibrary.co.uk; 43 Trinity Sq EC3; set meals £16.45; ⊗ 11.30am-2.30pm Mon-Fri, 5-8.30pm Tue; ⊖ Tower Hill

This is a great place for a light but boozy lunch in the City. Buy a bottle of wine at retail price (no mark-up; £6.50 corkage fee) from the large selection on offer at this vaulted-cellar restaurant and then snack on a set plate of delicious pâtés, cheeses and salads for £16.45.

### PLACE BELOW
Vegetarian £

☎ 7329 0789; www.theplacebelow.co.uk; St Mary-le-Bow Church, Cheapside EC2; dishes £3-8; ⊗ 7.30am-3pm Mon-Fri; ⊖ Mansion House

This atmospheric vegetarian restaurant is in the crypt of one of London's most famous old churches. The menu is a daily changing set of veggie dishes, from quiche to sourdough sandwiches.

# DRINKING

Catering to bankers, dealers and other suits, the City generally offers traditional pubs, most of which are only open Monday to Friday and are often deserted by 10pm. Despite this, the City has some magical places that positively ooze history and character.

### BLACK FRIAR
Pub

☎ 7236 5474; 174 Queen Victoria St EC4; ⊗ to 11.30pm Thu & Fri; ⊖ Blackfriars

It may look like Friar Tuck just stepped out of this 'olde pubbe' just north of Blackfriars tube station, but the interior is actually an Arts and Crafts makeover dating back to 1905. Not surprisingly, the Black Friar is the preserve of City suits during the week, but they disappear at the weekend, leaving it to the rest of us. There's a good selection of ales and bitters here.

### COUNTING HOUSE
Pub

☎ 7283 7123; 50 Cornhill EC3; ⊗ closed Sat & Sun; ⊖ Bank or Monument

They say that old banks – with their counters and basement vaults – make perfect homes for pubs, and this award-winner certainly looks and feels most comfortable in the former headquarters of NatWest with its domed skylight and beautifully appointed main bar. This is a City-boy favourite – they come for the good range of real ales (beer brewed in the traditional way) and the specialty pies (£9 to £10).

### YE OLDE CHESHIRE CHEESE
Pub

☎ 7353 6170; Wine Office Ct, 145 Fleet St EC4; ⊗ to 5pm Sun; ⊖ Blackfriars

The entrance to this historic pub is via a narrow alley off Fleet St. Locals over its long history have included Dr Johnson, Thackeray and Dickens. Despite (or

THE CITY

ENTERTAINMENT

Ornate interior of Black Friar (p127)

DOUG MCKIN

possibly because of) this, the Cheshire feels today like a bit of a museum piece, and a fairly shabby one at that, with saw-dust on the floors and a not inconsider-able smell in its warren of bars now that the cigarette smoke has disappeared. Nevertheless, it's one of London's most famous pubs and it's well worth popping in for a pint.

### YE OLDE WATLING                    Pub
☎ 7653 9971; 29 Watling St EC4; ☉ closed Sat & Sun; ⊖ Mansion House
This small strip back behind St Paul's has an almost villagelike feel to it, and the centre of the village is definitely Ye Olde Watling, an old-timer with a gorgeous wooden bar that is always busy from 5pm. Food is served and a there's a 'taste before you try' policy for the great selection of real ales.

# ENTERTAINMENT
## BARBICAN
Arts Centre
☎ information 7638 4141, bookings 7638 8891; www.barbican.org.uk; Silk St EC2; admission £7-50, Pit £15, student half-price Wed; ⊖ Moor gate or Barbican

Now approaching its third decade in showbiz the Barbican is looking a great as ever. Barbican International Theatre Events (bite) continues to find exciting overseas drama companies and it's a dream to watch a film here, with brilliant sloping seating that ensure full-screen view wherever you sit. The Barbican is also home to the wonderful London Symphony Orchestra, and stages dance performances within its eclectic program.

# THE SOUTH BANK

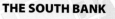

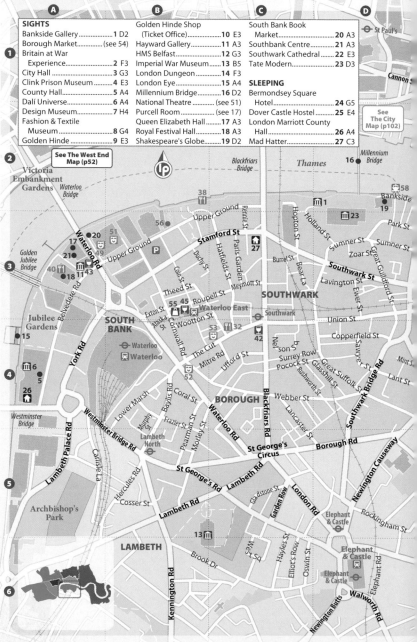

**SIGHTS**
Bankside Gallery ..................... 1 D2
Borough Market ............. (see 54)
Britain at War
  Experience ........................ 2 F3
City Hall .................................. 3 G3
Clink Prison Museum ......... 4 E3
County Hall ............................. 5 A4
Dalí Universe ........................ 6 A4
Design Museum ................... 7 H4
Fashion & Textile
  Museum .............................. 8 G4
Golden Hinde ......................... 9 E3

Golden Hinde Shop
  (Ticket Office) .................. 10 E3
Hayward Gallery ................ 11 A3
HMS Belfast ........................ 12 G3
Imperial War Museum ...... 13 B5
London Dungeon .............. 14 F3
London Eye ......................... 15 A4
Millennium Bridge ........... 16 D2
National Theatre ........... (see 51)
Purcell Room .................. (see 17)
Queen Elizabeth Hall ...... 17 A3
Royal Festival Hall ........... 18 A3
Shakespeare's Globe ........ 19 D2

South Bank Book
  Market ............................... 20 A3
Southbank Centre ............. 21 A3
Southwark Cathedral ....... 22 E3
Tate Modern ...................... 23 D3

**SLEEPING**
Bermondsey Square
  Hotel ................................. 24 G5
Dover Castle Hostel ......... 25 E4
London Marriott County
  Hall .................................... 26 A4
Mad Hatter ......................... 27 C3

THE SOUTH BANK

Orient Espresso.................**28** E3
Southwark Rose Hotel......**29** E3
St Christopher's Inn.........**30** E3
St Christopher's Village....**31** E4

**EATING**
Anchor & Hope..................**32** C4
Applebee's Fish Café.........**33** E3
Bermondsey Kitchen........**34** G5
Butler's Wharf Chop
    House.............................**35** H3
Champor-Champor..........**36** F4
Magdalen.........................**37** G3
Oxo Tower Restaurant &
    Brasserie.......................**38** B2
Roast................................**39** E3
Skylon..............................**40** A3

**DRINKING**
Anchor Bankside..............**41** E3
Baltic...............................**42** C4
Concrete..........................**43** A3
George Inn.......................**44** E3
King's Arms......................**45** B3
Rake.................................**46** E3
Royal Oak.........................**47** E4
Wine Wharf......................**48** E3

**ENTERTAINMENT &
ACTIVITIES**
BFI Southbank...................**49** A3
Menier Chocolate
    Factory.........................**50** E3
National Theatre...............**51** B3
Old Vic............................**52** B4

Shakespeare's
    Globe........................(see 19)
Southbank Centre.........(see 21)
Young Vic........................**53** C4

**SHOPPING**
Black + Blum................(see 38)
Borough Market...............**54** E3
Konditor & Cook..............**55** B3
South Bank Book
    Market......................(see 20)

**TRANSPORT**
London Bicycle
    Tour Company..............**56** B3
On Your Bike....................**57** F3
Tate Boat.........................**58** D2

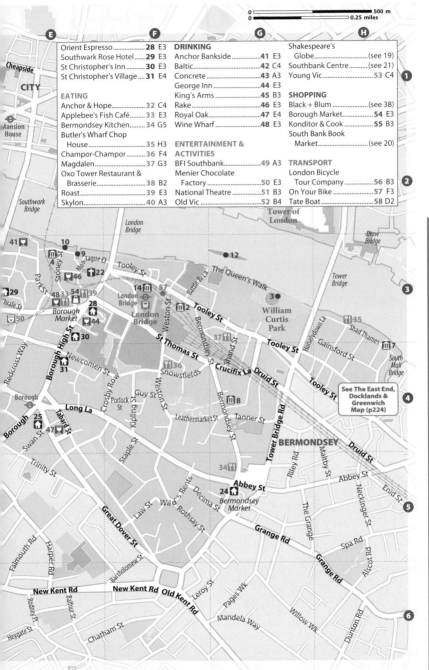

THE SOUTH BANK

# THE SOUTH BANK HIGHLIGHTS

**1**

# TATE MODERN

**London's world-class modern art museum remains a firm favourite with visitors as much for its superb Pritzker Prize-winning conversion of the former Bankside Power Station into London's most visited art gallery as for its contents. But while the conversion and the views are incomparable, there's no chance that they'll outshine the magnificent collection of international art. Here are just a few of our very favourite works on display:**

## ☟ OUR DON'T MISS LIST

**❶ WATER-LILLIES – CLAUDE MONET (1916)**

This oil painting is one of many Monet pictures of the water-lilly pond at his home in Giverny. In concentrating on the changing light and abstract surface of the water, the painting conveys a sense of being immersed in nature.

**❷ WEEPING WOMAN – PICASSO (1937)**

This extraordinarily vivid portrayal of loss and grief is the last in a series of paintings of individuals featured in *Guernica*,

Picasso's masterpiece of human suffering painted after a German bomb raid on the town of the same name during the Spanish Civil War. The painting is based on his lover Dora Marr.

**❸ TRIPTYCH, AUGUST 1972 – BACON (1972)**

This macabre masterpiece depicts a scene that would haunt Francis Bacon for the last two decades of his life: the suicide of his alcoholic lover George Dyer in Paris. Part of a series of paint-

Clockwise from top: Turbine Hall; Art installation; Inside the gallery; Turbine Hall detail; Tate Modern, Tate Modern from across the River Thames

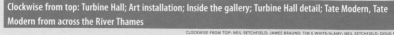

ngs known as the Black Triptychs, these are some of the most harrowing of even Bacon's work.

## ❹ DYNAMIC SUPREMATISM – MALEVICH (1915 OR 1916)

Malevich's paintings coincided with the unparalleled artistic experimentation brought about by the prelude to the 1917 Revolution in Russia. Malevich took up a form of representative painting he termed 'Supremetism'. This, one of his most famous works, depicts abstract forms pulling and pushing each other with no reference to the real world.

## ❺ UNTITLED – ROTHKO (1950-2)

This beautiful symphony of yellow and grey is typical of Rothko's later works in which fuzzy monochromatic forms float against contrasting backgrounds in a blissfully meditative style. The Tate Modern got egg on its face in 2008 when it was revealed that two of their Rothko friezes had been hung the wrong way round. In fairness, it's not hard to imagine how this mistake was made.

## ↘ THINGS YOU NEED TO KNOW

**Lunch with a view** Book a table at the top-floor restaurant to break up your visit in style **Top Tip** If you want to do both Tate galleries in one day, take the regular Tate Boat on to Tate Britain **Free tours** Free, thematic 45-minute tours leave throughout the day every day **For full details on Tate Modern, see p140**

# THE SOUTH BANK HIGHLIGHTS

**2**

## ⬈ FLY ON THE EYE

The **London Eye** (p139), erected, like the Eiffel Tower in Paris as a temporary structure, is now an integral part of the London skyline, and the city would now be almost unthinkable without it. But don't miss taking a 'flight' – the views are spectacular and the entire experience a highlight of many people's visit. Book online to avoid the lines.

**3**

## ⬈ VISIT THE GLOBE

History or drama lovers should look no further for their first stop on the South Bank. **Shakespeare's Globe** (p142), a painstaking reproduction of the theatre where the Bard worked and put on many of his plays for the first time, allows you to experience Elizabethan drama exactly as people four centuries ago would have done, including having to stand if you buy the cheapest tickets. Just hope it doesn't rain...

**4**

### ◤ SHOP AT BOROUGH MARKET

If you hear the way that some Londoners talk about Borough Market (p145), you'd think it was a holy site or shrine. It fulfils a similar role for serious London foodies. Come and peruse the freshest produce in the city here from Thursday to Saturday.

**5**

### ◤ CROSS THE MILLENNIUM BRIDGE

The delightful Millennium Bridge (p141) connects Bankside and the Tate Modern to the City and St Paul's. It was the first new bridge across the Thames for over a century when it opened in 2000, as well as the first ever pedestrian-only bridge in the city. Wander across for great views in all directions.

**6**

### ◤ DISCOVER THE SOUTHBANK CENTRE

Explore the various cultural attractions at the architecturally divisive Southbank Centre (p139). Here you'll find the fantastic Hayward Gallery, one of London's best art spaces, the awesome National Film Theatre and the gloriously revamped concert venue that is the Royal Festival Hall.

2 DENNIS JOHNSON; 3 NEIL SETCHFIELD; 4 RICK GERHARTER; 5 LAWRENCE WORCESTER; 6 DOUG MCKINLAY

2 London Eye (p139); 3 Shakespeare's Globe (p142); 4 Borough Market (p145); 5 Millennium Bridge (p141); 6 Southbank Centre (p139)

# THE SOUTH BANK WALK

**Beginning at Waterloo station, this relaxed one and a half mile walk will take you across the south bank of the River Thames and past some of London's most important cultural establishments. It can be done in under an hour, though it's much better not to rush this one.**

### ❶ COUNTY HALL

Across Westminster Bridge from the Houses of Parliament, this monumental building was the seat of London's local government from 1922 until Prime Minister Margaret Thatcher dissolved the Greater London Council in 1986. It now houses museums and hotels.

### ❷ BFI SOUTHBANK

The flashy headquarters of the **British Film Institute** (BFI; p151) in South Bank is a mecca for film buffs and historians alike. It screens thousands of films in four theatres each year, and archived films are available for watching in the new Mediatheque.

### ❸ TATE MODERN

London's most popular attraction, the wonderful **Tate Modern** (p140) is housed in a fantastically converted former power station overlooking the river. Its incredible permanent collection of modern art is free to visit and one of London's best treats. Don't miss the excellent installations in the main Turbine Hall.

### ❹ MILLENNIUM BRIDGE

This **pedestrian bridge** (p141) linking the north and south banks of the Thames, a slender 'blade of light' designed by Sir Norman Foster, is everything contemporary architecture should be: modern, beautiful and useful. It carries up to 10,000 pedestrians each day.

### ❺ SHAKESPEARE'S GLOBE

Now firmly entrenched as a London must, the **Globe** (p142) is a superb recreation of the theatre where Shakespeare worked and saw many of his plays first performed. It is definitely worth stopping to see, even if you don't see a play.

### ❻ GOLDEN HINDE

Now that the *Cutty Sark* is on sick leave, this **barge** (p141) is the only masted ship open to visitors in a city that was once the largest and richest port in the world. It's tiny but fascinating and well worth a visit.

# THE SOUTH BANK WALK

## **7** SOUTHWARK CATHEDRAL

Sometimes referred to as the 'Cinderella of English cathedrals', this **house of worship** (p143) is often overlooked but well worth a visit, especially for its historical associations. A monument to Shakespeare, whose great works were originally written for the Bankside playhouses nearby, takes pride of place here.

## **8** CITY HALL

Nicknamed 'the egg' (or, more cheekily, 'the testicle' because of its shape), this **glass-clad building** (The Queen's Walk SE1; admission free; 8.30am-6pm Mon-Thu, to 5.30pm Fri; Tower Hill or London Bridge; ) could also be likened to a spaceman wearing a helmet. It has an interior spiral ramp ascending above the assembly chamber to the building's roof, which has now been fitted with energy-saving solar panels.

# THE SOUTH BANK'S BEST...

## ↘ CULTURAL EXPERIENCES

- **See a play at the Globe** (p142) Experience Shakespeare as the Elizabethans did.
- **Exhibit at the Hayward Gallery** (p140) We're never disappointed by shows at this excellent art gallery.
- **Film at the BFI** (p151) New release, film festival or golden oldie – the FI has it all.
- **Concert at the Royal Festival Hall** (p139) See big names perform in an incredible venue.

## ↘ PLACES WITH A VIEW

- **London Eye** (p139) It's hard to get a better view of the whole city than from this iconic Ferris wheel.
- **Tate Modern** (p140) Head to the Level 4 Espresso Bar for great river views.
- **Millennium Bridge** (p141) Wander between the City and Bankside and see London all around you.

## ↘ THINGS FOR FREE

- **Tate Modern** (p140) The permanent collection here is completely free.
- **Borough Market** (p145) Get free samples from generous farmers at this temple to food.
- **Southwark Cathedral** (p143) Discover this ancient church with its wealth of London history.
- **Mediatheque** (p151) Watch films and TV shows from the BFI archive absolutely free.

## ↘ TABLES BY THE RIVER

- **Butlers Wharf Chop House** (p148) Fantastic views of Tower Bridge.
- **Oxo Tower** (p147) Combine lunch and great city views at this top notch restaurant.
- **Skylon** (p148) Unbeatable river views.

Left: Hayward Gallery (p140); Right: Borough Market (p145)

# DISCOVER THE SOUTH BANK

Until the late 1990s the southern part of central London was the city's forgotten underside – rundown, neglected and offering little to visitors once they'd been to the Southbank arts venues. That's all changed now, and the transformation of the so-called South Bank has been nothing short of astonishing. The London Eye 'wheel of good fortune' has been raised across the water from the neo-Gothic Parliament at Westminster, while the disused Bankside Power Station has morphed into Tate Modern (p140), London's most visited sight, opposite august St Paul's Cathedral.

The best way to see this neighbourhood is on foot. And if you follow the Silver Jubilee Walkway and the South Bank section of the Thames Path (p136) along the southern riverbank – one of the most pleasant strolls in town – you're in the perfect position to see it all. And always in sight is Father Thames himself.

# SIGHTS

## LONDON EYE

☎ 0870 500 0600; www.londoneye.com; Jubilee Gardens SE1; adult/4-15yr/senior £17/8.50/14; ☼ 10am-8pm Oct-Apr, to 9pm May, Jun & Sep, to 9.30pm Jul & Aug, closed 1 week in Jan; ⊖ Waterloo; ♿

It's difficult to remember what London looked like before the landmark London Eye began twirling at the southwestern end of Jubilee Gardens in 2000. Not only has it fundamentally altered the skyline of the South Bank but, standing 135m tall in a fairly flat city, it is visible from many surprising parts of the city (eg Kensington and Mayfair). A ride – or 'flight', as it is called here – in one of the wheel's 32 glass-enclosed gondolas holding up to 28 people is something you really can't miss if you want to say you've 'done' London; 3.5 million people a year give it a go. It takes a gracefully slow 30 minutes and, weather permitting, you can see 25 miles in every direction from the top of what is the world's tallest Ferris wheel.

## SOUTHBANK CENTRE

☎ 0871 663 2500; www.southbankcentre.co.uk; Belvedere Rd SE1; ⊖ Waterloo; ♿

The flagship venue of the **Southbank Centre**, the collection of concrete buildings and walkways shoehorned between Hungerford and Waterloo Bridges, is the **Royal Festival Hall**. It is the oldest building of the centre still standing, having been erected to cheer up a glum postwar populace as part of the 1951 Festival of Britain. Its slightly curved facade of glass and Portland stone always won it more public approbation than its 1970s neighbours, but a recent £90-million refit added new pedestrian walkways, bookshops, music stores and food outlets below it, including a restaurant called **Skylon** (p148).

Just north, **Queen Elizabeth Hall** is the second-largest concert venue in the centre and hosts chamber orchestras, quartets, choirs, dance performances and sometimes opera. It also contains the smaller **Purcell Room**. Underneath its elevated floor you'll find a real skateboarders' hangout, suitably decorated with masterful graffiti tagging.

The **Hayward Gallery** (☎ 0871 663 2509; www.southbankcentre.co.uk/visual-arts; admission £7-9; ⏲ 10am-6pm, to 10pm Fri) is one of London's premier exhibition spaces for major international art shows. The grey fortresslike building dating from 1968 makes an excellent hanging space for the blockbuster temporary exhibitions it puts on.

The **South Bank Book Market** (⏲ 11am-7pm), with prints and second-hand books, takes place daily immediately in front of the **BFI Southbank** (p151) under the arches of Waterloo Bridge.

## NATIONAL THEATRE

☎ 7452 3000; www.nationaltheatre.org.uk; South Bank SE1; ⊖ Waterloo; ♿

This is the nation's flagship theatre complex, comprising three auditoriums: the Olivier, the Lyttelton and the Cottesloe. Opened in 1976 and modernised to the tune of £42 million a decade back, it's been undergoing an artistic renaissance under the directorship of Nicholas Hytner. **Backstage tours** (adult/concession/family £5.90/4.90/12.70), lasting 1¼ hours, are also available. There are six daily Monday to Friday, two on Saturday and one on Sunday. Consult the website for exact times.

## TATE MODERN

☎ information & bookings 7887 8000; www.tate.org.uk/modern; Queen's Walk SE1; admission free, special exhibitions £8-10; ⏲ 10am-6pm Sun-Thu, to 10pm Fri & Sat; ⊖ St Paul's, Southwark or London Bridge; ♿

The public's love affair with this phenomenally successful modern art gallery shows no sign of waning a decade after it opened. Serious art critics have occasionally swiped at its populism, particularly the 'participatory art' exhibited in the **Turbine Hall**, but an average five million visitors a year appear to disagree, making it the world's most popular contemporary art gallery and – almost unbelievably – the most visited sight in London, just ahead of the British Museum.

The critics are right in one sense though: this 'Tate Modern effect' is really more about the building and its location than about the mostly 20th-century art inside. Swiss architects Herzog & de Meuron won the prestigious Pritzker Prize for their transformation of the empty Bankside Power Station, which was built between 1947 and 1963 and closed in 1981. Leaving the building's single central chimney, adding a two-storey glass box onto the roof and using the vast Turbine Hall as a dramatic entrance space were three strokes of genius. Then, of course, there are the wonderful views of the Thames and St Paul's, particularly from the restaurant-bar on the 7th level and the espresso bar on the 4th. There's also a cafe on the 2nd level, plus places to relax overlooking the Turbine Hall. An 11-storey sloping brick extension to the southwest corner, by the same architects, will be completed in 2012.

Tate Modern's permanent collection on levels 3 and 5 is now arranged by both theme and chronology. **States of Flux** is devoted to early-20th-century avant-garde movements, including cubism and futurism. **Poetry and Dream** examines surrealism through various themes and techniques. **Material Gestures** features European and American painting and sculpture of the 1940s and '50s. The new **Energy and Process** gallery will have Arte Povera, revolutionary art of the 1960s, as its main focus.

More than 60,000 works are on constant rotation here, and the curators have at their disposal paintings by Georges Braque, Henri Matisse, Piet

DOUG MCKINLAY
National Theatre (p140) at night

Mondrian, Andy Warhol, Mark Rothko, Roy Lichtenstein and Jackson Pollock, as well as pieces by Joseph Beuys, Marcel Duchamp, Damien Hirst, Rebecca Horn, Claes Oldenburg and Auguste Rodin. Audioguides, with four different tours, are available for £2. Free guided highlights tours depart at 11am, noon, 2pm and 3pm daily.

The **Tate Boat** (www.tate.org.uk/tatetotate; one-way adult/5-16yr/student £5/2.50/3.35; every 40min 10.10am-4.50pm) operates between the Bankside Pier at Tate Modern and the Millbank Pier at its sister-museum **Tate Britain** (p95). Services from the latter depart from 10.30am to 5.10pm daily also at 40-minute intervals. Discounts are available for Travelcard holders.

## MILLENNIUM BRIDGE

The Millennium Bridge pushes off from the south bank of the Thames in front of Tate Modern and berths on the north bank at the steps of Peter's Hill below St Paul's Cathedral. The low-slung frame designed by Sir Norman Foster and Antony Caro looks pretty spectacular, particularly lit up at night with fibre optics, and the view of St Paul's from the South Bank has swiftly become one of London's iconic images. The bridge got off on the wrong, err, footing when it had to be closed just three days after opening in June 2000 because of the alarming way it swayed under the weight of pedestrians. An 18-month refit costing £5 million eventually saw it right.

## GOLDEN HINDE
☎ 7403 0123, bookings 0870 011 8700; www.goldenhinde.org; St Mary Overie Dock, Cathedral St SE1; adult/concession/family £7/5/20; 10am-5.30pm; ❷ London Bridge

Okay, it looks like a dinky theme-park ride and kids do love it, but stepping aboard this replica of Sir Francis Drake's famous Tudor ship will inspire genuine admiration for the admiral and his rather short – average height: 1.6m – crew, which counted between 40 and 60. A tiny five-deck galleon just like this was home to Drake and his crew from 1577 to 1580 as they became the first sailors to circumnavigate

THE SOUTH BANK

SIGHTS

DOUG MCKINI

Shakespeare's Globe theatre

## ⬐ SHAKESPEARE'S GLOBE

Shakespeare's Globe consists of the reconstructed Globe Theatre and, beneath it, an exhibition hall, entry to which includes a **tour** (departing every 15 to 30 minutes) of the Globe Theatre, except when matinées are being staged in season.

The original Globe – known as the 'Wooden O' after its circular shape and roofless centre – was erected in 1599 with timber taken from the demolished Theatre (1576) on Curtain Rd in Shoreditch. The Globe was closed in 1642 after the English Civil War was won by the Puritans, who regarded the theatre as the devil's workshop, and it was dismantled two years later. Despite the worldwide popularity of Shakespeare over the centuries, the Globe was barely a distant memory when American actor (and later film director) Sam Wanamaker came searching for it in 1949. Undeterred by the fact that the foundations of the theatre had vanished, Wanamaker set up the Globe Playhouse Trust in 1970 and began fundraising for a memorial theatre. Work started only 200m from the original Globe site in 1987, but Wanamaker died four years before it opened in 1997.

The new Globe was painstakingly constructed with 600 oak pegs (there's not a nail or a screw in the house), specially fired Tudor bricks and thatching reeds from Norfolk that pigeons supposedly don't like; even the plaster contains goat hair, lime and sand as it did in Shakespeare's time.

**Things you need to know:** ☎ 7902 1400, bookings 7401 9919; www.shakespeares-globe.org; 21 New Globe Walk SE1; exhibition incl guided tour of theatre adult £7.50-10.50, 5-15yr £4.50-6.50, senior & student £6.50-8.50, family £20-28; ⏱ 9am-12.30 & 1-5pm Mon-Sat, 9am-11.30am & noon-5pm Sun late Apr–mid-Oct, 9am-5pm mid-Oct–late Apr; ⊖ St Paul's or London Bridge; ♿

the globe. Adult visitors wandering round stooped must also marvel at how the taller, modern-day crew managed to spend 20 years at sea on this 37m-long replica, after it was launched in 1973.

Tickets are available from the **Golden Hinde Shop** (Pickfords Wharf, 1 Clink St SE1). You can also spend the night aboard for £39.95 per person, including a supper of stew and bread and a breakfast of bread and cheese.

## CLINK PRISON MUSEUM

☎ 7403 0900; www.clink.co.uk; 1 Clink St SE1; adult/concession/family £5/3.50/12; ☉ 10am-6pm Mon-Fri, to 9pm Sat & Sun; ⊖ London Bridge

This one-time private jail in the park of Winchester Palace, a 32-hectare area known as the Liberty of the Clink and under the jurisdiction of the bishops of Winchester and not the City, was used to detain debtors, prostitutes, thieves and even actors. This was the notorious address that gave us the expression 'in the clink' (in jail). The poky little museum inside, which was getting a much needed refit at the time of research, reveals the wretched life of the prisoners who were forced to pay for their own food and accommodation and sometimes had to resort to catching and eating mice. There's a nice little collection of instruments of torture, too.

## SOUTHWARK CATHEDRAL

☎ 7367 6700; www.southwark.anglican.org/cathedral; Montague Close SE1; admission free, requested donation £4; ☉ 8am-6pm Mon-Fri, from 9am Sat & Sun; ⊖ London Bridge; ♿

The earliest surviving part of this relatively small cathedral is the **retrochoir** at the eastern end, which contains four chapels and was part of the 13th-century Priory of St Mary Overie (from 'St Mary over the Water'). However, most of the cathedral is Victorian, including the nave (1897).

You enter via the southwest door and immediately to the left is the **Marchioness memorial** to the 51 people who died when a pleasure cruiser on the Thames hit a dredger and sank near Southwark Bridge in 1989. Walk up the north aisle of the nave and on the left you'll see the brightly coloured and canopied **tomb of John Gower**, the 14th-century poet who was the first to write in English. In the north transept you'll see a **memorial tablet to Lionel Lockyer**, a quack doctor celebrated for his patent medicines; note its humorous epitaph. On the eastern side of the north transept is the **Harvard Chapel**, named after John Harvard, founder of the namesake university in Cambridge, Massachusetts, who was baptised here in 1607.

Cross into the choir to admire the 16th-century **Great Screen** separating the choir from the retrochoir, a gift of the bishop of Winchester in 1520. On the choir floor below the organ is a tablet marking the **tomb of Edmond Shakespeare**, actor-brother of the Bard, who died in 1607.

In the south aisle of the nave have a look at the green alabaster **monument to William Shakespeare** with depictions of the original Globe Theatre and Southwark Cathedral; the stained-glass window above shows characters from *A Midsummer Night's Dream, Hamlet* and *The Tempest*. Beside the monument is a **plaque to Sam Wanamaker** (1919-93), the American film director and actor who was the force behind the rebuilt Globe Theatre.

## LONDON DUNGEON

☎ 7403 7221, bookings 0871 423 2240; www.thedungeons.com; 28-34 Tooley St SE1; adult/5-15yr/concessions £21.95/15.95/19.95; ☉ 10.30am-5pm; ⊖ London Bridge

Under the arches of the Tooley St railway bridge, the London Dungeon was

THE SOUTH BANK

SIGHTS

KEVIN FOY/ALAMY

Design Museum (p145)

supposedly developed after some-body's kid didn't find Madame Tussauds Chamber of Horrors frightening enough. Well, it failed in that endeavour but the place has been minting money ever since.

It all starts with a stagger through a mirror maze (the Labyrinth of the Lost); followed by a waltz through Bedlam; a push through a torture chamber; a run 'through' the Great Fire of London (where wafting fabric makes up the 'flames'); a close shave with Sweeney Todd, the demon barber of Fleet St; and an encounter with Jack the Ripper: the Victorian serial killer is shown with the five prostitutes he sliced and diced, their entrails hanging out in full gory display. A new attraction called Surgery: Blood & Guts takes its cue from the Old Operating Theatre Museum just aroun the corner.

The best bits are the vaudevillian de lights of being sentenced by a mad, be wigged judge on trumped-up charge the fairground-ride boat to Traitor's Gat and the Extremis Drop Ride to Doom tha has you 'plummeting' to your death b hanging from the gallows.

It's a good idea to buy tickets onlin for this camped-up 90-minute gore fest to avoid the mammoth queue Depending on the time slot you choos the cost of tickets can drop to as low a £16.95/10.95/13.95 for adults/childre 5-15 years/concessions. Hours vary ac cording to season; check the website.

## HMS BELFAST

☎ 7940 6300; www.hmsbelfast.iwm.org.uk; Morgan's Lane, Tooley St SE1; adult/under 16yr/ concession £10.70/free/8.60; ☺ 10am-6pm Mar Oct, to 5pm Nov-Feb; ⊖ London Bridge; ⓖ Moored on the Thames opposite Potter Fields Park, HMS *Belfast* is a big toy tha kids of all ages generally love. Of course for most of its commissioned life thi large, light cruiser had a rather more seri ous purpose. Launched in 1938 she serve in WWII, most noticeably in the Normand landings, and during the Korean War.

It probably helps to be keen on thing naval, but the HMS *Belfast,* spread ove five decks and four platforms, is surpris ingly interesting for what it shows of th way of life on board a cruiser, from boile room to living quarters. The operation room has been reconstructed to show its role in the 1943 Battle of North Cap off Norway, which ended in the sinkin of the German battleship *Scharnhors* On the bridge you can visit the admiral' cabin and sit in his chair, and you can pee through the sights of the 4in HA/LA gun on the open deck.

## BRITAIN AT WAR EXPERIENCE

☎ 7403 3171; www.britainatwar.co.uk; 64-66 Tooley St SE1; adult/5-15yr/concession/family £11.45/5.50/6.50/29; ☉ 10am-5pm Apr-Oct, to 4.30pm Nov-Mar; ⊖ London Bridge

Under another Tooley St railway arch, the Britain at War Experience aims to educate the younger generation about the effect WWII had on daily life, while simultaneously playing on the nostalgia of the war generation. In general it's a tribute to ordinary people and comes off fairly well – though the rather musty displays make it feel like you're on a low-budget TV stage-set.

You descend by lift to a reproduction of an Underground station fitted with bunks, tea urns, gas masks and even a lending library (as some stations were, for use as air-raid shelters) and then progress through rooms that display wartime newspaper front pages, posters and Ministry of Food ration books. The BBC Radio Studio allows you to hear domestic and international broadcasts by everyone from Winston Churchill and Edward Murrow to Hitler and Lord Haw Haw. The Rainbow Corner, a mock-up of a club frequented by American GIs 'overpaid, oversexed and over here'. Finally, you emerge amid the wreckage of a shop hit by a bomb during the Blitz, with the smoke still eddying around and the injured – or dead – being carried from the rubble.

## DESIGN MUSEUM

☎ 7403 6933, recorded information 0870 833 9955; www.designmuseum.org; 28 Shad Thames SE1; adult/under 12yr/student/concession £8.50/free/5/6.50; ☉ 10am-5.45pm; ⊖ Tower Hill or London Bridge; &

Founded by Sir Terence Conran and housed in a 1930s-era warehouse, the Design Museum has a revolving program of special exhibitions devoted to contemporary design. Both populist and popular, past shows

have dealt with everything from Manolo Blahnik shoes to Formula One racing cars, the Model T Ford in its centenary year and that miracle material, Velcro.

## BOROUGH MARKET

☎ 7407 1002; www.boroughmarket.org.uk; cnr Southwark & Stoney Sts SE1; ☉ 11am-5pm Thu, noon-6pm Fri, 9am-4pm Sat; ⊖ London Bridge

On this spot in some form or another since the 13th century, 'London's Larder' has enjoyed an enormous renaissance in recent years. It's overflowing with food-lovers, both experienced and wannabes, and has become quite a tourist destination.

# SLEEPING
## WATERLOO
### LONDON MARRIOTT COUNTY HALL
Hotel £££

☎ 7928 5200; www.marriott.co.uk/lonch; Westminster Bridge Rd SE1; r from £240, with river views from £270, breakfast £18.95-20.95; ⊖ Westminster; ✖ 🖳 🐾 &

This elegant 200-room hotel is famed for its fabulous close-up views of the Thames and the Houses of Parliament. It was formerly the headquarters of the Greater London Council; the atmosphere in the traditional rooms remains somewhat stuffy in a wood-panelled kind of way. There's a well-equipped fitness centre on the 5th floor and a 25m-long pool on the 6th floor.

# BANKSIDE & SOUTHWARK
### SOUTHWARK ROSE HOTEL
Boutique Hotel ££

☎ 7015 1480; www.southwarkrosehotel.co.uk; 47 Southwark Bridge Rd SW1; d & tw £125-190, breakfast £9-13, weekend rate incl breakfast £95; ⊖ London Bridge; ✖ 🖳 &

Billed as London's first 'budget boutique' hotel, this 84-room place just minutes

Dalí Universe next to the London Eye

ORIEN HARVEY

## ↘ IF YOU LIKE...

If you liked the Tate Modern (p140) then we think you'll like some of the South Bank's other galleries and museums:

- **Dalí Universe** Within the cavernous walls of County Hall next to the London Eye is this museum devoted to everyone's favourite surrealist. With over 500 Dalí paintings on display, it's actually worth the steep entry fee.
- **Bankside Gallery** Home of the Royal Watercolour Society, this friendly place has no permanent collection, but there are frequently changing exhibitions of watercolours, prints and engravings.
- **Fashion & Textile Museum** This original and interesting museum, founded by British fashion icon Zandra Rhodes, is one of the world's first museums devoted to fashion. There is no permanent collection, but quarterly exhibitions on wide-ranging subjects.

from the Thames is very versatile. Service is good, prices are reasonable and while the rooms are compact, they're stylish in a vaguely minimalist way, with plum-coloured headboards, white fluffy duvets and silver lampshades.

**MAD HATTER** Hotel £

☎ 7401 9222; www.madhatterhotel.com; 3-7 Stamford St SE1; r £145-165, breakfast £7.50-11 weekend rate incl breakfast £90-100; ⊖ Southwark; ✺ ▯ &

Its 30 rooms across three floors are quit generic, but the Mad Hatter feels slight homier than most chain hotels – belongs to the Fuller's brewery group thanks to its traditionally styled receptio area and (surprise, surprise) an adjacer pub with the same name.

# BOROUGH & BERMONDSEY

## BERMONDSEY SQUARE HOTEL Boutique Hotel £

☎ 0870 111 2525, 0774 884 3350; www.ber mond seysquarehotel.co.uk; Bermondsey Sq, Tower Bridge Rd SE1; r £119-299; ⊖ London Bridge; ✺ ▯ &

Just the ticket for this up-and-coming are of South London crying out for quality ac commodation is this stunner of a purpose built boutique hotel with 79 rooms. Th smallish standard rooms make good us of space with an excellent work area an Apple TVs that link with your laptop an iPod, a rainforest of a shower and grea modern art on the walls.

## ST CHRISTOPHER'S VILLAGE Hostel

☎ 7407 1856; www.st-christophers.co.uk; 161-163 Borough High St SE1; dm £12.50-21, d & tw £46-56; ⊖ Borough or London Bridge; ▯

This 185-bed place is the flagship of a hos tel chain with basic, but cheap and clea accommodation totalling eight proper ties across London. There's a roof garde with bar, barbecue and excellent view of the Thames, as well as a cinema an Belushi's bar below for serious partyin to 2am weekdays and 4am at the week end. Dorms have four to 14 beds. Its tw

THE SOUTH BANK

EATING

nearby branches (same contact details) are **St Christopher's Inn** (121 Borough High St SE1), with 50 beds, another pub below and a small veranda, and the **Orient Espresso** (59-61 Borough High St SE1), with 40 beds, a laundry, cafe, and a dormitory for women only.

## DOVER CASTLE HOSTEL Hostel £
☎ 7403 7773; www.dovercastlehostel.co.uk; 6a Great Dover St SE1; dm £12-19.50, per week £80; ⊖ Borough; 🖳

This 80-bed hostel in a four-storey Victorian terrace house has a welcoming bar below it as well as a lounge with TV, kitchen facilities, luggage storage and laundry (£5). It's a somewhat frayed but friendly place to stay. Dorms have between three and 12 beds. It also organises flat shares from single/double £119/150 per week, including bills.

# EATING

The revitalised South Bank, with the Tate Modern, the replicated Globe Theatre and the splendid Millennium Bridge its major drawcards, now has an interesting array of restaurants. Many, including the Oxo Tower and Butlers Wharf Chop House, take full advantage of their riverine locations, offering a titbit of romance as a prelude to the main course. Borough and Bermondsey, historically important but run-down and almost forgotten in modern times, are no longer just the provinces of smoked and jellied eel; you're just as likely to find yourself sitting in a Victorian market pavilion and enjoying fresh oysters or a perfectly grilled steak.

## WATERLOO
### OXO TOWER RESTAURANT & BRASSERIE Modern International £££
☎ 7803 3888; www.harveynichols.com; 8th fl, Barge House St SE1; mains £17-33, brasserie 2-/3-course set lunch £21.50/24.50, restaurant 3-course set lunch £33.50; ⊖ Waterloo

The conversion of the old Oxo Tower on the South Bank into housing with this restaurant on the 8th floor helped spur much of the dining renaissance south of the river. In the stunning glassed-in terrace you have a front-row seat for the

DOUG MCKINLAY

Stunning view from the Oxo Tower restaurant

The Anchor Bankside pub (p150)

GUIDO DONATI/ALAMY

best view in London, and you pay for this (not the fusion food) handsomely in the brasserie and stratospherically in the restaurant.

## SKYLON                 Modern International ££
☎ 7654 7800; www.skylonrestaurant.co.uk; 3rd fl, Royal Festival Hall, Southbank Centre, Belvedere Rd SE1; restaurant 2-/3-course meal £37.50/42.50, grillroom mains £11.50-16.50; ⏰ grillroom noon-11pm, restaurant lunch daily, dinner to 10.30pm Mon-Sat; ⊖ Waterloo
This cavernous restaurant on the top of the refurbished Royal Festival Hall is divided into grillroom and fine-dining sections with a large bar (open 11am to 1am) separating the two. Floor-to-ceiling windows offer views of the Thames and the City, and the decor of muted colours and

period chairs harkens back to the 195 Festival of Britain, when the hall opened

## ANCHOR & HOPE           Gastropub £
☎ 7928 9898; 36 The Cut SE1; mains £11.50-16; ⏰ closed lunch Mon & dinner Sun; ⊖ Southwark or Waterloo
The hope is that you'll get a table withou waiting hours because you can't book a this quintessential gastropub, except fo Sunday lunch at 2pm. The anchor is gutsy unashamedly carnivorous British food The critics love this place but, with dishe such as salt marsh lamb shoulder cooked for seven hours and soy-braised shin o beef, it's decidedly not for vegetarians.

# BOROUGH & BERMONDSEY
## ROAST                    Modern British £
☎ 7940 1300; www.roast-restaurant.com; 1st fl, Floral Hall, Borough Market, Stoney St SE1; mains £14-25; ⏰ closed dinner Sun; ⊖ London Bridge
The focal point at this unique restauran and bar perched directly above Borough Market is the glassed-in kitchen with an open spit, where ribs of beef, suckling pigs, birds and game (no doubt sourced from the stalls below) are roasted. The emphasis is on roasted meats (feather blade of beef, lamb's kidneys) and seasonal vegetables, though there are lighte dishes from salads to grilled fish.

## BUTLERS WHARF CHOP HOUSE               Modern British ££
☎ 7403 3403; www.chophouse.co.uk; Butlers Wharf Bldg, 36e Shad Thames SE1; mains £15.50-22.50, 2-/3-course set lunch £19.50/24.50, set dinner £22/26; ⊖ Tower Hill
A poster child for early Modern British cuisine, the Chop House continues to create upmarket variants on bangers and mash bubble and squeak, and fish pie, as well a 'new-old' arrivals like Old Spot pork and

patchcock chicken. A great view of Tower Bridge (which may be your main reason for visiting) is part of the deal but best enjoyed from an outdoor table.

## MAGDALEN                    Modern British ££
☎ 7403 1342; www.magdalenrestaurant.co.uk; 152 Tooley St SE1; mains £13.50-17, 2-/3-course set lunch £15.50/18.50; ☾ closed lunch Sat & all day Sun; ⊖ London Bridge

This stylish dining room on two levels seems somewhat out of place in hardcore Tooley St but any port in a storm will do in these parts. The Modern British fare takes familiar dishes and puts a spin on them (roast pork loin with sage and lentils, smoked haddock choucroute). The welcome is warm and the service impeccable. A winner in its class and neighbourhood.

## CHAMPOR-CHAMPOR    Asian Fusion ££
☎ 7403 4600; www.champor-champor.com; 62-64 Weston St SE1; 2-/3-course set meal 25/29; ☾ lunch Thu & Fri, dinner Mon-Sat; ⊖ London Bridge

Not surprisingly, a restaurant whose name means 'mix and match' in Malay serves up some unusual creations. East-West cuisine includes ostrich sausages in Sichuan pepper-and-peanut sauce, and pigeon-and-plum hotpot, as well as vegetarian options such as roast aubergine teriyaki. Some dishes are successful, others less so. The eclectic Asian decor is a delight.

## APPLEBEE'S FISH CAFÉ        Seafood ££
☎ 7407 5777; 5 Stoney St SE1; mains £12.50-19, 2-course set lunch £13.50; ☾ closed Sun & Mon; ⊖ London Bridge

If you are tempted by the offerings of the fishmongers of Borough Market and must have a fix of iodine right then and there, head for this excellent fishmongers with a cafe-restaurant attached. You'll find all manner of fresher-than-fresh fish and

shellfish dishes on the ever-changing chalkboard, but we always go for the meal-in-itself fish soup (£8.50).

## BERMONDSEY KITCHEN        Modern European ££
☎ 7407 5719; www.bermondseykitchen.co.uk; 194 Bermondsey St SE1; mains £9.50-16.50; ☾ closed dinner Sun; ⊖ London Bridge

As this is a great place to curl up on the sofas with the Sunday newspapers or enjoy brunch at the weekend, it's hardly surprising that many locals seem to have made BK their second living room. The Modern European food (with a nod towards the Mediterranean) that comes from the open grill is as homely and unpretentious as the butcher-block tables, and the refreshingly brief menu (six starters and as many mains) changes daily. Set lunch can cost below £10 on weekdays.

# DRINKING
## WATERLOO
### BALTIC                                    Bar
☎ 7928 1111; www.balticrestaurant.co.uk; 74 Blackfriars Rd SE1; ☾ noon to midnight Mon-Sat, to 10.30pm Sun; ⊖ Southwark

This very stylish bar at the front of an Eastern European restaurant specialises – not surprisingly – in vodkas; some 50-plus, including bar-infused concoctions, are on offer. The bright and airy, high-ceilinged dining room, with a glass roof and lovely amber wall, is just behind, should you need some blotter.

### CONCRETE                              Cafe-Bar
☎ 7928 4123; www.southbankcentre.co.uk; Hayward Gallery, Southbank Centre, Belvedere Rd SE1; 10am-6pm Sun & Mon, 10am-11pm Tue-Thu, to 1am Fri & Sat; ⊖ Waterloo

By day this outlet in the **Hayward Gallery** (p140) is a discreet cafe serving tea and cake to an earnest art-loving crowd. By night this Cinderella transforms into a wicked step-sister, with late-night bar, DJs and live music from Thursday to Saturday and neon-pink cement mixers as props.

## KING'S ARMS                          Pub
☎ 7928 4334; 25 Roupell St SE1; ⊖ Waterloo or Southwark

A relaxed and charming neighbourhood boozer at the corner of a terraced Waterloo backstreet, the award-winning King's Arms was a funeral parlour in a previous life, so show some respect. The large traditional bar area, serving up a good selection of ales and bitters, gives way to a fantastically odd conservatory bedecked with junk-store eclectica of local interest, which has decent Thai food.

## ANCHOR BANKSIDE                      Pub
☎ 7407 1577; 34 Park St SE1; ⊖ London Bridge
This pub dating back to the early 17th century (but subsequently rebuilt after the Great Fire and again in the 19th century) has superb views across the Thames from its terrace and is the most central – and most popular – riverside boozer in London; expect a scrum at almost all times. Dictionary writer Samuel Johnson, whose brewer friend owned the joint, drank here as did diarist Samuel Pepys.

## GEORGE INN                           Pub
☎ 7407 2056; Talbot Yard, 77 Borough High St SE1; ⊖ Borough
The always-popular George Inn is London's last surviving galleried coaching inn. It dates from 1676 and is mentioned in Dickens' *Little Dorrit*. No wonder it falls under the protection of the National Trust. It is on the site of the Tabard Inn (thus the Talbot Yard ad

dress), where the pilgrims in Chaucer' *Canterbury Tales* gathered before setting out (well lubricated, we suspect) on the road to Canterbury, Kent.

## RAKE                                 Pub
☎ 7407 0557; 14 Winchester Walk SE1; noon-11pm Mon-Fri, from 10am Sat; ⊖ London Bridge
The place of superlatives – it's the only pub actually in Borough Market and supposedly the smallest boozer in London the Rake has one of the best line-ups of bitters and real ales in town. The outside deck is a plus and has more than doubled the pub's seating capacity.

## ROYAL OAK                            Pub
☎ 7357 7173; 44 Tabard St SE1; noon-11pm Mon-Sat, to 6pm Sun; ⊖ Borough
This authentic Victorian establishment, owned by a small independent brewery in Sussex, is tucked away down a side street and is a mecca for serious beer drinkers. The literati might find their way here too; it's just a hop, skip and a handful of rice south of the Church of St George the Martyr, where Little Dorri (aka Amy) got married in Dickens' eponymous novel.

## WINE WHARF                          Wine Bar
☎ 7940 8335, 0870 899 8856; www.wine wharf co.uk; Stoney St SE1; closed Sun; ⊖ London Bridge
Located in an erstwhile Victorian ware house close to the culinary joys of Borough Market, this very smart wine bar's selection will delight oenophiles as well as people just coming along for a drink. The range is truly enormous, and the staff is more than happy to advise and let you taste. There's live jazz on Monday evenings.

# ENTERTAINMENT & ACTIVITIES

THE SOUTH BANK

## BFI SOUTHBANK                                    Film

☎ information 7633 0274, bookings 7928 3232; www.bfi.org.uk; Belvedere Rd SE1; ⊖ Waterloo

Tucked almost out of sight under the arches of Waterloo Bridge is the British Film Institute, containing four cinemas that screen thousands of films each year, a gallery devoted to the moving image and the **Mediatheque** ( ☎ 7928 3535; admission free; 🕑 1-8pm Tue, 11am-8pm Wed-Sun), where you watch film and TV highlights from the BFI National Archive.

## SOUTHBANK CENTRE          Classical Music

☎ 0871 663 2500; www.southbankcentre.co.uk; Belvedere Rd SE1; admission £8-45; ⊖ Waterloo

The **Royal Festival Hall**, which reopened in 2007 after an extensive two-year overhaul, is London's premier concert venue and seats 3000 in a now acoustic amphitheatre. You can see music and dance performances here and more eclectic gigs at the smaller **Queen Elizabeth Hall** and **Purcell Room**.

## MENIER CHOCOLATE FACTORY
Theatre

☎ 7907 7060; www.menierchocolatefactory.com; 53 Southwark St SE1; ⊖ London Bridge

Theatre and chocolate, two of many Londoners' major passions, have never been as gloriously paired up as they have here – a theatre inside a gorgeous conversion of a 19th-century chocolate factory. To make matters better, the theatre's superb restaurant makes for great combination deals (from around £24 per person for a two-course dinner and a ticket).

## NATIONAL THEATRE                  Theatre

☎ 7452 3000; www.nationaltheatre.org.uk; South Bank SE1; admission £10-41; ⊖ Waterloo

England's flagship theatre showcases a mix of classic and contemporary plays performed by excellent casts. Its outstanding artistic director, Nicholas Hytner, is not only using exciting stagings and plays to attract new audiences but has also slashed

ENTERTAINMENT & ACTIVITIES

DOUG MCKINLAY

BFI Southbank

ticket prices. Sell-out performances allow for some standing room (£5).

### OLD VIC                                    Theatre
☎ 0870 060 6628; www.oldvictheatre.com; Waterloo Rd SE1; ⊖ Waterloo
Never has there been a London theatre with a more famous artistic director. American actor Kevin Spacey looks after this glorious theatre's program and he just keeps going from strength to strength, with such recent pickings as Brian Friel's *Dancing at Lughnasa* with singer Andrea Corr (who knew?) and a new version of Chekhov's *Cherry Orchard* by Tom Stoppard and directed by ex-Donmar Warehouse honcho Sam Mendes.

### SHAKESPEARE'S GLOBE                  Theatre
☎ information 7902 1400, bookings 7401 9919; www.shakespeares-globe.org; 21 New Globe Walk SE1; adult £15-33, concession £12-30, standing £5; ⊖ St Paul's or London Bridge
If you love Shakespeare and the theatre, the Globe will knock you off your feet. This is authentic Shakespearean theatre, and a near-perfect replica of the building the Bard worked in from 1598 to 1611, that follows Elizabethan staging practices. The theatre season runs from late April to mid-October and includes works by Shakespeare and his contemporaries such as Christopher Marlowe.

### YOUNG VIC                                 Theatre
☎ 7922 2922; www.youngvic.org; 66 The Cut SE1; ⊖ Waterloo
One of the capital's most respected theatre troupes – bold, brave and talented

– the Young Vic grabs audiences with ar resting plays such as *Vernon God Little* (a adapted from DBC Pierre's novel) and th English Touring Theatre's foot-stompir soul-funk musical *Been So Long*. There' a lovely two-level bar-restaurant with ar open-air terrace upstairs.

# SHOPPING
### KONDITOR & COOK                    Food & Drin
☎ 7261 0456; www.konditorandcook.com; 22 Cornwall Rd SE1; ⏰ 7.30am-8.30pm Mon-Fri, 8.30am-3pm Sat; ⊖ Waterloo
This elegant cake shop and bakery produces wonderful cakes – lavender anc orange, and lemon and almond – mas sive raspberry meringues, cookies (in cluding gingerbread men!), and loave of warm bread with olives, nuts anc spices.

### BLACK + BLUM                           Homeware
☎ 7633 0022; www.black-blum.com; Unit 2.07, 2nd fl, Oxo Tower, Barge House St SE1; ⏰ 9am-5pm Mon-Fri, from 11am Sat; ⊖ Southwark or Waterloo
You might see 'James the doorman bookend' (a human-shaped doorstop bookend) and 'Mr and Mrs Hangup' (an thropomorphic coat hooks that can indi cate your mood through a choice of eyes in numerous gift shops across town, bu this Anglo-Swiss partnership produce more wonderful stuff in its shop, such a the intricate wire 'bowl' called a Fruit Loop or the Spudski potato masher inspired by a ski pole.

BLOOMSBURY TO REGENT'S PARK

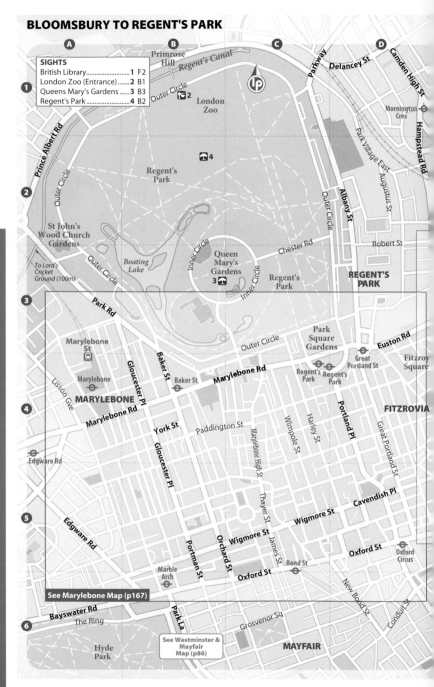

**SIGHTS**
| | | |
|---|---|---|
| British Library | **1** | F2 |
| London Zoo (Entrance) | **2** | B1 |
| Queens Mary's Gardens | **3** | B3 |
| Regent's Park | **4** | B2 |

Primrose Hill

Regent's Canal

London Zoo

Regent's Park

Prince Albert Rd

Outer Circle

St John's Wood Church Gardens

To Lord's Cricket Ground (100m)

Boating Lake

Inner Circle

Queen Mary's Gardens

Chester Rd

Regent's Park

REGENT'S PARK

Robert St

Parkway

Delancey St

Camden High St

Mornington Cres

Hampstead Rd

Park Village East

Augustus St

Albany St

Outer Circle

Park Square Gardens

Euston Rd

Fitzroy Square

Great Portland St

Regent's Park

Regent's Park

FITZROVIA

Park Rd

Marylebone St

Marylebone

Outer Circle

Baker St

Baker St

Marylebone Rd

Portland Pl

Great Portland St

Lisson Gve

Marylebone

MARYLEBONE

Gloucester Pl

Marylebone Rd

York St

Paddington St

Gloucester Pl

Marylebone High St

Harley St

Winpole St

Cavendish Pl

Edgware Rd

Thayer St

Wigmore St

Wigmore St

Wigmore St

James St

Oxford St

Oxford St

Edgware Rd

Portman St

Orchard St

Oxford St

Oxford St

Bond St

New Bond St

Oxford Circus

Marble Arch

See Marylebone Map (p167)

Bayswater Rd

The Ring

Park La

See Westminster & Mayfair Map (p86)

Grosvenor Sq

MAYFAIR

Conduit St

Hyde Park

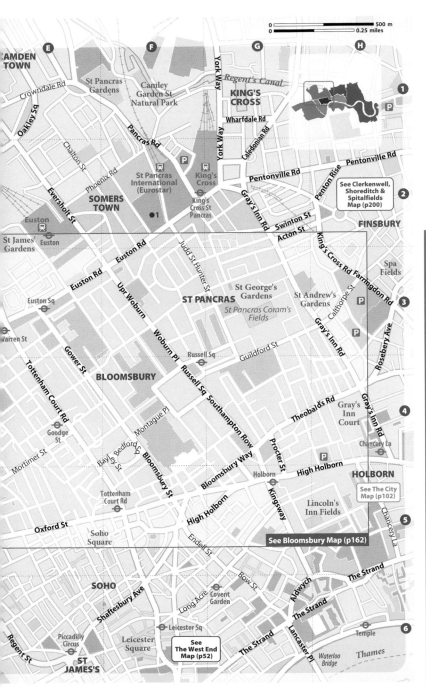

0  500 m
0  0.25 miles

**E** | **F** | **G** | **H**

AMDEN TOWN

Crowndale Rd

Oakley Sq

Chalton St

St Pancras Gardens

Camley Garden St Natural Park

York Way

Regent's Canal

**KING'S CROSS**

Wharfdale Rd

**1**

P

Pancras Rd

York Way

Phoenix Rd

St Pancras International (Eurostar)

King's Cross

Caledonian Rd

Pentonville Rd     Pentonville Rd

Penton Rise

Eversholt St

**SOMERS TOWN**

King's Cross St Pancras

●1

Gray's Inn Rd

See Clerkenwell, Shoreditch & Spitalfields Map (p200)

**2**

Euston

St James' Gardens

Euston

Swinton St

Acton St

King's Cross Rd

**FINSBURY**

Euston Rd

Judd St

Hunter St

Upr Woburn

Euston Sq

Euston Rd

**ST PANCRAS**

St George's Gardens

St Pancras Coram's Fields

St Andrew's Gardens

Calthorpe St

Farringdon Rd

Spa Fields

**3**

P

Warren St

Woburn Pl

Russell Sq

Guildford St

Gray's Inn Rd

P

Roseberry Ave

Gower St

Tottenham Court Rd

**BLOOMSBURY**

Montague Pl

Russell Sq

Southampton Row

Theobald's Rd

Gray's Inn Court

Gray's Inn Rd

**4**

Goodge St

Bayley St

Bedford Sq

Bloomsbury St

Bloomsbury Way

Procter St

High Holborn

Chancery La

Mortimer St

Holborn

**HOLBORN**

Kingsway

P

See The City Map (p102)

Oxford St

Tottenham Court Rd

High Holborn

Lincoln's Inn Fields

Chancery La

**5**

Soho Square

Endell St

See Bloomsbury Map (p162)

**SOHO**

Shaftesbury Ave

Long Acre

Bow St

Covent Garden

Aldwych

The Strand

The Strand

**6**

Regent St

Piccadilly Circus

Leicester Sq

Leicester Square

See The West End Map (p52)

The Strand

Lancaster Pl

Waterloo Bridge

Temple

Thames

**ST JAMES'S**

BLOOMSBURY TO REGENT'S PARK

HIGHLIGHTS

# HIGHLIGHTS

## 1 BRITISH MUSEUM

### BY PAUL COLLINS, CURATOR IN THE MIDDLE EAST AT THE BRITISH MUSEUM

The British Museum is one of London's great wonders. As our slogan suggests, it's truly a museum of the world; in the space of a day you can explore the history and culture of all the world's great civilisations. It's a real privilege to work here.

## ➦ PAUL COLLINS' DON'T MISS LIST

### ❶ ENLIGHTENMENT GALLERY (ROOM 1)

This magnificent room contains an informative display that shows how collectors, antiquaries and travellers viewed and classified objects at the time the museum was founded (1753). It's an excellent introduction to the British Museum.

### ❷ ASSYRIAN LION HUNT FROM NINEVEH (ROOM 10)

These are some of the greatest carvings from the ancient world. They originate from the city of Nineveh, i what is now modern-day Iraq. They'v become especially important given th events of recent years in Iraq.

### ❸ CLOCKS & WATCHES GALLERY (ROOMS 38–9)

These rooms contain a collection of me chanical devices for telling the time. M favourite clock is driven by a ball tha rolls back and forward along a groove plate that releases the mechanism. It' quite a strange experience to be sur

Clockwise from top: The Great Court;  External columns; Domed library of the British Museum; Elgin Marbles

ounded by the ticking, striking and himing of hundreds of clocks!

## EAST STAIRS

n impressive collection of casts of ersian, Mayan and Egyptian reliefs ne the stairs. These were made in the 9th and early 20th centuries, and are istorically important as the original bjects left at the sites have been damged or have disappeared.

## NATIONAL PORTRAIT GALLERY

'd encourage everyone to pay a visit to his wonderful **art gallery** (p69), which ontains Britain's finest collection of istoric portraits, from the early Tudors ight through to the modern day; the ooftop cafe has the most wonderful iew over Trafalgar Sq.

❶ Enlightenment Gallery (Room 1)
❷ Assyrian Lion Hunt from Nineveh (Room 10)
❸ Clocks & Watches Gallery (Rooms 38–9)
❹ East Stairs
❺ National Portrait Gallery

0 ———— 50 m
0 ■■■ 0.02 miles

## ⬎ THINGS YOU NEED TO KNOW

**Best time to visit** Weekdays are quieter than weekends **How long will I need?** At least half a day **Top tips** Audioguides (£3.50) let you explore at your own pace **Tours** Free thirty-minute guided tours are offered throughout the day **For full details on the British Museum, see p161**

# HIGHLIGHTS

**2**

## ↘ LONDON ZOO

The world's oldest zoo has in recent years reinvented itself as one of the best and most progressive zoos in the world, with fewer animals being given more space and comprehensive conservation programs being undertaken. No visit to **London Zoo** (p170) is complete however, without seeing the fantastic Gorilla Kingdom, the modernist Penguin Pool and the replica Rainforest where the monkeys rule!

**3**

## ↗ WANDER THROUGH REGENT'S PARK

London's royal parks are simply superb, and though each one is unique in its own way, we can't think of anywhere more pleasant for a stroll than beautiful **Regent's Park** (p167) where the combination of formal gardens, public art, lakes and the beautiful Regent's Canal that runs along the park's northern edge make this a blissful green space in the middle of London's daily chaos.

BLOOMSBURY TO REGENT'S PARK

## ◢ DISCOVER THE WALLACE COLLECTION

The **Wallace Collection** (p164) is housed in this impressive Marylebone mansion. As well as a fantastic selection of 18th-century art from such masters as Titian, Rubens and Rembrandt, there are some spectacular interiors, a collection of armour and a superb courtyard restaurant to boot.

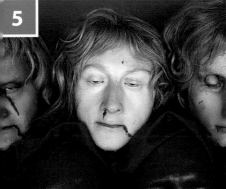

## ◢ SEE MADAME TUSSAUD'S

**Madame Tussaud's** (p163) is rightly on many first-time visitors' must-see list. Here you can get your photo taken with any one of hundreds of stars, whose likeness varies from staggeringly accurate to amusingly unconvincing, you can take a walk through the Chamber of Horrors and even ride a taxi through London history.

## ◢ EAT AROUND MARYLEBONE

London has undergone a total food revolution in the past decade. Nowhere is this more evident than around **Marylebone** (p173) where some of London's very best restaurants are concentrated, particularly on and around Marylebone High St. Book ahead for the most famous of these or just try your luck and wander by.

2 MARTIN MOOS; 3 JANE SWEENEY; 4 NEIL SETCHFIELD; 5 NEIL SETCHFIELD; 6 PAT TUSON/ALAMY

2 London Zoo (p170); 3 Regent's Park (p167); 4 Wallace Collection (p164); Madame Tussauds (p163); 6 Eating and drinking on Marylebone High Street (p173)

# BEST...

## ⬎ PLACES TO GET LOST IN

- **British Museum** (p161) You can quite literally get lost in this massive collection.
- **Heal's** (p176) Lose yourself in sumptuous interiors and design nirvana.
- **Regent's Park** (p167) This is the perfect place to retreat from central London for an hour or two.
- **Selfridges** (p175) High fashion escapism doesn't come much better than this huge Oxford St department store.

## ⬎ QUIRKY SIGHTS

- **Penguin Pool** (p170) London Zoo's most famous structure is this modernist marvel.
- **Lindow Man** (p165) Want to see a garrotted man's corpse from the 1st century? Thought so.
- **Hunterian Museum** (p166) Look no further for the strangest museum in London.

- **Mosaic Mask of Tezcatlipoca** (p165) Another British Museum treasure – an Aztec human skull overlaid in mosaic.

## ⬎ INTELLECTUAL HANGOUTS

- **Museum Tavern** (p175) The favoured Bloomsbury pub of academics.
- **Daunt Books** (p175) London's best travel bookshop is a magnet for interesting types.
- **Wallace** (p174) Have lunch at the excellent restaurant inside the fabulous Wallace Collection.

## ⬎ CHIC RETREATS

- **King's Bar** (p174) A stone's throw from the University of London, this bar is for intellectuals with style.
- **Sanderson** (p171) A palace of design rather than a mere hotel.
- **Locanda Locatelli** (p173) The neighbourhood's most exclusive restaurant, bar none.

DOUG MCKINLA

Books for sale at Daunt Books (p175)

# DISCOVER BLOOMSBURY TO REGENT'S PARK

orth of Covent Garden – but worlds away in look and atmosphere – Bloomsbury, a leafy quarter and the academic and intellectual heart f London. Here you will find the University of London and its many aculties and campuses scattered along the uniform Georgian streets and legant green squares. Surrounded by grand town houses is what must e one of the world's best museums: the British Museum.

Fitzrovia – located to the west of Bloomsbury – was a forerunner o Soho as a bohemian enclave populated by struggling artists and vriters who frequented its numerous pubs, particularly the Fitzroy avern. Today it's a largely tourist-free area and is still full of great ubs and restaurants. To the north of here is stately Regent's Park, erhaps London's single smartest open space, ringed by the charming egent's Canal and fantastic London Zoo, the world's oldest.

# SIGHTS
## BLOOMSBURY
### BRITISH MUSEUM

ap p162

☎ 7323 8000, tours 7323 8181; www.thebritish useum.ac.uk; Great Russell St WC1; admission ee, £3 donation suggested; ☼ galleries 10am-.30pm Sat-Wed, to 8.30pm Thu & Fri, Great ourt 9am-6pm Sun-Wed, to 11pm Thu-Sat; ◆ Tottenham Court Rd or Russell Sq; ☺

ne of London's most visited attrac-ons, this museum draws an average of ve million punters each year through s marvellous porticoed main gate on reat Russell St (a few go through the uieter Montague Pl entrance). One of he world's oldest and finest museums, he British Museum started in 1749 in he form of royal physician Hans Sloane's abinet of curiosities' – which he later equeathed to the country – and car-ed on expanding its collection (which ow numbers some seven million items) hrough judicious acquisition and the ontroversial plundering of empire. It's n exhaustive and exhilarating stampede

through world cultures, with galleries devoted to Egypt, Western Asia, Greece, the Orient, Africa, Italy, the Etruscans, the Romans, prehistoric and Roman Britain and medieval antiquities.

The museum is huge, so make a few focused visits if you have time, and con-sider the choice of tours. There are nine free 50-minute **eyeOpener tours** of indi-vidual galleries throughout the day, and 20-minute **eyeOpener spotlight talks** at 1.15pm focusing on different themes from the collection. Ninety-minute **high-lights tours** (adult/concession £8/5) leave at 10.30am, 1pm and 3pm. If you want to go it alone, **audioguide tours** (£3.50) are available at the information desk, includ-ing a family-oriented one narrated by co-median, writer and TV presenter Stephen Fry. One tour specific to the Parthenon Sculptures (aka the Parthenon Marbles or Elgin Marbles) is available in that gal-lery. You could also check out Compass, a multimedia public access system with 50 computer terminals that lets you take a virtual tour of the museum, plan your

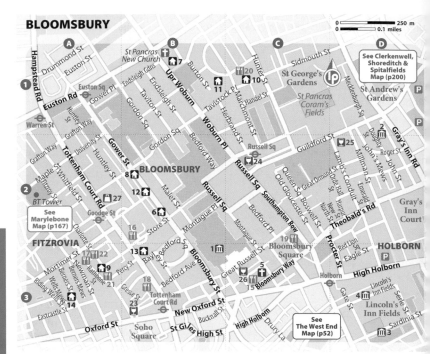

## BLOOMSBURY

**SIGHTS**

| | | |
|---|---|---|
| British Museum | **1** | B3 |
| Dickens House Museum | **2** | D1 |
| Hunterian Museum | **3** | D3 |
| Sir John Soane's Museum | **4** | D3 |
| St George's Bloomsbury | **5** | C3 |

**SLEEPING**

| | | |
|---|---|---|
| Academy Hotel | **6** | B2 |
| Ambassadors Bloomsbury | **7** | B1 |
| Arosfa | **8** | B2 |
| Charlotte Street Hotel | **9** | A3 |
| Generator | **10** | C1 |
| Harlingford Hotel | **11** | B1 |

| | | |
|---|---|---|
| Jesmond Hotel | **12** | B2 |
| Myhotel Bloomsbury | **13** | B3 |
| Sanderson | **14** | A3 |

**EATING**

| | | |
|---|---|---|
| Abeno | **15** | C3 |
| Busaba Eathai | **16** | B2 |
| Fino | **17** | A3 |
| Hakkasan | **18** | B3 |
| Hummus Bros | **19** | C2 |
| North Sea Fish Restaurant | **20** | C1 |

| | | |
|---|---|---|
| Rasa Samudra | **21** | A3 |
| Roka | **22** | A3 |

**DRINKING**

| | | |
|---|---|---|
| Bradley's Spanish Bar | **23** | B3 |
| King's Bar | **24** | C2 |
| Lamb | **25** | D2 |
| Museum Tavern | **26** | C3 |

**SHOPPING**

| | | |
|---|---|---|
| Habitat | **27** | A3 |
| Heal's | | (see 27 |

own circuit or get information on specific exhibits.

The British Museum is planning to build a major new extension in its north-western corner, to be completed in 2012. The new building will have, among other things, a gallery dedicated to special exhibitions and a conservation and science centre.

## DICKENS HOUSE MUSEUM Map p16

☎ 7405 2127; www.dickensmuseum.com; 48 Doughty St WC1; adult/under 16yr/concession £5/3/4; ⊙ 10am-5pm Mon-Sat, 11am-5pm Sun; ⊖ Russell Sq

The great Victorian novelist lived a nomadic life in the big city, moving around London so often that he left behind a unrivalled trail of blue plaques. Thi handsome four-storey house is his sol surviving residence before he upped and moved to Kent. Not that he stayed here for very long – he lasted a mere 2½ years (1837–39) – but this is where his work really flourished: he dashed off *The Pickwick Papers, Nicholas Nickleby* and *Oliver Twist* despite worry over debts, deaths and his ever-growing family. The house was saved from demolition and the fascinating museum opened in 1925, showcasing the family drawing room (restored to its original condition) and 10 rooms chock-a-block with memorabilia. In the dressing room you can see texts Dickens had prepared for his reading tours, which include funny notes-to-self such as 'slapping the desk'. The said slapped desk is on display, a velvet-topped bureau purpose-made for his public readings.

## ST GEORGE'S BLOOMSBURY

Map p162

☎ 7405 3044; Bloomsbury Way WC1; ⊙ 9.30am-5.30pm Mon-Fri, 10.30am-12.30pm Sun; ⊖ Holborn or Tottenham Court Rd

Superbly restored in 2005, this Nicholas Hawksmoor church (1731) is distinguished by its classical portico of Corinthian capitals and a steeple that was inspired by the Mausoleum of Halicarnassus. It is topped with a statue of George I in Roman dress.

# MARYLEBONE

## MADAME TUSSAUDS Map p167

☎ 0870 400 3000; www.madame-tussauds.com; Marylebone Rd NW1; adult/under 16yr £25/21; ⊙ 9.30am-5.30pm Mon-Fri, 9am-6pm Sat & Sun; ⊖ Baker St; ♿

What can one say about Madame Tussauds? It's unbelievably kitsch and terribly overpriced, yet it draws more than three million people every year and sits high on the 'must-do' list of any visitor to London. Different strokes for different folks, as they say, but if you like the idea of wax celebrities, movie stars and fantastically lifelike figures of the Windsors, you're in for a treat.

Madame Tussauds dates back more than two centuries when the eponymous Swiss model-maker started making death masks of the people killed during the French Revolution. She came to London in 1803 and exhibited around 30 wax models in Baker St, on a site not far from this building, which has housed the waxworks since 1885. The models were an enormous hit in Victorian times, when they provided visitors with their only glimpse of the famous and infamous before photography was widespread and long before the advent of TV.

Madame Tussauds is very keen on public surveys telling it who the punters would like to see most, resulting in such highlights as a photo op with the **Kate Moss** figure (a poor likeness), an eco **Prince Charles** statue, the **Blush Room** where A-listers stand listlessly and where the J-Lo figure blushes if you whisper in her ear.

Permanent photo opportunities include the political leaders in **World Stage** and the array of celebrities in **Premiere Room**. The famous **Chamber of Horrors** details the gory exploits of Jack the Ripper and is usually a huge hit with children. Finally you can take a ride in the **Spirit of London 'time taxi'**, where you sit in a mock-up of a London black cab and are whipped through a five-minute historical summary of London, a mercifully short time to endure the god-awful scripts and hackneyed commentary. The old Planetarium is now the **Stardome**, which screens an entertaining and educational animation by Nick Park, creator of *Wallace and Gromit* (it involves aliens and celebrities).

In case you were wondering what happens to the models of those people whose 15 minutes have passed, contrary to popular belief, they are never melted down, but simply rest in storage.

If you want to avoid the queues (particularly in summer) book your tickets online and get a timed entry slot. They are cheaper this way too.

### WALLACE COLLECTION Map p167

☎ 7563 9500; www.wallacecollection.org; Hertford House, Manchester Sq W1; admission free; 🕙 10am-5pm; ⊖ Bond St; ♿

Arguably London's finest small gallery (relatively unknown even to Londoners),

the Wallace Collection is an enthralling glimpse into 18th-century aristocratic life. The sumptuously restored Italianate mansion houses a treasure-trove of 17th- and 18th-century paintings, porcelain, artefacts and furniture collected by generations of the same family and bequeathed to the nation by the widow of Sir Richard Wallace (1818-90) on condition it should always be on display in the centre of London.

Among the many highlights here – besides the warm and friendly staff – are paintings by Rembrandt, Hals, Delacroix, Titian, Rubens, Poussin, Van Dyck, Velázquez, Reynolds and Gainsborough in the stunning **Great Gallery**. There's

## BRITISH MUSEUM HIGHLIGHTS (& CONTROVERSIES)

The first and most impressive thing you'll see is the museum's **Great Court**, covered with a spectacular glass-and-steel roof designed by Norman Foster in 2000; it is the largest covered public square in Europe. In its centre is the world-famous **Reading Room**, formerly the British Library, which has been frequented by all the big brains of history: George Bernard Shaw, Mahatma Gandhi, Oscar Wilde, William Butler Yeats, Karl Marx, Vladimir Lenin, Charles Dickens and Thomas Hardy.

The northern end of the courtyard's lower level houses the terrific new **Sainsbury African Galleries**, a romp through the art and cultures of historic and contemporary African societies.

Check out the 1820 **King's Library**, the most stunning neoclassical space in London, which hosts a permanent exhibition 'Enlightenment: Discovering the World in the 18th Century'.

One of the museum's major stars is the **Rosetta Stone** (room 4), discovered in 1799. It is written in two forms of ancient Egyptian and Greek and was the key to deciphering Egyptian hieroglyphics.

A major star is the **Parthenon Sculptures** (aka Parthenon Marbles; room 18). The marble works are thought to show the great procession to the temple that took place during the Panathenaic Festival, on the birthday of Athena, one of the grandest events in the Greek world.

They are better known as the Elgin Marbles (after Lord Elgin, the British ambassador who shipped them to England in 1806), though this name is fraught with controversy due to the British Museum's dispute with the Greek government, who want to see the pieces back in Athens. The New Acropolis Museum in Athens was built especially to house the works in 2009, after objections that there was no suitable venue for them to be displayed in Greece. The British Museum has a spectacular array of medieval and Renaissance armour (including some to try on), a Minton-tiled smoking room, stunning chandeliers and a sweeping staircase that is reckoned to be one of the best examples of French interior architecture (including in France) in existence.

## SHERLOCK HOLMES MUSEUM
Map p167

☎ 7935 8866; www.sherlock-holmes.co.uk; 221b Baker St; adult/child £6/4; ⏱ 9.30am-6pm; ⊖ Baker St

Though the museum gives its address as 221b Baker St, the actual fictional abode of Sherlock Holmes is the Abbey National building a bit further south. Fans of the books will enjoy examining the three floors of reconstructed Victoriana, deerstalkers, burning candles and flickering grates, but may baulk at the dodgy waxworks of Professor Moriarty and 'the Man with the Twisted Lip'. The only disappointment is the lack of material and information on Arthur Conan Doyle.

## BROADCASTING HOUSE Map p167

☎ 0870 603 0304; www.bbc.co.uk; Portland Pl; ⏱ shop 9.30am-6pm Mon-Sat, 10am-5.30pm Sun; ⊖ Oxford Circus

This is the iconic building from which the BBC began radio broadcasting in 1932,

---

since offered to lend the marbles to Athens for a period of three or four months, as is customary with loaned objects. The Greek government rejected the idea. The majority of voters in a *Guardian* newspaper online survey in June 2009 thought the marbles should go back to Greece – but the final outcome is anyone's guess.

Prepare for a bit of gore in the Mexican Gallery (room 27), at the foot of the eastern staircase. The room features the 15th-century Aztec **Mosaic Mask of Tezcatlipoca (The Skull of the Smoking Mirror)**, which has a turquoise mosaic laid over a human skull.

On a calmer note, rooms 33 and 34 host the Asian collections with the wonderful **Amaravati Sculptures** (room 33a), Indian goddesses, dancing Shivas and serene cross-legged Buddhas in copper and stone.

The story goes that bandits tried to steal the 7th- to 4th-century BC pieces of Persian gold known as the **Oxus Treasure** (room 52), which originated in the ancient Persian capital of Persepolis, but the British rescued the impressive collection and brought it to the museum.

The **Lindow Man** (room 50) is a 1st-century unfortunate who appears to have been smacked on the head with an axe and then garrotted. His remains were preserved in a peat bog until 1984 when a peat-cutting machine sliced him in half.

The old **Percival David Foundation of Chinese Art** (room 95) is now housed in the museum. With some 1700 pieces, it's the largest collection of Chinese ceramics from the 10th to 18th centuries outside China. Sir Percival David donated it to the University of London in 1950 on the condition that every single piece be displayed at all times, and the collection was moved to the British Museum from its own space nearby in 2009. Among the highlights are the David Vases (1351), the earliest dated and inscribed blue-and-white Chinese porcelain, named after Sir Percival himself.

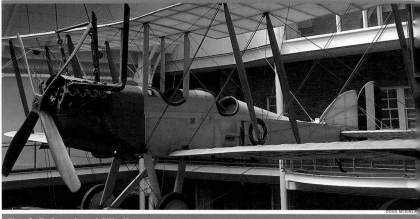

DOUG MCKINLAY

Aircraft display at Imperial War Museum

## ⬎ IF YOU LIKE...

If you liked the British Museum (p161) then spare some time for some of London's large array of lesser known museums:

- **Imperial War Museum** (Map p130) This outstanding Lambeth museum is most famous for its main hall that contains numerous combat aircraft, tanks and other pieces of large-scale military equipment. A must for any military history fans.
- **Hunterian Museum** (Map p162) The museum of the Royal College of Surgeons on Lincoln's Inn Fields contains a collection of human and animal anatomical samples collected by surgeon John Hunter in the 18th century. They survive today in one of London's best, weirdest and least-known museums.
- **Sir John Soane's Museum** (Map p162) Many Londoners will tell you that this gem of a place is their favourite small museum in the capital. Soane was a tireless collector of just about everything and his eccentric taste can be seen on display in every inch of this enormous Lincoln's Inn Fields townhouse.

and from where much of its radio output still comes. There's a shop stocking any number of products relating to BBC programs, even though the majority of the Beeb's output is produced in the corporation's glassy complex in Shepherd's Bush (hop on the website if you want to get tickets to a recording).

**ALL SOULS CHURCH** Map p167
☎ 7580 3522; www.allsouls.org; Langham Pl W1; 🕒 9am-6pm, closed Sat; ⊖ Oxford Circus

A John Nash solution for the curving northern sweep of Regent St was this delightful church, which features a circular columned porch and distinctive needle-like spire, reminiscent of an ancient Greek temple. Built from Bath stone, the church was very unpopular when completed in 1824. It was bombed during the Blitz and renovated in 1951, and is now one of the most distinctive churches in central London.

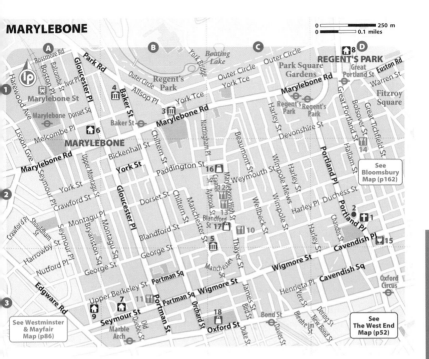

# REGENT'S PARK

### REGENT'S PARK Map p154

☎ 7486 7905; ⏰ 5am-dusk; ⊖ Baker St or Regent's Park

The most elaborate and ordered of London's many parks, this one was created around 1820 by John Nash, who planned to use it as an estate to build palaces for the aristocracy. Although the plan never quite came off – like so many at the time – you can get some idea of what Nash might have achieved from the buildings along the Outer Circle, and in particular from the stuccoed Palladian mansions he built on Cumberland Tce.

Like many of the city's parks, this one was used as a royal hunting ground, and then as farmland, before it was used as a place for fun and leisure during the 18th century. These days it's a well-organised but relaxed, lively but serene, local but cosmopolitan haven in the heart of the city. Among its many attractions are the London Zoo, the Grand Union Canal along its northern side, an ornamental lake, an open-air theatre in Queen Mary's Gardens where Shakespeare is performed during the summer months, ponds and colourful flowerbeds, rose gardens that look spectacular in June, football pitches and summer games of softball.

### LORD'S CRICKET GROUND
off Map p154

☎ 7616 8595; bookings 7432 1000; www.lords. org; St John's Wood Rd NW8; tours adult/child & concession/family £14/8/38; ⏱ tours when no play 10am, noon & 2pm Apr-Sep, noon & 2pm Oct-Mar; ⊖ St John's Wood; ♿

The 'home of cricket' is a must for any devotee of this peculiarly English game: book early for the test matches here, but it's also worth taking the absorbing and anecdotal 90-minute tour of the ground and facilities. This interesting tour takes in the famous Long Room, where members watch the games surrounded by por-

traits of cricket's great and good, and museum featuring evocative memorabili that will appeal to fans old and new. Th famous little urn containing the Ashe the prize of the most fiercely conteste competition in cricket, resides here whe in English hands.

The ground itself is dominated by striking media centre that looks like clock radio, but you should also keep a eye out for the famous weather vane i the shape of Father Time and the remark able tentlike modern Mound Stand.

# SLEEPING
## BLOOMSBURY
### MYHOTEL BLOOMSBURY
Map p162                          Boutique Hotel ££

☎ 7667 6000; www.myhotels.com; 11-13 Bayle St WC1; s £120-205, d & tw £205-250, ste from £355, weekend rates from £130; ⊖ Tottenham Court Rd or Goodge St; ⌘

Its less-than-inspired name notwith standing, this stylish Conran-designe hotel was one of London's first boutiqu

Lord's Cricket Ground

NEIL SETCHFIE

otels and still bears the classic boutique combination of colours (blacks, greys and reds) in its 78 guestrooms. The library is a welcome retreat for chilling.

## AMBASSADORS BLOOMSBURY

Map p162                                    Hotel ££

☎ 7693 5400; www.ambassadors.co.uk; 12 Upper Woburn WC1; r £99-155; ⊖ Euston; ♿

This 100-room hotel in a gem of a belle époque building just south of Euston Rd has been beautifully renovated. The emphasis here is on comfort, the style is contemporary and the attached Number 12 bar a welcome addition to the area. Weekend rates are cheaper and worth checking.

## ACADEMY HOTEL

Map p162                            Boutique Hotel ££

☎ 7631 4115; www.theetoncollection.com; 21 Gower St WC1; s/d £120-205, weekend rate incl breakfast from £150; ⊖ Goodge St; ▓

This terribly English 49-room hotel is set across five Georgian town houses but has a slight Regency feel. Quality rooms are kitted out with fluffy duvets, plump cushions and bolster pillows. There's a conservatory overlooking a leafy back garden with fish pond, and a contemporary-looking bar in blue tones called the Library.

## HARLINGFORD HOTEL

Map p162                                    Hotel ££

☎ 7387 1551; www.harlingfordhotel.com; 61-63 Cartwright Gardens WC1; s/d/tr/q £85/110/125/135; ⊖ Russell Sq

With its 'H' logo proudly sewn on your bedroom cushion, and a modern interior design with lots of lavender and mauve and green-tiled bathrooms, this stylish Georgian hotel with 43 rooms is arguably the best on the street. You'll recognise it from all the ivy at the front.

DOUG MCKINLAY
Georgian houses in Russell Square, Bloomsbury

## JESMOND HOTEL  Map p162          B&B £

☎ 7636 3199; www.jesmondhotel.org.uk; 63 Gower St WC1; s/d/tr/q/f £50/75/95/110/120, with shared bathroom £40/60/80/100/110; ⊖ Goodge St; 🛜

We've received lots of letters from readers singing the praises of this B&B in Bloomsbury. The guestrooms – a dozen with bathroom – are basic but clean, and it's a good choice if you're travelling in a small group. There's laundry service and internet's free, but wi-fi is £10 flat rate.

## AROSFA  Map p162                  Hotel £

☎ 7636 2115; www.arosfalondon.com; 83 Gower St WC1; s/d/tr/q £60/90/102/145; ⊖ Euston Sq or Goodge St

The new owners have really spanked up old Arosfa, decking out the lounge with

Pelican, London Zoo

NEIL SETCHFIE

## ⬊ LONDON ZOO

Established in 1828, these zoological gardens are among the oldest in the world. This is where the word 'zoo' originated and London Zoo has become one of the most progressive in the world. It is in the process of implementing a long-term modernisation plan and the emphasis is now firmly placed on conservation, education and breeding, with fewer species and more spacious conditions.

The newest developments have brought **Gorilla Kingdom**, a project that involves a gorilla conservation program in Gabon with the aim of providing habitat for Western gorillas and protecting them by providing the local communities and former poachers with work in the program. The zoo has three gorillas – Zaire, Effie and Mjukuu – who live on their own island; their space measures 1600 sq metres.

The **Clore Rainforest Lookout and Nightzone** is an excellent installation – a slice of the South American rainforest complete with marmosets, monkeys, fruit bats and other creatures wandering and flying freely among the visitors inside the humid, tropical-climate room. The monkeys are especially happy to roam – they see it as their territory, so watch out!

The elegant and cheerful **Penguin Pool**, designed by Berthold Lubetkin in 1934, is one of London's foremost modernist structures, although the penguins didn't like it and are now bathing at a more ordinary round pool.

Other highlights include **Butterfly Paradise**, **Into Africa** and **Meet the Monkeys**. In 2008 the Mappin Terrace (which was formerly home to London Zoo's polar bears) reopened as the **Outback** exhibit, a slice of Australia, home to wallabies and emus, and focusing on the challenges that climate change will present to animals living in already hot climates.

**Things you need to know:** Map p154; ☎ 7722 3333; www.zsl.org/london-zoo; Outer Circle, Regent's Park NW1; adult/child/concession £16.80/13.30/15.30 plus optional £1.70 donation to protect endangered species; ☯ 10am-5.30pm mid-Mar–Oct, to 4pm Nov-Jan, to 4.30pm Feb–mid-Mar; ⊖ Baker St or Camden Town

hilippe Starck furniture, blow-ups of ve Manhattan skyline on the wall and a enerally modern look. The rooms are less vish, however, with cabinlike bathrooms each that the owners say they are going o change and update. It's good value, in vy case, though watch out for the tiny ngles.

## ENERATOR

ap p162                                      Hostel £

7388 7655; www.generatorhostels.com; impton Pl, opp 37 Tavistock Pl WC1; dm £15-17, tw/tr/q £5/50/60/80; ↔ Russell Sq

/ith its industrial decor, blue neon ghts and throbbing techno, the huge enerator is one of the grooviest budget laces in central London and not for the int-hearted. The bar stays open until am and there are frequent drinking competitions. Along with 214 rooms, which ave dorm rooms of between four and 14 eds, there are pool tables, safe-deposit oxes and a large eating area, but no itchen.

# ITZROVIA

## ANDERSON

ap p162                          Boutique Hotel £££

7300 1400; www.sandersonlondon.com; 0 Berners St W1; d from £235, loft ste £600; ↔ Oxford Circus

Don't let yourself be deterred by the ight of the white aluminium and grey-reen glass facade of a 1960s-era corpolate HQ: this uber-designed 'urban spa' omes with a lush bamboo-filled garden, rtworks and installations, bed sheets vith a 450-thread count and a jumble of personality furniture, including a Dalí ips' sofa and swan-shaped armchairs. t's a quirky, almost surreal place, with 50 rooms, and decadent enough to lie for.

## CHARLOTTE STREET HOTEL

Map p162                          Boutique Hotel £££

☎ 7806 2000; www.charlottestreethotel.com; 15-17 Charlotte St W1; s/d from £220/310, ste from £375; ↔ Tottenham Court Rd; ⚏ ♿

This wonderful hotel, where Laura Ashley goes postmodern and comes up smelling of roses, is a favourite of visiting media types. The bar buzzes by night, while the Oscar restaurant is a delightful spot any time of day, but particularly for afternoon tea.

# MARYLEBONE

## DORSET SQUARE HOTEL

Map p167                                      Hotel £££

☎ 7723 7874; www.dorsetsquare.co.uk; 39 Dorset Sq NW1; d from £240, ste from £350; ↔ Baker St

Two combined Regency town houses contain this hotel overlooking Dorset Sq, where the very first cricket ground was laid in 1814 (which explains the cricket memorabilia in glass cases in the lobby). Guestrooms are small but dreamily decorated with a blend of antiques, sumptuous fabrics and crown-canopied or four-poster beds.

## SUMNER HOTEL Map p167          Hotel ££

☎ 7723 2244; www.thesumner.com; 54 Upper Berkeley St W1; r £155-193; ↔ Marble Arch; ⚏

This five-star town house hotel offers incomparable value for such a central location. The 20 rooms are contemporary, comfortable and of a good size, but the focal point of the hotel is the sitting room with an original fireplace and hardwood flooring.

## EDWARD LEAR HOTEL

Map p167                                      Hotel £

☎ 7402 5401; www.edlear.com; 28-30 Seymour St W1; s £72-91, d & tw £89-113, f £115-145, with shared bathroom s £52-60, d & tw £60-74, f £89-113; ↔ Marble Arch

Once the home of a Victorian painter and poet (well, composer of limericks), the

31 rooms of this flower-bedecked terrace hotel offer basic accommodation at spectacular prices. Indeed, never undersold, the management claims that 'if you can find a hotel as close to Oxford St that quotes a lower price, we will match it'.

# REGENT'S PARK
## MELIÃ WHITE HOUSE
Map p167        Hotel ££

☎ 7391 3000; www.solmelia.com; Albany St NW1; r £99-265; ⊖ Great Portland St; ⊠ ⚶ ▯ ☎

This enormous 545-room hotel in a stylish white-tile art deco building is unsurprisingly popular with groups, and its rooms are rather on the flouncy side. But the location, just west of Regent's Park and within easy walking distance of Soho and three Underground stations, and the reasonable price make it a great option.

# EATING
## BLOOMSBURY
### NORTH SEA FISH RESTAURANT
Map p162        Fish & Chips ££

☎ 7387 5892; 7-8 Leigh St WC1; mains £9-19; ⊗ closed Sun; ⊖ Russell Sq

The North Sea sets out to cook fresh fish and potatoes, a simple ambition in which it succeeds admirably. Look forward to jumbo-sized plaice or halibut steaks, deep-fried or grilled, and a huge serving of chips. There's takeaway next door if you can't handle the soulless dining room.

### ABENO Map p162        Japanese £

☎ 7405 3211; 47 Museum St WC1; mains £6.50-12.80; ⊖ Tottenham Court Rd

This understated Japanese restaurant specialises in *okonomiyaki*, a savoury pancake of cabbage, egg and flour combined with the ingredients of your choice (there are more than two dozen varieties, including

anything from sliced meats and vegetabl to egg, noodles and cheese) and cooked c the hotplate at your table. There's a rang of set lunches (£7.80 to £12.80).

### HUMMUS BROS
Map p162        Middle Easterr

☎ 7404 7079; www.hbros.co.uk; Victoria Hous 37-63 Southampton Row WC1; mains £2.50-6; ⊖ Holborn

The deal at this very popular minichain a bowl of filling hummus with your choic of topping (beef, chicken, chickpeas et eaten with warm pita bread.

## FITZROVIA
### HAKKASAN Map p162        Chinese ££

☎ 7907 1888, 7927 7000; 8 Hanway Pl W1; mains £9.50-42; ⊖ Tottenham Court Rd

This basement restaurant – hidden dow a most unlikely back alleyway – succes fully combines celebrity status, stunnin design, persuasive cocktails and surpri ingly sophisticated Chinese food. It wa the first Chinese restaurant to receive Michelin star. The low, nightclub-styl lighting (lots of red) makes it a good spc for dating, while the long, glitzy bar is great place for truly inventive cocktail For dinner in the formal main dining roor you'll have to book far in advance and n doubt be allocated a two-hour slot. D what savvy Londoners do and have lunc in the more informal Ling Ling lounge.

### ROKA Map p162        Japanese £

☎ 7580 6464; www.rokarestaurant.com; 37 Charlotte St W1; mains £10-19; ⊖ Goodge St or Tottenham Court Rd

This stunner of a Japanese restaurant mixe casual dining (wooden benches) with sa voury titbits from the *robatayaki* (grill kitchen in the centre. It has modern deco with the dominating materials grey stee and glass. Sushi is £5 to £9, set lunch is £3

DOUG MCKINLAY

Bloomsbury Sq

**INO** Map p162      Spanish ££
☎ 7813 8010; www.finorestaurant.com; 33
arlotte St (enter from Rathbone St) W1; tapas
2-17; ⊖ Goodge St or Tottenham Court Rd
ritically acclaimed (and it's easy to see
hy), Fino represents an example of good
panish cuisine in a London all too dom-
ated by dreary and uninventive tapas
ars. Set in a glamorous basement, Fino
a tapas restaurant with a difference.
ry the Jerusalem artichoke cooked with
int, the prawn tortilla with wild garlic
r the foie gras with chilli jam for a feast
f innovative and delightful Spanish
ooking.

**ASA SAMUDRA** Map p162     Indian £
☎ 7637 0222; www.rasarestaurants.com; 5
harlotte St W1; mains £6.25-12.95; ⏰ closed
nch Sun; ⊖ Goodge St or Tottenham Court Rd
his bubblegum-pink eatery just up from
xford St showcases the seafood cuisine
f Kerala state on India's southwest coast,
upported by a host – eight out of 14 main
ourses – of more familiar vegetarian
ishes. The fish soups are outstanding,

the breads superb and the various cur-
ries divinely spiced.

**BUSABA EATHAI** Map p162     Thai £
☎ 7299 7900; 22 Store St WC1; mains £6.40-
8.90; ⊖ Goodge St
We prefer the less hectic Store St premises
of this West End favourite, but there are
also a couple more locations, including a
**Wardour St branch** (Map p70; ☎ 7255 8686;
106-110 Wardour St; ⊖ Tottenham Court Rd). Here
the sumptuous Thai menu greets you via
an electronic screen outside and the uber-
styled interior is softened by communal
wooden tables. This isn't the place to come
for a long and intimate dinner, but it's a superb option for an excellent and (usually)
speedy meal of stir-fries and noodles.

## MARYLEBONE
### LOCANDA LOCATELLI
Map p167        Italian £££
☎ 7935 9088; www.locandalocatelli.com; 8 Seymour St W1; mains £20-29.50; ⊖ Marble Arch
This dark but quietly glamorous restaurant
in an otherwise unremarkable Marble Arch

hotel is still one of London's hottest tables, and you're likely to see some famous faces being greeted by celebrity chef Giorgio Locatelli at some point during your meal. Locatelli is renowned for its pasta dishes, which are sublime, but still rather over-priced for what they are (£20 to £25 for a pasta main course). Still, the smart interna-tional crowd doesn't seem to mind one bit. Booking a few weeks ahead is essential.

### PROVIDORES & TAPA ROOM
Map p167                                    Fusion £££

☎ 7935 6175; www.theprovidores.co.uk; 109 Marylebone High St W1; mains £18-26; ⊖ Baker St or Bond St

This place is split over two levels: tapas (£2.80 to £15) on the ground floor; full meals along the same innovative lines – Spanish and just about everything else – in the el-egant and understated dining room. It's popular enough to be frenetic at the busi-est times; don't come for quiet conversation over your plate of chorizo and chillies.

### WALLACE Map p167                     French ££

☎ 7563 9505; www.wallacecollection.org; Hertford House, Manchester Sq W1; mains £12.50-18; ⏱ 10am-5pm Sun-Thu, to 11pm Fri & Sat; ⊖ Bond St; &

There are few more idyllically placed res-taurants than this French brasserie in the courtyard of the **Wallace Collection** (p164), London's finest small gallery and virtually unknown to most Londoners. Michelin-starred chef Thierry Laborde's seasonal menus are a veritable *tour de France* and cost £32 to £36 for three courses.

### VILLANDRY Map p167   Modern European ££

☎ 7631 3131; www.villandry.com; 170 Great Portland St W1; mains #12-24; ⏱ closed dinner Sun; ⊖ Great Portland St

This excellent Modern European restau-rant with a strong Gallic slant has an at-

tractive market-delicatessen attache (not to mention a bar) so freshness ar quality of ingredients is guaranteed. T the cassoulet or one of the several dai fish dishes.

### NATURAL KITCHEN Map p167   Organi

☎ 7486 8065; 77-78 Marylebone High St W1; mains £8-10; ⊖ Bond St

This is a decent, practical place to drop for a relaxing pit stop in between raidin the shops on Marylebone High St. The o ganic shop – with fresh produce, butcher deli and wine – has a restaurant on the 1 floor. It offers good-value breakfasts (£3 t £5) of porridge, fruit and granola yoghur and eggs with soldiers (toast cut in strip to dip), and an all-day brunch (around £7 in addition to lunches.

### GOLDEN HIND Map p167     Fish & Chips

☎ 7486 3644; 73 Marylebone Lane W1; mains £6.90-10.60; ⏱ closed lunch Sat & all day Sun; ⊖ Bond St

This 90-year-old chippie has a classic in terior, chunky wooden tables and build ers sitting alongside suits. And from th vintage fryer comes some of the best co and chips available in London.

# DRINKING
## BLOOMSBURY
### KING'S BAR Map p162                          Ba

☎ 7837 6470; Hotel Russell, Russell Sq WC1; ⊖ Russell Sq

Nestled behind the awesome Victoria Gothic facade of the Hotel Russell, th King's Bar is an oasis of booze in a neigh bourhood sorely lacking decent bars. Th grand Edwardian decor, huge leathe armchairs and table service make th prices worthwhile. There's a great selec tion of cocktails and wines, and you'r always guaranteed a seat.

**AMB** Map p162          Pub

☎ 7405 0713; 94 Lamb's Conduit St WC1; ⏰ to midnight Mon-Sat, to 10.30pm Sun; ⊖ Russell Sq

The Lamb's central mahogany bar with beautiful Victorian dividers has been its *pièce de résistance* since 1729, when the screens used to hide the music stars from the punters' curious gaze. Just like three centuries ago, the pub is still wildly popular, so come early to bag a booth.

**MUSEUM TAVERN** Map p162      Pub

☎ 7242 8987; 49 Great Russell St WC1; ⊖ Tottenham Court Rd or Holborn

This is where Karl Marx used to retire for a well-earned pint after a hard day's inventing communism in the British Museum Reading Room, and where George Orwell boozed. A lovely traditional pub set around a long bar, it has friendly staff and is popular with academics and students alike.

## FITZROVIA

**BRADLEY'S SPANISH BAR**

Map p162            Bar

☎ 7636 0359; 42-44 Hanway St W1; ⊖ Tottenham Court Rd

Hanway St is home to several Spanish-style tapas-and-flamenco and speakeasy bars that open until dawn and serve beer from crates. Bradley's is vaguely Spanish in decor, though it's really Spanish in its choice of booze: San Miguel, Cruzcampo and some decent wines.

**SOCIAL** Map p167           Bar

☎ 7636 4992; www.thesocial.com; 5 Little Portland St W1; ⏰ to 1am Thu-Sat, to midnight Mon-Thu, to 12.30am Sun, closed Sun; ⊖ Oxford Circus

The Social remains one of the best places for a good night out in central London thanks to the fact that it steers clear of catering to the regular West End crowd. Revel in live or DJ music and £6 cocktails until late.

# SHOPPING

**DAUNT BOOKS** Map p167      Books

☎ 7224 2295; www.dauntbooks.co.uk; 83-84 Marylebone High St W1; ⊖ Baker St

An original Edwardian bookshop, with oak panels and gorgeous skylights, Daunt is one of London's loveliest travel bookshops. It has two floors and the ground level is stacked with fiction and nonfiction titles; the lower ground contains travel books.

**SELFRIDGES** Map p167    Department Store

☎ 7629 1234; www.selfridges.com; 400 Oxford St W1; ⏰ 10am-8pm Mon-Fri, 9.30am-8pm Sat, noon-6pm Sun; ⊖ Bond St

Selfridges loves innovation – it's famed for its inventive window displays by international artists, gala shows and above all an

DOUG MCKINLAY

Daunt Books

amazing range of products. It's the funkiest and most vital of London's one-stop shops, with an unparalleled food hall and Europe's largest cosmetics department.

### HABITAT Map p162  Homewares
☎ 7631 3880; www.habitat.net; 196 Tottenham Court Rd W1; 🕙 10am-6.30pm Mon-Sat, to 8pm Thu, noon-6pm Sun; ⊖ Goodge St

Started by the visionary designer and restaurateur Terence Conran in the 1950s, Habitat still does what it originally set out to do – brighten up your home with inventive and inspiring furniture and decorations. Artists, actors, musicians and fashion designers are employed to design items.

### HEAL'S Map p162  Homewares
☎ 7636 1666; www.heals.co.uk; 196 Tottenham Court Rd W1; 🕙 10am-6pm Mon-Wed, to 8pm Thu, to 6.30pm Fri & Sat, noon-6pm Sun; ⊖ Goodge St

Heal's is more serious, classical and expensive than Habitat, serving a more conservative, yet practical clientele. It a long-established furniture and homewares store.

### MONOCLE SHOP
Map p167  Jewellery & Accessorie
☎ 7486 8770; www.monocle.com; 2a George S W1; 🕙 10am-6pm Mon-Sat, to 7pm Thu, noon-6pm Sun; ⊖ Bond St

Run by the people behind the design an international current affairs magazin *Monocle,* this shop is pure understate heaven. True, most things cost mor than many spend in a year, but if you'r a fan of minimalist, quality design acros the board (there are bicycles, clothe bags and so on), you won't regret drop ping in. Beautifully bound first edition are on sale here, as well as stunnin photography.

# HYDE PARK & SOUTH KENSINGTON

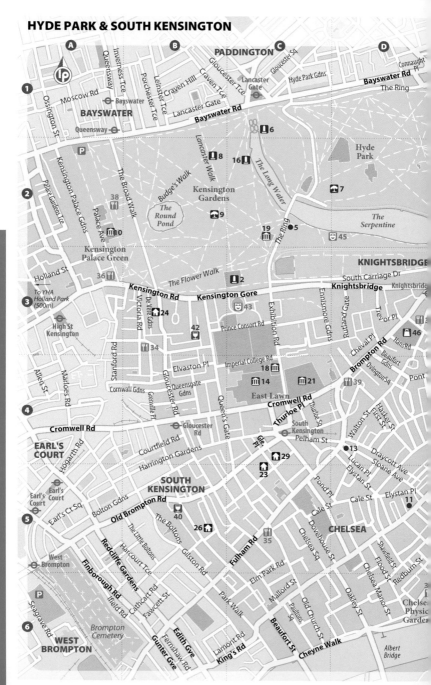

HYDE PARK SOUTH KENSINGTON

**INFORMATION**
Irish Embassy.............................. **1** F3

**SIGHTS**
Albert Memorial........................ **2** C3
Apsley House.............................. **3** E2
Australian War Memorial.... **4** F3
Diana, Princess of Wales
  Memorial Fountain .............. **5** C2
Edward Jenner Statue........ **6** C1
Hyde Park ................................... **7** D2
John Hanning Speke
  Sculpture................................ **8** B2
Kensington Gardens............ **9** B2
Kensington Palace...............**10** A2
Kings Road ..............................**11** D5
Marble Arch ............................**12** E1

Michelin House .................**13** D4
Natural History
  Museum ...........................**14** C4
New Zealand War
  Memorial ..........................**15** F3
Peter Pan Statue .............**16** C2
Royal Albert Hall.............(see 43)
Saatchi Gallery.................**17** E5
Science Museum................**18** C4
Serpentine Gallery ..........**19** C2
Speaker's Corner..............**20** E1
Victoria & Albert
  Museum ............................**21** C4
Wellington Arch................**22** F3

**SLEEPING**
Aster House ......................**23** C5
Astor Hyde Park ...............**24** B3
B+B Belgravia....................**25** F4
Blakes .................................**26** B5
Cadogan Hotel ..................**27** E4
Halkin ................................**28** E3
Number Sixteen ................**29** C4

**EATING**
Bibendum.......................... (see 13)
Capital................................ **30** D3
Gordon Ramsay ................. **31** D6
Jenny Lo's Tea
  House................................ **32** F4
La Poule au Pot ................ **33** F5
Launceston Place.............. **34** B3
Lucio.................................... **35** C5
Min Jiang ........................... **36** A3
Olivo ................................... **37** F4
Orangery............................ **38** A2
Racine ................................ **39** D4

**DRINKING**
Drayton Arms.................... **40** B5
Nag's Head ........................ **41** E3
Queen's Arms .................... **42** B3

**ENTERTAINMENT &
ACTIVITIES**
Royal Albert Hall............... **43** C3
Royal Court Theatre ......... **44** E4
Serpentine Lido ................. **45** D2

**SHOPPING**
Harrods............................... **46** D3
Harvey Nichols.................. **47** E3

**TRANSPORT**
Green Line Bus
  Station............................. **48** F4
Victoria Coach
  Station............................. **49** F4
Victoria Coach
  Station (Arrivals)............ **50** F4

See Westminster &
Mayfair
Map (p86)

# HIGHLIGHTS

## ⬑ CHECK OUT THE V&A

South Kensington's extraordinary **Victoria & Albert Museum** (p185) is a true one-off and will be a hit with anyone interested in decorative art and design. Within its vast Cromwell Rd premises the museum contains a staggering 145 galleries that include everything from ancient Chinese ceramics to Vivienne Westwood gowns. Make time for this collection – it's without question the best of its kind in the world.

## ⬐ SHOP IN KNIGHTSBRIDGE

If you've ever wanted to re-enact *Absolutely Fabulous* then **Knightsbridge** (p198) is your set – here you can visit two of Britain's most famous department stores – touristy but world-famous Harrods and the rather chicer Harvey Nichols before bombing down Sloane St or Brompton Rd with your credit card to find the month's fashion must-haves in the boutiques of this most luxurious corner of London.

## ↘ EXPLORE HYDE PARK

There's nowhere like Hyde Park (p190) – central London's largest open space is criss-crossed with things to do: feed the ducks, admire the rose garden, listen to the ranters at Speakers' Corner, swim at the Serpentine Lido, admire Princess Diana's last home or just wander the open spaces and settle in the shade for a picnic.

## ↘ NATURAL HISTORY MUSEUM

This Cromwell Rd institution will thrill those with an interest in the natural world with its collection of life forms and natural phenomena on display. Even if the Victorian pursuit of collecting doesn't appeal, the Central Hall of the National History Museum (p187) with its incredible diplodocus skeleton may well win you over!

## ↘ SNOOP AROUND KENSINGTON PALACE

Access to royal property is a fleeting affair in London – only accessible in the summer months when they're on holiday. But Kensington Palace (p189), last home to Princess Diana, is open all year round and is a fascinating place to look around for anyone interested in how royalty once lived.

1 NEIL SETCHFIELD; 2 VERONICA GARBUTT; 3 PHILIP GAME; 4 GLENN BEANLAND; 5 DOUG MCKINLAY

1 Victoria & Albert Museum (p185); 2 Harrods in Knightsbridge (p198); 3 Diana, Princess of Wales Memorial Fountain (p182); 4 Natural History Museum (187); 5 Kensington Palace (p189)

# THE HYDE PARK WALK

Start at Hyde Park Corner tube station and embark on this leisurely two-mile walk around central London's enormous green lung. The walk takes in all of the main sights of the Park, and ends up at a great pub by Lancaster Gate. As ever, take your time!

### ❶ HYDE PARK CORNER

Climb monumental **Wellington Arch** for great views and, in the same small square of grass, you will find the rather tasteful wall of eucalypt green granite of the **Australian War Memorial** and the 16 'standards' of the **New Zealand War Memorial**.

### ❷ THE SERPENTINE

Keep to the lake's northern side and interrupt your walk by renting a paddle boat from the **Serpentine boathouse** ( ☎ 7262 1330; adult/child per 30min £6/2, per 1hr £8/3; ☻ 10am-4pm Feb & Mar, 10am-6pm Apr-Jun, 10am-7pm Jul & Aug, 10am-5pm Sep & Oct, 10am-5pm Sat & Sun Nov). The **Serpentine solar shuttle boat** (single/return adult £2.50/4.50, child £1/1.50, family £6/10; ☻ every 30min noon-5pm), uses only solar power to get you from the boathouse to the Diana, Princess of Wales Memorial Fountain.

### ❸ DIANA, PRINCESS OF WALES MEMORIAL FOUNTAIN

Despite early teething problems, this Cornish granite memorial fountain sitting on a perfectly manicured lawn is a popular chill-out spot today. Water flows from the highest point in both directions, into a small pool at the bottom. Bathing is forbidden, although you are allowed to dip your feet. Near here you can take a break at the **Lido Café**.

### ❹ SERPENTINE GALLERY

This former teahouse is now one of the city's best contemporary **art galleries** (p190) and houses interesting exhibitions and summer pavilions designed by the world's leading architects. Recent years have seen the pavilion designed by such architectural luminaries as Jean Nouvel and Frank Gehry.

### ❺ ALBERT MEMORIAL

Gilded and enormous, the **Albert Memorial** (p190) is in stark contrast with the humility of the real Prince Albert, Queen Victoria's much-loved husband. It has recently been completely renovated at enormous expense and glimmers almost indecently in the sun.

# THE HYDE PARK WALK

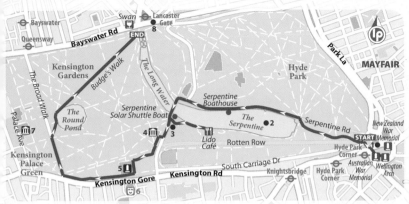

## ROYAL ALBERT HALL

Another memorial to Queen Victoria's beloved husband, this is Britain's most famous **concert hall** (p190). It has seen more big names and significant performances in its time than most others, including the choral version of Blake's *Jerusalem,* held to celebrate the granting of the vote to women in 1928.

## KENSINGTON PALACE

Princess Diana's former home and a long-standing **royal residence** (p189), this is where you can stop off and take a look at the permanent and temporary exhibitions and the stunning interior, before surrendering to one of the park's many stretches of grass.

## LANCASTER GATE

There's plenty more to see in the park, if you have time, stamina and the strength of will to resist merely having a snooze on the grass. For an end-of-walk drink, stop in at the **Swan** ( ☎ 7262 5204; 66 Bayswater Rd W2), with its beer garden in back.

HYDE PARK & SOUTH KENSINGTON

BEST...

# BEST...

## ꕔ ROYAL SIGHTS

- **Kensington Palace** (p189) Check out Princess Diana's last home.
- **Albert Memorial** (p190) Marvel at this over-the-top monument to Queen Victoria's husband.
- **Royal Albert Hall** (p190) Queen Victoria's last-minute dedication of this exhibition hall to her late husband completely changed its fate.

## ꕔ SHOPPING STRIPS

- **Knightsbridge** (p198) Home to two of London's world-famous department stores.
- **Kensington High St** (p198) Full of excellent high street shopping.
- **King's Rd** (p185) Chelsea's up-market shopping mecca.

## ꕔ THINGS FOR FREE

- **V&A** (p185) Arguably the best design museum in the world.
- **Serpentine Gallery** (p190) There's always something interesting on at this Hyde Park favourite.
- **Science Museum** (p187) Making science fun for all.
- **Natural History Museum** (p187) From dinosaurs to volcanoes – it's all free here.

## ꕔ FASHIONABLE RETREATS

- **Harvey Nichols** (p198) Forget Harrod's, the top floor bar here is the haunt of the true fashionista.
- **Orangery** (p196) Afternoon tea in the shadow of Kensington Palace always appeals.
- **Blakes** (p192) This temple of minimalist design still attracts the in-the-know crowd.

LEFT: DOUG MCKINLAY; RIGHT: DOUG MCKINLA

Left: Royal Albert Hall and Albert Memorial (p190); Right: Serpentine Gallery (p190), Hyde Park

# DISCOVER HYDE PARK & SOUTH KENSINGTON

The area stretching from Hyde Park – the largest of London's so-called royal Parks – to Chelsea is high-class territory. But it's not all about multimillion-pound properties and glitzy shopping here. This area can boast some of the capital's most important attractions, particularly museums, and its communities are among the most cosmopolitan.

Thanks to Prince Albert and the 1851 Great Exhibition, South Kensington is first and foremost museumland, boasting three of London's richest all on the same street: the Natural History Museum, the Science Museum and the Victoria & Albert Museum. Splendid Hyde Park and Kensington Gardens – just one big sprawling green mass – separate the glitz of Knightsbridge and Kensington from the noise and havoc of the West End, shooing the hoi polloi away with exclusive hotels and expensive shopping.

# SIGHTS

## CHELSEA & BELGRAVIA

### KING'S ROAD

◉ Sloane Sq or South Kensington

In the 17th century, Charles II set up a love nest here for himself and his mistress Nell Gwyn, an orange-seller turned actress at the Drury Lane Theatre. Heading back to Hampton Court Palace of an evening, Charles would make use of a farmer's track that inevitably came to be known as the King's Rd. The street was at the forefront of London fashion during the technicolour 60s and anarchic '70s, and continues to be trendy now, in a more self-conscious way.

## KNIGHTSBRIDGE, KENSINGTON & HYDE PARK

### VICTORIA & ALBERT MUSEUM

☎ 7942 2000; www.vam.ac.uk; Cromwell Rd SW7; admission free; ◷ 10am-5.45pm, to 10pm Fri; ◉ South Kensington; ♿

The Museum of Manufactures, as the V&A was known when it opened in 1852, specialises in decorative art and design, with some

4.5 million objects reaching back as far as 3000 years, from Britain and the world. Part of Prince Albert's legacy to the nation in the aftermath of the successful Great Exhibition of 1851, its original aims – which still hold today – were the 'improvement of public taste in design' and 'applications of fine art to objects of utility'. It's done a fine job so far.

As you enter under the stunning blue-and-yellow blown glass **chandelier by Dale Chihuly** you can pick up a museum map (free; £1 donation requested) at the information desk. (If the 'Grand Entrance' on Cromwell Rd is too busy, there's another around the corner on Exhibition Rd.) Consider one of the free **introductory guided tours**, which last 45 minutes to an hour and leave the main reception area every hour from 10.30am to 3.30pm.

Spread over 145 galleries, the museum houses the world's greatest collection of **decorative arts**, including ancient Chinese ceramics, modernist architectural drawings, Korean bronze and Japanese swords, cartoons by Raphael, spellbinding Asian and Islamic art, Rodin sculptures, gowns from the Elizabethan era, dresses straight from this year's Paris fashion shows, ancient jewellery, a 1930s wireless set – and a lot more. Choose the section(s) you want to visit and stick to that plan.

Level 1 – the floor at street level – is mostly devoted to art and design from India, China, Japan, Korea and Southeast Asia, as well as European art. The museum has the best collection of Italian Renaissance sculpture outside Italy, as well as excellent French, German and Spanish pieces. Some of the museum's highlights are the **Cast Courts** in room 46a, containing plaster casts collected in the Victorian era, such as Michelangelo's David, which was acquired in 1858. The

**Victoria & Albert Museum (p185)**
ORIEN HARVEY

museum's then director, Henry Cole, commissioned casts of Europe's finest work to be used by art students.

The **Photography collection** (room 38a) is one of the country's best, with more than 500,000 images collected since 1852. Among the highlights are the 19th-century photographs of London by Lady Clementina Hawarden. Room 40, the museum's **Fashion Room**, is among the most popular, with displays ranging from Elizabethan costumes to Vivienne Westwood gowns, dated 1980s Armani outfits and designs from this year's catwalks. A fascinating display of women's undergarments shows the 'progress' from the stifling and life-endangering corset from Victorian times to present-day Agent Provocateur's sexy (and comfortable) versions.

The **Jameel Gallery** (room 42) contains more than 400 objects from the Islamic Middle East, including ceramics, textiles, carpets, glass and woodwork from the 8th-century caliphate up to the year before WWI. The pieces were collected from Spain to Afghanistan, though the exhibition's highlight is the gorgeous mid-16th-century **Ardabil Carpet**, the world's oldest (and one of the largest) dated carpet, from Iran.

The **British Galleries**, featuring every aspect of British design from 1500 to 1900, are on levels 2 and 4. They include Henry VIII's writing desk and the so-called Great Bed of Ware from the late 16th century, big enough to sleep five and designed as an early advertising gimmick for an inn in Hertfordshire. Shakespeare mentions it in *Twelfth Night*. The **Architecture gallery** (rooms 127 to 128a) is also on level 4, with descriptions of architectural styles, videos, models and plans. In rooms 70 to 73 on level 4 is part of the **Gilbert Collection** of gold, silver, mosaics, gold boxes and amel miniatures, which was housed in merset House until 2008.

## ATURAL HISTORY MUSEUM
7942 5000; www.nhm.ac.uk; Cromwell SW7; admission free; 10am-5.50pm; South Kensington;

is mammoth institution is dedicated the Victorian pursuit of collecting and taloguing. Walking into the **Life galries** (Blue Zone) in the 1880 Gothic evival building off Cromwell Rd evokes e musty moth-eaten era of the Victorian entleman scientist. The main museum uilding, with its blue and sand-coloured rick and terracotta, was designed by fred Waterhouse and is as impressive the towering **diplodocus dinosaur keleton** in the Central Hall just ahead the main entrance. It's hard to match ny of the exhibits with this initial sight, xcept perhaps the huge **blue whale** just eyond it.

Children, who are the main fans of this useum, are primed for more primeval ildlife by the dinosaur skeleton, and ank their parents to the **dinosaur galry** to the left of the Central Hall to see e roaring and tail-flicking animatron-s T-rex dinosaur, the museum's star ttraction.

The Life galleries to the right of the entral Hall (Green Zone) are full of fos-ls and glass cases of taxidermied birds, nd the antiquated atmosphere is mes-erising. There is also a stunning **Creepy rawlies** room, the Ecology gallery's ideo wall and the vast **Darwin Centre** Orange Zone) which focuses on taxon-my (the study of the natural world), with me 450,000 jars of pickled specimens, cluding an 8.6m-long giant squid called rchie, shown off during free guided tours very half-hour (book in advance). The entre's new feature showcases some 28 million insects and six million plants in 'a giant cocoon'.

The second part of the museum, the **Earth galleries** (Red Zone) can be reached most easily from the Exhibition Rd entrance. Here Victorian fustiness is exchanged for sleek, modern design and the black walls of its **Earth Hall** are lined with crystals, gems and precious rocks. An escalator slithers up through a hollowed-out globe into displays about earth's geological make-up.

Volcanoes, earthquakes and storms are all featured on the upper floors, but the star attraction inside the **Restless Surface gallery**, is the **mock-up of the Kobe earthquake**, a facsimile of a small Japanese grocery shop that trembles in a manner meant to replicate the 1995 earthquake that killed 6000 people. Exhibitions on the lower floors focus on ecology, look at gems and other precious stones and explore how planets are formed.

The **Wildlife Garden** (open April to September) displays a range of British lowland habitats. A stunning temporary exhibit that may become permanent is the **Butterfly Jungle** (adult/child & senior/family £6/4/17; 10am-6pm May-late Sep), a tunnel tent on the East Lawn swarming with what must originally have been called 'flutter-bys'.

## SCIENCE MUSEUM
☎ 0870 870 4868; www.sciencemuseum.org. uk; Exhibition Rd SW7; admission free, adult/concession IMAX Cinema £8/6.25, Motionride simulator £2.50/1.50; 10am-6pm; South Kensington;

With seven floors of interactive and educational exhibits, the Science Museum is highly informative, entertaining and comprehensive.

The **Energy Hall**, on the ground floor as you enter, concentrates on full-sized machines of the Industrial Revolution, showing how the first steam engines such as Puffing Billy, a steam locomotive dating from 1813, helped Britain become 'the workshop of the world' in the early 19th century. Animations show how the machines worked and are accompanied by detailed overall explanations, including a section on the Luddites who opposed the march of technology.

Of course, it's impossible to miss the **Energy Ring**, a huge interactive sculpture that hangs in the space next to the gallery called **Energy: Fuelling the Future** on the 2nd floor. Kids can enter their names then ask energy questions: the answers appear like electronic tickertape messages, running around the inside of the ring. On the same level you will also find a re-creation of **Charles Babbage's Analytical Engine** (1834), now considered the forerunner to the computer.

The 3rd-floor **Flight** and **Launchpad galleries** are favourite places for children, with its gliders, hot-air balloon and varied aircraft, including the *Gipsy Moth,* in which Amy Johnson flew to Australia in 1930. This floor also features an adapted **flight simulator** that's been turned into a 'Motionride' (admission fees apply). The 1st floor has displays on food and time, while the 4th and 5th floors offer exhibits on medical and veterinary history.

## APSLEY HOUSE

☎ 7499 5676; www.english-heritage.org.uk; 149 Piccadilly W1; adult/5-15yr/concession/family £5.70/2.90/4.80/17.50, with Wellington Arch £7/3.50/6/17.50; ☺ 11am-5pm Wed-Sun Apr-Oct, to 4pm Wed-Sun Nov-Mar; ⊖ Hyde Park Corner

This stunning house, which contains exhibits devoted to the life and times of the Duke of Wellington, was once the first building to come into view when enter-

ing the city from the west and was there-fore known as 'No 1 London'. Still one London's finest but overlooking the night-marish Hyde Park Corner roundabout Apsley House was designed by Robe Adam for Baron Apsley in the late 18 century, but was later sold to the first Du of Wellington, who cut Napoleon dov to size in the Battle of Waterloo and live here for 35 years until his death in 1852

In 1947 the house was given to the n tion, which must have come as a surpri to the duke's descendants who still live a flat here; 10 of its rooms are open to th public and visited on a self-paced audi guide tour. **Wellington memorabili** including the Iron Duke's medals, some e tertaining old cartoons and his death mas fill the basement gallery, while there's a astonishing collection of china, includir some of his personal silverware, on th ground floor. The stairwell is dominate by Antonio Canova's staggering 3.4m-hig statue of a fig-leafed Napoleon, adjudge by the subject as 'too athletic'. The 1st-flo **Wellington Gallery** contains paintings b Velázquez, Rubens, Van Dyck, Brueghel an Murillo, but the most interesting is Goya portrait of the duke, which some yea ago was discovered to have the face c Napoleon's brother, Joseph Bonapart beneath the duke's. Apparently, the arti had taken a punt on Napoleon winning th Battle of Waterloo and had to do a quic 'about face' when news of Wellington victory arrived.

## KENSINGTON GARDENS

☎ 7298 2000; www.royalparks.org.uk; ☺ 6am dusk; ⊖ Queensway, High St Kensington or Lancaster Gate

Immediately west of Hyde Park and acros the Serpentine, these gardens are techni cally part of Kensington Palace. The palac and the gardens have become somethin

Gardens at Kensington Palace

# ↘ KENSINGTON PALACE

Kensington Palace already had a long history when Diana moved in after her separation from Prince Charles. Built in 1605, the palace became the favourite royal residence under William and Mary of Orange in 1689, and remained so until George III became king and relocated to Buckingham Palace. Even after that the royal family stayed here occasionally, with Queen Victoria being born here in 1819.

A self-paced audio tour leads you through the surprisingly small, wood-panelled State Apartments dating from William's time and then the grander apartments by William Kent. For most visitors, however, the highlight is the **Royal Ceremonial Dress Collection**, which contains costumes and outfits dating from the 18th century to the present day, including some of Diana's most impressive frocks.

Most beautiful of all the quarters is the **Cupola Room**, where the ceremony initiating men into the exclusive Order of the Garter took place and where Victoria was christened; you can see the order's crest painted on the trompe l'œil 'domed' ceiling, which is actually flat.

The **King's Gallery**, the largest and longest of the State Apartments displays some of the royal art collection, including the only known painting of a classical subject by Van Dyck. On the ceiling Kent painted the story of Odysseus but slipped up by giving the Cyclops two eyes.

**Things you need to know:** ☎ 0844 482 5170; www.hrp.org.uk; Kensington Gardens W8; adult/5-16yr/concession/family £12.50/6.25/11/34, park & gardens free; ☽ 10am-6pm Mar-Oct, to 5pm Nov-Feb; ⊖ Queensway, Notting Hill Gate or High St Kensington

of a shrine to the memory of Princess Diana since her death in 1997.

Art is also characteristic of these gardens. George Frampton's celebrated **Peter Pan statue** is close to the lake. On the opposite side is a **statue of Edward Jenner**, who developed a vaccine for smallpox. To the west of the Serpentine is a **sculpture of John Hanning Speke**, the explorer who discovered the Nile.

## SERPENTINE GALLERY

☎ 7402 6075, recorded information 7298 1515; www.serpentinegallery.org; Kensington Gardens W2; admission free; ⏰ 10am-6pm; ⊖ Knightsbridge; ♿

What looks like an unprepossessing 1930s-style tearoom in the midst of the leafy Kensington Gardens is one of London's most important contemporary art galleries. Artists including Damien Hirst, Andreas Gursky, Louise Bourgeois, Gabriel Orozco, Tomoko Takahashi and Jeff Koons have all exhibited at the Serpentine Gallery, and the gallery's huge windows beam natural light onto the pieces, making the space perfect for sculpture and interactive displays.

Every year a leading architect (who has never built in the UK) is commissioned to build a new 'Summer Pavilion' nearby, which is open from May to October. Reading, talks and open-air cinema screenings take place here as well.

## ALBERT MEMORIAL

☎ 7495 0916; www.royalparks.org.uk/parks/kensington_gardens; 45min tours adult/concession £5/4.50; ⏰ tours 2pm & 3pm 1st Sun of the month Mar-Dec; ⊖ Knightsbridge or Gloucester Rd

On the southern edge of Kensington Gardens and facing the Royal Albert Hall on Kensington Gore, this memorial is as ostentatious as the subject, Queen Victoria's German husband Albert (1819–61), was purportedly humble. Albert explicitly said he did not want a monument and 'if (as is very likely) it became an artistic monstrosity like most of our monuments, it would upset my equanimity to be permanently ridiculed and laughed at in effigy'. Ignoring the good prince's wishes, the Lord Mayor (with Victoria's consent) got George Gilbert Scott to build the 53m-high, gaudy Gothic monument in 1872; the 4.25m-tall gilded statue of the

prince, thumbing through a catalogue his Great Exhibition and surrounded 187 figures representing the continer (Asia, Europe, Africa and America), t arts, industry and science, was erecte in 1876.

## ROYAL ALBERT HALL

☎ 7589 3203, tour bookings 0845 401 5045; www.royalalberthall.com; Kensington Gore SW ⊖ South Kensington; ♿

This huge, domed, red-brick amphithe tre adorned with a frieze of Minton til is Britain's most famous concert venu The hall, built in 1871, was never intende as a concert venue but as a 'Hall of Ar and Sciences'; Queen Victoria added th 'Royal Albert' when she laid the found tion stone, much to the surprise of thos attending. Consequently it spent th first 133 years of its existence tormen ing concert performers and audience with its terrible acoustics. It was said th a piece played here was assured of an in mediate second hearing, so bad was th reverberation around the oval structure. massive refurbishment was completed i 2004, however, installing air-conditionin modernising the backstage areas, movir the entrance to the south of the buildin and fixing the acoustics.

## HYDE PARK

☎ 7298 2000; www.royalparks.org.uk; ⏰ 5.30am-midnight; ⊖ Hyde Park Corner, Marble Arch, Knightsbridge or Lancaster Gate

London's largest royal park spreads itse over a whopping 142 hectares of neatl manicured gardens and wild, deserte expanses of overgrown grass. Sprin prompts the gorgeous Rose Garden: added in 1994, into vivacious bloom, an summers are full of sunbathers, picnick ers, frisbee-throwers and general Londo populace who drape themselves acros

NEIL SETCHFIELD

Kenwood House

## ➘ IF YOU LIKED...

If you like the history, grand decor and smart gardens of Kensington Palace (p189) then we think you will like these other grand London addresses:

- **Chiswick House** Frequently overlooked by visitors, this stunner of a place is a Palladian mansion with an octagonal dome and a colonnaded portico. Inside, some of the rooms are so grand as to be almost overpowering. The expansive landscape garden of Chiswick Park, restored in 2009, surrounds the house.

- **Kenwood House** This grand home at the northern edge of wonderful Hampstead Heath was gifted to the nation, along with its wonderful art collection, by Lord Iveagh Guinness in 1927. Remodelled by Robert Adam in the 18th century, the house is a wonderful combination of historic stately home and art gallery.

- **Syon House** Across the Thames from Kew Gardens, this was the sometime residence of Lady Jane Grey, Queen of England for nine days in 1553. It was remodelled in the 18th century and the main house is stuffed full of Adam furniture, while the gardens were landscaped by Capability Brown.

- **Linley Sambourne House** Tucked away behind High St Kensington, this Victorian family home is full of collected treasures and trinkets, and the entire place is swathed in glorious Turkish carpets and bathed in multicoloured beams of light from the stained-glass windows.

he green. It is also a magnificent backdrop for open-air concerts, demonstrations and royal occasions. Gun salutes are fired here and soldiers ride through the park each morning on their way to Horse Guards Parade in Whitehall.

### SPEAKERS' CORNER

⊖ Marble Arch

The northeastern corner of Hyde Park is traditionally the spot for soapbox ranting. It's the only place in Britain where demonstrators can assemble without police permission, a concession granted in 1872 as a response to serious riots 17 years before when 150,000 people gathered to demonstrate against the Sunday Trading Bill before Parliament. Speakers' Corner was frequented by Karl Marx, Vladimir Lenin, George Orwell and William Morris; if you've got something to get off your chest, you can get rid of it here on Sunday, although it'll be largely loonies, religious fanatics and hecklers you'll have for company.

### MARBLE ARCH
⊖ Marble Arch

John Nash designed this huge arch in 1827. It was moved here, to the north-eastern corner of Hyde Park, from its original spot in front of Buckingham Palace in 1851, when it was adjudged too small and unimposing to be the entrance to the royal manor. A plaque on the traffic island at Marble Arch indicates the spot where the infamous **Tyburn Tree**, a three-legged gallows, once stood. An estimated 50,000 people were executed here between 1571 and 1783, many having been dragged from the Tower of London.

# SLEEPING

Gracious Chelsea and Kensington present London at its elegant best, though count on very little in the midrange and budget categories. Accommodation is more modest in Victoria and Pimlico. The former may not be the most attractive part of London, but you'll be very close to major transport links and the hotels in this area are better value than those in Earl's Court. Pimlico is more residential, though convenient for the Tate Britain at Millbank.

# CHELSEA & BELGRAVIA
## B+B BELGRAVIA
B&B ⊞

☏ 7259 8570; www.bb-belgravia.com; 64-66 Ebury St SW1; s/d/tw/tr/q £99/120/130/150/160 ⊖ Victoria; ▯ ♿

This B&B, stunningly remodelled in con temporary style, boasts a chic black-and white lounge where you can relax befor a fire or watch a DVD, and 17 earth-tone rooms that aren't enormous but have fla screen TV. There's a lovely back garde and guests get to use hotel bicycles fc free.

# KNIGHTSBRIDGE, KENSINGTON & HYDE PARK
## HALKIN
Hotel ££

☏ 7333 1000; www.halkin.como.bz; Halkin St SW1; r from £390, ste from £600, breakfast £20-25; ⊖ Hyde Park Corner; ▦ ▯

The chichi Halkin is for business trave lers of a minimalist bent. Bedroom door are hidden within curved wooden hal ways, and the 41 rooms are filled wit natural light, cream walls, burlwoo panelling and large all-marble bathroom Gratefully they are as stylishly uncluttere as the staff, who wear Armani-designe uniforms.

## BLAKES
Hotel ££

☏ 7370 6701; www.blakeshotels.com; 33 Roland Gardens SW7; s £175, d £225-375, ste from £565, breakfast £17.50-25; ⊖ Gloucester Rd; ▦ ▯

For classic style (and celebrity spotting) one of your first choices in London shoulc be Blakes: five Victorian houses cobblec into one hotel, painted an authoritative very serious dark green and designed by the incomparable Anouska Hempel. It 41 guestrooms are elegantly decked ou with four-poster beds (with and withou nopies), rich fabrics and antiques set on eached hardwood floors.

## ADOGAN HOTEL                    Hotel ££

7235 7141; 75 Sloane St SW1; r £180-335, from £395, breakfast £20-25; Sloane Sq;

his 64-room hotel is a wonderful hybrid, ith two lower floors contemporary in yle and the recently refurbished top o a wonderful vestige from Edwardian mes, filled with polished oak panels, ing chairs, rich heavy fabrics and a re-ned drawing room for afternoon tea. Not urprisingly, the two rooms that are the ost indulgent (and coveted) are No 118 here Oscar Wilde was arrested for 'inde-ent acts' in 1895 and the Lillie Langtry om (No 109) – all rose wallpaper, feather oas and pink lace – where the epony-ous actress (and mistress to Edward VII) nce laid her head.

## UMBER SIXTEEN        Boutique Hotel ££

7589 5232; www.numbersixteenhotel.co.uk; Sumner Pl SW7; s £120, d £165-270, breakfast 6-17.50; South Kensington;

ith cool grey muted colours, tasteful arity and choice art throughout, Number ixteen is a stunning place to stay, with 42 dividually designed rooms, a cosy draw-ng room and fully stocked library. And ait til you see the idyllic back garden set round a fishpond with a few cosy snugs, r have breakfast in the conservatory.

## STER HOUSE                        B&B ££

7581 5888; www.asterhouse.com; 3 Sumner SW7; s £100-120, d & tw £145-250; South ensington;

hat has made this Singaporean-run roperty the winner of Visit London's best &B award not just once but three times? o doubt the quintessential English aura, he welcoming staff, the comfortable

Science Museum (p187)

DOUG McKINLAY

rooms with good-quality furnishings and sparkling bathrooms, and the reason-able price all had something to do with it. Oh, and that's not to mention the lovely garden and the delightful plant-filled Orangerie where breakfast is served on the 1st floor.

## ASTOR HYDE PARK                 Hostel £

7581 0103; 191 Queen's Gate SW7; www. astorhostels.co.uk; dm £20-31, tw £70-80, d £80-90; Gloucester Rd or High St Kensington;
It's fairly unlikely you've ever seen a hos-tel like this one, with its wood-panelled walls, bay windows with leaded lights, 19th-century vibe and ever-so-posh ad-dress just over from the Royal Albert Hall. It has 150 beds in rooms over five floors (no lift), including dorms with three to 12

Main hall, Natural History Museum (p187)

DOUG MCKIN

beds, and a fabulous kitchen complete with incongruous pool tables.

### YHA HOLLAND HOUSE — Hostel £

☎ 7937 0748; www.yha.org.uk; Holland Walk W8; dm £20.95-27.50; ⊖ High St Kensington; ▯ Built into the Jacobean wing of Holland House (1607) in Holland Park, this hostel has 201 beds in large rooms with between six and 20 beds. It's large, always busy and rather institutional, but the position is unbeatable. There's a cafe and kitchen.

# EATING

The influx of foreign migrants to 18th-century London, already Europe's largest city, led to the expansion of the working-class areas to the east and the south while the more affluent headed north and west. Quality tends to gravitate to where the money is, and you'll find some of London's finest establishments in the swanky hotels and mews of Chelsea, Belgravia and Knightsbridge. The king of them all, Gordon Ramsay, has three Michelin stars

in its crown and resides in Chelsea. Chic ar cosmopolitan South Kensington has alway been reliable for pan-European options.

### GORDON RAMSAY — Modern European ££

☎ 7352 4441; www.gordonramsay.com; 68 Royal Hospital Rd SW3; 3-course lunch/dinner £45/90; ☺ lunch & dinner Mon-Fri; ⊖ Sloane S One of Britain's finest restaurants an still the only one in the capital with thre Michelin stars, this is hallowed turf fc those who worship at the altar of the stov It's true that it is a treat right from the taste to the truffles, but you won't get muc time to savour it all. Bookings are made i specific sittings and you dare not linge The blow-out tasting Menu Prestige (£12C is seven courses of absolute perfection.

### CAPITAL — Modern European ££

☎ 7589 5171, 7591 1202; www.capitalhotel. co.uk; Capital Hotel, 22-23 Basil St SW3; 2-/3-course set lunch £27.50/33, dinner £55/63; ⊖ Knightsbridge Of the eight restaurants in London to hav been awarded two Michelin stars, th apital behind Harrods is the least known, nd so much the better. The modern yet armth-inducing decor, welcoming nd accommodating staff and chef Eric havot's award-winning dishes (roasted bster with chilli and coconut broth, a addle of rabbit seared calamari and to- ato risotto) all remain our secret. And ow yours. Tasting menu is £70 (add £55 r accompanying wines).

## BENDUM                    Modern European £££
☎ 7581 5817, 7589 1480; www.bibendum. .uk; Michelin House, 81 Fulham Rd SW3; ains £23-27, 2-/3-course set lunches £25/29; ⊖ South Kensington

ocated in listed art nouveau Michelin ouse, Bibendum offers upstairs dining a spacious and light room with stained- lass windows, where you can savour bulous and creative food, and what, must be said, is fairly ordinary service. he Bibendum Oyster Bar on the ground oor offers a front-row seat from which to dmire the building's architectural finery hile lapping up terrific native and rock ysters (per half-dozen £12; mains £7.50 o £10.50)

## IN JIANG                    Chinese £££
☎ 7361 1988; www.minjiang.co.uk; 10th fl, oyal Garden Hotel, 2-24 Kensington High St W8; ains £12-48; ⊖ High St Kensington

his stunner of a Chinese restaurant, erched on the top of a hotel owned y a Hong Kong-based group, offers illion-dollar views of Kensington Palace nd Gardens as well as arguably the best eking duck (half/whole £25/48) in all f London. You'll consume everything om the skin and feet to the shredded eat and then get the bill. It's cooked in wood-burning stove. There's excellent eafood here, too.

## LAUNCESTON PLACE
Modern European ££
☎ 7937 6912; www.launcestonplace-restaurant. co.uk; 1a Launceston Pl W8; 3-course lunch/Sun lunch/dinner £18/24/42; ⊗ closed lunch Mon; ⊖ Gloucester Rd or Kensington High St

This exceptionally handsome restaurant on a picture-postcard Kensington street of Edwardian houses is about the chic-est address in this part of town at the mo- ment. The food, prepared by chef Tristan Welsh, a protégé of Marcus Wareing, tastes as divine as it looks. The adven- turous (and flush) will go for the tasting menu (£52).

## RACINE                    French ££
☎ 7584 4477; 239 Brompton Rd SW3; mains £12.50-26.25, 2-/3-course set lunch £17.50/19.50; ⊖ Knightsbridge or South Kensington

Regional French cooking is the vehicle at this brasserie that looks like it just stepped off the Eurostar. Expect the likes of *tête de veau* (the classic French veal dish; £16.50), grilled rabbit with mustard (£19.95), and veal kidneys with Fourme d'Ambert (a blue cheese from the Auvergne) and wal- nut butter. Being French and very classic, dishes might feel heavy to some, but the sauces and the desserts are all spot on.

## LUCIO                    Italian ££
☎ 7823 3007; www.luciorestaurant.com; 257-259 Fulham Rd SW3; mains £18.50-20.50, 2-/3-course set lunch £15.50/19; ⊖ South Kensington

One of our favourite Italian eateries in London, Lucio is decidedly top end but not overly so. Try the exquisitely cooked pasta with clams, the crab ravioli or, when in season, the deep-fried zucchini. The surrounds are understatedly stylish, the clientele subdued and the service seamless.

## ORANGERY
Teahouse ££

☎ 0844 482 7777; www.hrp.org.uk; Kensington Palace, Kensington Gardens W8; mains £9.95-12.95, tea £13.50-28.50; ☺ 10am-6pm Mar-Oct, to 5pm Nov-Feb; ⊖ Queensway, Notting Hill Gate or High St Kensington

The Orangery, housed in an 18th-century conservatory on the grounds of Kensington Palace, is a great place for lunch, especially in fine weather, but nothing beats this place for tea. Choose from several varieties, which start with a 'normal' tea (sandwiches, desserts and tea) and end with a champagne one (the same but with champagne) at £28.50, which you're almost certain not to be able to finish.

## LA POULE AU POT
French

☎ 7730 7763; 231 Ebury St SW1; mains £15.50 21, 2-/3-course set lunches £18.75/22.75; ⊖ Sloane Sq

Illuminated with candlelight eve at lunch, the 'Chicken in the Pot' is long-established country-style Frenc restaurant that is long on romance an cosiness and somewhat shorter on th quality of what it serves. Still, the a fresco front terrace is a lovely spot the warmer months. Expect dishes lik onion tarte, rabbit casserole and roa guinea fowl.

## OLIVO
Italian ££

☎ 7730 2505; 21 Eccleston St SW1; mains £13.75-17.50; ☺ closed lunch Sat & Sun; ⊖ Victoria or Sloane Sq

This colourful restaurant specialises in th food and wine of Sardinia and Sicily, an has a dedicated clientele who, frankl would rather keep it to themselves. No surprising, really, because this place nea Victoria station is a true gem. As a gen eral rule, drink Sicilian and eat Sardinia Excellent pasta dishes (£10.75 to £15.50

## JENNY LO'S TEA HOUSE
Chinese £

☎ 7259 0399; 14 Eccleston St SW1; mains £6.9 8.50; ☺ lunch & dinner Mon-Fri; ⊖ Victoria

This is a good-value place in Victoria fo rice and noodles. It was set up by th daughter of the late Chinese cookery book author Kenneth Lo, who introduce the UK to Chinese food in the 1950s.

# DRINKING

This is where high style and traditiona pubs meet and coexist in surprisin harmony. You can choose betwee the sultry lights of expensive cockta

JONATHAN SMITH
Gordon Ramsay restaurant (p194)

ars, frequented by the deep-pocketed Knightsbridge and Chelsea dwellers, or join the area's ale lovers in some of the most beautiful of London's old pubs.

## DRAYTON ARMS                                    Pub
☎ 7835 2301; 153 Old Brompton Rd SW5; ♨ noon-midnight; ⊖ West Brompton or South Kensington; ☒ 430

This vast Victorian corner boozer is as delightful on the inside as out, with some bijou art nouveau features (sinuous tendrils and curlicues above the windows and the doors), interesting contemporary art on the walls and a fabulous coffered ceiling. The crowd is both hip and down-to-earth, young and been around a bit, in that relaxing sort of way. There's a good beer and wine selection.

## NAG'S HEAD                                      Pub
☎ 7235 1135; 53 Kinnerton St SW1; ⊖ Hyde Park Corner

Located in a serene mews not far from bustling Knightsbridge, this gorgeously genteel early-19th-century drinking den has eccentric decor (think 19th-century cricket prints), a sunken bar and a 'no mobile phones' rule. A dreamy delight, this one.

## QUEEN'S ARMS                                    Pub
☎ 7581 7741; 30 Queen's Gate Mews SW7; ⊖ Gloucester Rd

The Queen's Arms wouldn't get much of a look-over if elsewhere. But location, location, location, as they say: tucked down a quiet mews off Queen's Gate, this place wins bouquets from the many students living in the area as well as from concert-goers heading for the **Royal Albert Hall** (p190), just around the corner. Add to that four hand pumps and a decent (mostly gastropub) menu.

# ENTERTAINMENT & ACTIVITIES

## ROYAL ALBERT HALL          Classical Music
☎ information 7589 3203, bookings 7589 8212, www.royalalberthall.com; Kensington Gore SW7; admission £5-150, Proms admission £5-75; ⊖ South Kensington

This splendid Victorian concert hall hosts many classical-music, rock and other performances, but it is most famous as the venue for the BBC-sponsored Proms – one of the world's biggest classical-music festivals. Booking is possible, but from mid-July to mid-September Proms punters also queue for £5 standing (or 'promenading') tickets that go on sale one hour before curtain up. Otherwise, the box office and prepaid ticket collection counter are both through door 12 on the south side of the hall.

## SERPENTINE LIDO                    Swimming
☎ 7298 2100; Hyde Park W2; ⊖ Hyde Park Corner or Knightsbridge

Perhaps the ultimate London pool inside the Serpentine lake, this fabulous lido is usually open in July and August. Admission prices and opening times are always subject to change, so it's essential to call ahead.

## ROYAL COURT THEATRE              Theatre
☎ 7565 5000; www.royalcourttheatre.com; Sloane Sq SW1; admission free-£25; ⊖ Sloane Sq

Equally renowned for staging innovative new plays and old classics, the Royal Court is among London's most progressive theatres. Starting with its inaugural piece in 1956, John Osborne's *Look Back In Anger*, now considered the starting point of modern British theatre, under its inspirational artistic director Dominic Cooke it has continued to discover major writing talent across the UK. Recent triumphs were a star-studded performance of *The Seagull,* a sassy new musical about drag queens and a retrospective of plays by American actor and playwright Wallace Shawn.

Tickets for concessions are £6 to £10, and £10 for everyone on Monday. At the same time, under 25s can get into selected performances at the Jerwood Theatre Downstairs for free. Standby tickets are sold an hour before the performance, but normally at full price.

# SHOPPING

This well-heeled part of town is all about high fashion, glam shops and groomed shoppers and is home to Chelsea's chic King's Rd. Knightsbridge draws the hordes with high-end department stores and glamorous boutiques. Among the glitz, venerable and atmospheric stores survive thanks to centuries of catering to the whims and vanities of the rich and refined folk who live here. High St Kensington has a good mix of chains and boutiques.

## HARRODS                           Department Sto

☎ 7730 1234; www.harrods.com; 87-135 Brompton Rd SW1; ⏰ 10am-8pm Mon-Sat, 11.30am-6pm Sun; ⊖ Knightsbridge

It's garish and stylish at the same tim and sure to leave you reeling with consumer-rush after you've spent a fe hours within its walls. Harrods is an obliga tory stop for many of London's tourist always crowded and with more rules tha an army barracks. And despite the tack elements, you're bound to swoon over th spectacular food hall and impeccable 5th floor perfumery. **Harrods 102** ( ☎ 7730 123 102 Brompton Rd SW1; ⏰ 9am-9pm Mon-Sat, noo 6pm Sun), across the street, contains a luxur food shop and several casual restaurant:

## HARVEY NICHOLS                    Department Sto

☎ 7235 5000; www.harveynichols.com; 109-12 Knightsbridge SW1; ⏰ 10am-8pm or 9pm Mon-Sat, 11.30am-6pm Sun; ⊖ Knightsbridge

London's temple of high fashion is wher you'll find Chloé and Balenciaga bag; London's best denim range, a massiv make-up hall with exclusive lines, grea jewellery and the restaurant Fifth Floo with a three-course set lunch from £19.5C

# ↘ CLERKENWELL, SHOREDITCH & SPITALFIELDS

ITALIAN
COFFEES

# CLERKENWELL, SHOREDITCH & SPITALFIELDS

| SIGHTS | |
|---|---|
| Brick Lane | **1** H4 |
| Geffrye Museum | **2** G2 |
| Old Truman Brewery | **3** H5 |
| Spitalfields Market | **4** G5 |
| St John's Gate | **5** C5 |
| Vat House | **6** H5 |
| White Cube Gallery | **7** F3 |

| SLEEPING | |
|---|---|
| Hoxton Hotel | **8** F4 |
| Rookery | **9** C5 |
| Zetter | **10** C4 |

| EATING | |
|---|---|
| Brick Lane Beigel Bake | **11** H4 |
| Coach & Horses | **12** B4 |
| Eyre Brothers | **13** F4 |
| Fifteen | **14** E3 |
| Furnace | **15** F3 |
| Green & Red | **16** H4 |
| Medcalf | **17** B4 |
| Mesón Los Barriles | (see 4) |
| Modern Pantry | **18** C4 |
| Moro | **19** B4 |
| Smiths of Smithfield | **20** C5 |
| St John | **21** H5 |

| DRINKING | |
|---|---|
| Bar Kick | **22** G3 |
| Bricklayers Arms | **23** G3 |
| Dreambagsjaguarshoes | **24** G3 |
| Filthy McNasty's | **25** B3 |
| George & Dragon | **26** G3 |
| Golden Heart | **27** H5 |
| Jerusalem Tavern | **28** C5 |
| Mother Bar | (see 33) |
| Old Blue Last | **29** G4 |

| | |
|---|---|
| Red Lion | **30** G3 |
| Ten Bells | **31** H5 |
| Ye Olde Mitre | **32** C5 |

| ENTERTAINMENT & ACTIVITIES | |
|---|---|
| 333 | **33** G3 |
| 93 Feet East | **34** H5 |
| Cargo | **35** G3 |
| Catch | **36** G3 |
| East Village | **37** F4 |
| Fabric | **38** C5 |
| Favela Chic | **39** F4 |
| Last Days of Decadence | **40** G4 |
| Sadler's Wells | **41** C3 |

| SHOPPING | |
|---|---|
| Absolute Vintage | **42** H5 |
| Antoni & Alison | **43** B4 |
| Columbia Road Flower Market | **44** H3 |
| Hoxton Boutique | **45** G3 |
| Laden Showrooms | **46** H4 |
| Magma | **47** B5 |
| No-one | **48** G3 |
| Spitalfields Market | (see 4) |
| Start | **49** F4 |
| Start Made to Measure | (see 49) |
| Start Menswear | **50** G4 |
| Sunday UpMarket | (see 3) |
| Tatty Devine | **51** H4 |

See Bloomsbury
To Regents Park
Map (p154)

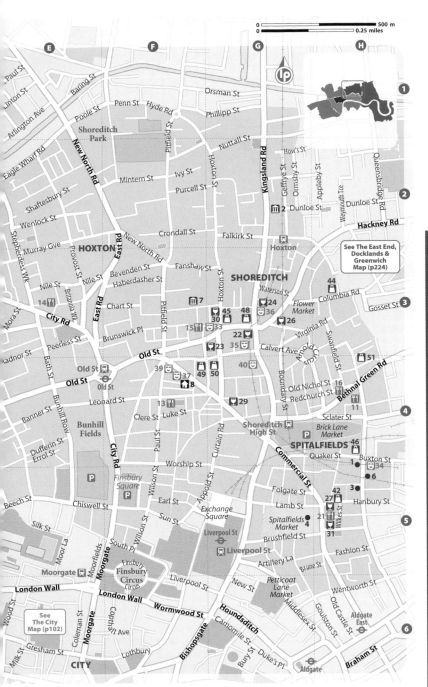

# HIGHLIGHTS

## ↘ GET TO KNOW BANGLATOWN

Take a wander down **Brick Lane** (p213) and its surroundings (including the Truman Brewery) to find the heart of London's thriving Bangladeshi community, commonly known as Banglatown. Grab a cheap and filling spicy meal, stop into some of the many interesting shops or just soak up the atmosphere. You might want to steer clear of Brick Lane at the weekends though, as crowds can be huge.

## ↘ CLUBBING IN SHOREDITCH

Nowhere in London can rival the creative maelstrom of the capital's coolest quarter. True, prices have risen hugely over the past decade and many of the original creators of the 'Hoxton scene' may have moved on to the still ungentrified fringes of Hackney, but you still can't beat an evening out in **Shoreditch** (p218), where the best and most unruly of the capital's clubs can be found.

**3**

## ⬆ GEFFRYE MUSEUM

An institution devoted to interiors may not exactly set your imagination on fire, but this charming and idiosyncratic **museum** (p210) succeeds on all levels and is a fascinating insight into the evolution of interiors in Britain. It's also housed in a beautiful old row of almshouses, well worth seeing for themselves alone.

**4**

## ⬆ SHOP AT SPITALFIELDS MARKET

The **market** (p212) at Spitalfields has long been a London favourite – and even though (inevitably given its position on some of London's prime real estate) the developers have finally moved in and 'regenerated' much of the old market, this place still has its fair share of great shopping, eating and atmosphere.

**5**

## ⬆ EAT OUT IN CLERKENWELL

Chic little sister to Shoreditch, Clerkenwell is richer, more gentrified and steeped in history. It also has some of the best **eating options** (p212) in the entire city concentrated in its quaint streets. Come here for an exciting and memorable meal before heading east to Shoreditch or west to the West End.

1 KARL BLACKWELL; 2 ROBERTO HERRETT/ALAMY; 3 TRAVIS DREVER; 4 RICHARD I'ANSON; 5 JONATHAN SMITH

1 Brick Lane (p213); 2 333 club (p218); 3 Geffyre Museum (p210); 4 Spitalfields Market (p212);
5 Moro restaurant (p213)

# SUNDAY WALK AT SPITALFIELDS & SHOREDITCH

You can of course do this walk at anytime to get to know one of London's most exciting and creative neighbourhoods, but for the very best experience try to come on Sunday mornings when two of the biggest markets are in full swing. This one-mile walk will take you from Liverpool St station all the way to Old Street tube station.

## ❶ SPITALFIELDS MARKET

This is one of London's best **markets** (p212), and a great weekend trea for clothing, records and food. As you approach from Liverpool St, you see the new development, which, although trying to maintain an inde pendent spirit, lacks the old market's rugged and spontaneous atmos phere. Enter the old market building and get lost among the many stall

## ❷ ABSOLUTE VINTAGE

Check out the tons of vintage shoes in this excellent **shop**. There ar colours and sizes for all, with shoes ranging from designer vintage t something out of your grandma's attic. Clothes for men and wome line the back of the shop.

## ❸ SUNDAY UPMARKET

Having lost valuable stall space with the new development a Spitalfields Market, the young designers moved their **market** (p212 inside the Old Truman Brewery. The new space is brilliant – not a crowded, and with wonderful clothes, music and crafts. Its excellen food hall (at the Brick Lane end) has worldwide grub, from Ethiopia veggie dishes to Japanese delicacies.

## ❹ OLD TRUMAN BREWERY

This was the biggest **brewery** (p213) in London by the mid-18th cen tury, and the Director's House on the left dates from 1740. Next to the 19th-century Vat House is the 1830 Engineer's House and a ro of former stables. The brewery shut down in 1989 and is now part o Sunday UpMarket.

## ❺ BRICK LANE

In 1550 this was just a country road leading to brickyards; by th 18th century it had been paved and lined with houses and cottage inhabited by the Spitalfields weavers. Today the southern part of thi vibrant **street** (p213) is taken up by touristy curry houses and all th street names are in Bengali as well as English.

# SUNDAY WALK AT SPITALFIELDS & SHOREDITCH

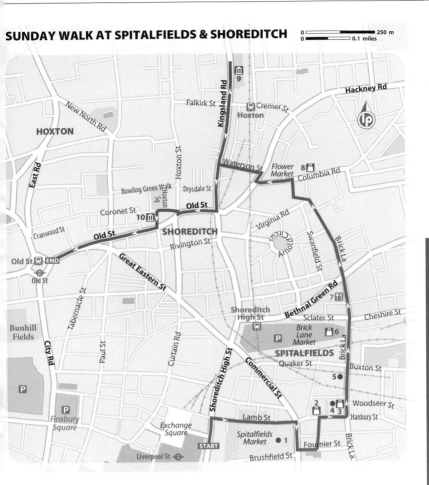

## ❻ BRICK LANE MARKET

Sundays at Brick Lane around the newly reopened Shoreditch tube station are the best place to find good bargains for clothes, but the market is particularly good for furniture. Saunter down Cheshire St for little boutiques featuring new designers and vintage collections.

## ❼ BRICK LANE BEIGEL BAKE

At the far end of Brick Lane, this excellent **bagel business** (p214) was started by some of the Jewish families who originally settled in the neighbourhood and still live here. It operates 24 hours a day and is always busy: with market shoppers on Sunday and Shoreditch clubbers by night.

### ❽ COLUMBIA ROAD FLOWER MARKET

Every Sunday from dawn market stalls sell freshly cut flowers, plan
and orchids for Londoners' gardens and window sills. The earlier yc
arrive, the better the **market**, though the best bargains are to be ha
later on (around noon) as things wrap up. Make a beeline for the foc
stalls behind the main flower sellers for a mid-morning snack.

### ❾ GEFFRYE MUSEUM

A small estate of Victorian houses, this fascinating **museum** (p21(
is devoted to English interiors through the ages. End your walk i
the lovely glass cafe in the back, and have a look at the museum
aromatic herb garden.

### ❿ HOXTON SQUARE

Pop into Hoxton Sq on the way to Old Street tube. Check out th
small park where there's always something going on and join th
crowds having a drink outside if the weather is good. Don't miss th
**White Cube Gallery** (p210) where there's always something fun c
controversial hanging on its pristine white walls.

White Cube Gallery (p210)

# BEST...

## ◥ THINGS FOR FREE

- **Geffrye Museum** (p210) See the history of London interiors at this great little museum.
- **White Cube Gallery** (p210) Take the temperature of contemporary international art at Jay Joplin's gleaming gallery.
- **Spitalfields Market** (p212) Great eating and shopping at one of London's best-loved market spaces.

## ◥ TRENDIEST DRINKING HOLES

- **George & Dragon** (p216) Have a drink at Shoreditch's hipster epicentre.
- **Red Lion** (p217) Kick back with a pint at this off-the-wall DJ pub.
- **Golden Heart** (p218) Infiltrate Spitalfields' notoriously raucous art scene.
- **Old Blue Last** (p217) Get down and dirty with the Vice magazine crew.

## ◥ QUIRKY PLACES

- **Jerusalem Tavern** (p215) Drink unusual beers in this tiny little curiosity of a pub.
- **Tatty Devine** (p222) Shoreditch's funkiest jewellery and accessories store.
- **Antoni & Alison** (p220) The gods of quirky T-shirts, Antoni & Alison is always worth a visit.

## ◥ HOT TABLES

- **Moro** (p213) This fantastic Moorish establishment never fails to impress.
- **Fifteen** (p214) Jamie Oliver's training restaurant is still in huge demand.
- **St John** (p213) Book ahead for the original 'nose to tail' dining experience.
- **Eyre Brothers** (p214) Iberia meets Africa at this superb Shoreditch restaurant.

LEFT: TRAVIS DREVER; RIGHT: RICHARD I'ANSE

Left: Geffrye Museum (p210); Right: Glass wall inside Spitalfields Market (p212)

# DISCOVER CLERKENWELL, SHOREDITCH & SPITALFIELDS

These three redeveloped post-industrial areas northeast of the city remain London's creative engine room and, for many visitors, its current throbbing heart. These are undoubtedly the best areas for discovering London's legendary nightlife, hippest shopping and most innovative eating options.

The three adjoining but very different districts are Clerkenwell, just north of the City; Shoreditch and its northern extension Hoxton, an area (roughly) between Old St tube station and just east of Shoreditch High St; and Spitalfields, centred around the market of that name and Brick Lane, its heaving main thoroughfare. There is a smattering of interesting off-piste sights in these areas, but the main attraction is the fun you'll usually have here, from clubbing at Fabric and from shopping at Spitalfields Market to drinking cocktails at a Shoreditch dive bar – this is London's coolest quarter and shouldn't be missed.

# SIGHTS
## CLERKENWELL
### ST JOHN'S GATE

⊖ Farringdon

This surprisingly out-of-place medieval gate across St John's Lane is not a modern folly, but the real deal. It dates from the early 16th century and was heavily restored 300 years later. During the Crusades, the Knights of St John of Jerusalem, soldiers who took on a nursing role, established a priory in Clerkenwell that originally covered around 4 hectares. The gate was built in 1504 as a grand entrance to their church, St John's Clerkenwell in St John's Sq.

Although most of the buildings were destroyed when Henry VIII dissolved every priory in the country between 1536 and 1540, the gate lived on. It had a varied afterlife, not least as a Latin-speaking coffee house run, without much success, by William Hogarth's father during Queen Anne's reign. The restoration dates from the period when it housed the Old Jerusalem Tavern in the 19th century. A pub of (almost) that name can now be found a round the corner on Britton St (see p215).

Inside St John's Gate is the small **Order of St John Museum** ( ☎ 7324 40005; www.sja.org.uk/museum; admission free; 🕑 10am-5pm Mon-Fri, to 4pm Sat) which recounts the history of the knights and their properties around the world and of their successors.

Definitely try to time your visit for one of the **guided tours** (adult/senior £5/4; 🕑 tours 11am & 2.30pm Tue, Fri & Sat) of the gate and the restored church remains, though. This includes the fine Norman crypt with a sturdy alabaster monument commemorating a Castilian knight (1575); a battered monument portraying the last prior, William Weston, as a skeleton in a shroud; and stained-glass windows showing the main figures in the story. You'll also be shown the sumptuous **Chapter Hall** where the Chapter General of the Order meets every three months.

# SHOREDITCH & HOXTON

## WHITE CUBE GALLERY

☎ 7930 5373; www.whitecube.com; 48 Hoxton Sq N1; admission free; ⏱ 10am-6pm Tue-Sat; ⊖ Old St

Jay Jopling, dealer to the stars of the Brit Art firmament, made his reputation in the 1990s by exhibiting then-unknown artists such as Damien Hirst, Antony Gormley and Tracey Emin. This Hoxton Sq cube is aptly named and, while the gallery is now part of Britain's 'new establishment', it's always worth a visit just to have a look at the latest shows. There's another **White Cube** (p64) in St James's.

## GEFFRYE MUSEUM

☎ 7739 9893; www.geffrye-museum.org.uk; 136 Kingsland Rd E2; admission by donation; ⏱ 10am-5pm Tue-Sat, noon-5pm Sun; ⊖ Old St or Liverpool St; ♿

Definitely Shoreditch's most accessible sight, this 18th-century ivy-clad series of almshouses with a herb garden draws you in immediately. The museum inside is devoted to domestic interiors, with each room of the main building furnished to show how the homes of the relatively affluent middle class would have looked from Elizabethan times right through to the end of the 19th century. A postmodernist extension completed in 1998 contains several 20th-century rooms (a flat from the 1930s, a room in the contemporary style of the 1950s and a 1990s converted warehouse complete with Ikea furniture). There is also a lovely herb garden, gallery for temporary exhibits, a design centre with works from the local community, a shop and restaurant.

Another development has been the exquisite restoration of a **historic almshouse interior** (adult/under 16yr £2/free). It's the absolute attention to detail that impresses, right down to the vintag newspaper left open on the breakfa table. The setting is so fragile, howeve that this small almshouse is only ope twice a month (usually on a Wednesda and Saturday).

# SPITALFIELDS

Crowded around its eponymous marke and the marvellous Hawksmoor Chri Church, Spitalfields, this wedge of th capital between the City and Shoreditc is a layer cake of immigration from a over the world. Waves of Hugueno (French Protestants persecuted i France), Jews, Irish and, more recentl Indian and Bangladeshi immigrants hav made Spitalfields home and it remain one of the capital's most multicultura areas.

# SLEEPING

Clerkenwell, Spitalfields and especiall Shoreditch, with its northern extensio Hoxton, are very popular neighbou hoods, and there are a few good place to stay here. Accommodation choices ar for the most part, at the top end, with th exception of the superb-value Hoxto Hotel, for which you should book as fa ahead as possible!

## ROOKERY

Hotel £££

☎ 7336 0931; www.rookeryhotel.com; Peter's Lane, Cowcross St EC1; s £200, d & tw £240-340, ste £570; ⊖ Farringdon; ▧ ☎

This absolute charmer of a hotel is warren of 33 rooms that has been buil within a row of 18th-century Georgia houses and fitted out with antique fur niture (including a museum-piece co lection of Victorian baths, showers an toilets), original wood panelling, statue

DOUG MCKINLAY

Columbia Road Flower Market

## ☙ IF YOU LIKE...

If you liked **Spitalfields Market** (p212) then don't miss out on some of our other favourite London markets:

- **Portobello Market** Though shops and stalls open daily, the busiest days are Friday, Saturday and Sunday. There's an antiques market on Saturday, and a flea market on Portobello Green on Sunday morning. Antiques, jewellery, paintings and ethnic stuff are concentrated at the Notting Hill Gate end of Portobello Rd.
- **Camden Market** The place is busiest at weekends, especially Sunday, when the crowds elbow each other all the way north from Camden Town tube station to Chalk Farm Rd. It's composed of several separate markets, which tend to merge.
- **Columbia Road Flower Market** London's most fragrant market shouldn't be missed. Merchants lay out their blooms, from everyday geraniums to rare pelargoniums, between Gosset St and the Royal Oak pub every Sunday morning.
- **Brixton Market** A heady, cosmopolitan mix, ranging from silks, wigs, knock-off fashion and the occasional Christian preacher on Electric Ave to the foodstuffs in the covered Brixton Village.
- **Riverside Walk** Great for cheap second-hand books long out of print, this is held in all weather outside the National Film Theatre, under the arches of Waterloo Bridge every weekend.

n the bathrooms and artworks selected personally by the owner. There's a small courtyard garden and a wonderfully private and whimsical feel to the whole place.

**ZETTER** Boutique Hotel ££
☎ 7324 4444; www.thezetter.com; 86-88 Clerkenwell Rd EC1; r £170-270, ste from £276; ⊖ Farringdon; ⚒ 🛜
The Zetter is a special place – a temple of cool with an overlay of kitsch on

**Tasty treats at Spitalfields Market**

## ↘ SPITALFIELDS MARKET

This market was originally the place to snaffle the latest street wear at good prices, with young fashion designers joined by jewellers, furniture makers and a variety of fresh-produce stalls. Unfortunately, with big businesses wanting a piece of the action, part of the old market was converted into a new restaurant and shopping complex in 2006. The old market still stands, thankfully, and much of the young designer stalls have moved up the road to the Old Truman Brewery's **Sunday UpMarket** (www.sunday|upmarket. co.uk; 🕙 10am-6pm), basically a Spitalfields Market extension.

**Things you need to know:** Spital-fields Market (www.visitspitalfields. com; Commercial St, btwn Brush-field & Lamb Sts E1; 🕙 9.30am-5.30pm Sun; ⊖ Liverpool St)

Clerkenwell's titular street. Its rooms are small but perfectly formed, with Penguin Classics on the bookshelves and hi-tech flat screens and air-conditioning (using water from the hotel's very own bore hole). It's worth investigating the superb weekend deals, which make some rooms available for as little as £99.

**HOXTON HOTEL**   Hotel #

☎ 7550 1000; www.hoxtonhotels.com; 81 Great Eastern St EC2; r £1-199; ⊖ Old St; 🔀 🕭 🛜

This is hands down the best hotel deal i London. In the heart of Shoreditch, th sleek 205-room hotel aims to make it money by being full each night, rathe than ripping its guests off. Rooms ar small but stylish, with flat-screen TV, des and fridge. Best of all is the price – whil you have to be very lucky to get one c the £1 rooms, it's quite normal to find room for £59 or £79 – still excellent dea for this level of comfort.

# EATING

Shoreditch offers some of the best eatin in London these days – the neighbou hood's creative flair has attracted sim larly minded, independent restaurateur and there seems to be a new additio every week. Clerkenwell has a more tra ditional feel, but continues to host som of London's most celebrated eaterie while Spitalfields is home to other gem including several of London's best-love bagel bakeries and a slew of often rathe lacklustre balti houses.

## CLERKENWELL

**MEDCALF**   British £-£

☎ 7833 3533; www.medcalfbar.co.uk; 40 Exmouth Market EC1; mains £8.50-19.50; 🕙 **closed dinner Sun;** ⊖ **Farringdon or Angel** Medcalf is far and away one of the best value hangouts in Exmouth Marke Housed in a beautifully converte butcher shop dating back to 1912, i serves up innovative and well-realise British fare, such as handpicked Devor crab and Welsh rarebit.

## MITHS OF SMITHFIELD

Modern British ££

☎ 7251 7950, 7236 6666; www.smithsofsmith eld.co.uk; 67-77 Charterhouse St EC1; mains £10-7; ⏱ breakfast, lunch & dinner; ⊖ Farringdon

his Clerkenwell institution packs in a mix-ure of locals, city workers and clubbers for s rightly celebrated breakfast in the cav-rnous ground-floor canteen. Elsewhere in 1e building, the food quality and prices 1crease with each staircase. The linking 1ctor between them all is a focus on top-uality British meat and organic produce.

## T JOHN

British ££

☎ 7251 0848; www.stjohnrestaurant.co.uk; 6 St John St EC1; mains £12.50-22; ⏱ closed inner Sun; ⊖ Farringdon

his London classic is wonderfully sim-le – its surprisingly small dining room /as one of the places that launched ondoners on the quest to rediscover 1eir culinary past. Don't miss the signa-ure roast bone-marrow salad with pars-ey; follow it with one of the tasty daily pecials – roast kid, fennel and green

sauce, for example, or smoked eel with beetroot and horseradish. The traditional British puddings are similarly superb.

## MORO

North African, Spanish ££

☎ 7833 8336; www.moro.co.uk; 34-36 Exmouth Market EC1; mains £15.50-18.50; ⊖ Farringdon or Angel

The best-known restaurant in Clerkenwell and still a frequent award winner a decade after it launched, Moro serves 'Moorish' cuisine, a fusion of Spanish, Portuguese and North African flavours. The restaurant doesn't look like anything special, though it's full and buzzing, but the food is fabu-lous with such dishes on its constantly evolving menu as charcoal-grilled lamb with deep-fried aubergine. Reserve ahead.

## MODERN PANTRY

Fusion ££

☎ 7553 9210; www.themodernpantry.co.uk; 47-48 St John's Sq EC1; mains £12.50-18.50; ⏱ 8am-11pm Mon-Fri, 9am-11pm Sat, 10am-10pm Sun; ⊖ Farringdon

This three-floor Georgian town house in the heart of Clerkenwell has a

## ↘ BRICK LANE

Brick Lane is the centrepiece of a thriving Bengali community in an area nick-named Banglatown. The lane itself, south of the Old Truman Brewery is one long procession of curry and balti houses intermingled with fabric shops and Indian supermarkets. Sadly, the once-high standard of cooking in the curry houses is a distant memory, so you're probably better off trying subcontinental cuisine in Whitechapel (p235).

Just past Hanbury St is the converted **Old Truman Brewery** which was once London's largest brewery. The Director's House on its left harks back to 1740, the old **Vat House** across the road with its hexagonal bell tower is early 19th century, and the Engineer's House next to it dates from 1830. The brewery stopped producing beer in 1989, and in the 1990s became home to a host of independent music businesses, small shops and hip clubs and bars. North of here Brick Lane is a very different place, stuffed with great clothing, book and record stores, some of London's best bagel bakeries and plenty of cafes and bars.

cracking all-day menu, which gives almost as much pleasure to read as to eat from. Ingredients are combined sublimely into dishes such as grilled whole mackerel, aubergine, currant and coriander *harasume* noodles and sweet soy sauce.

### COACH & HORSES
Gastropub £

☎ 7278 8990; www.thecoachandhorses.com; 26-28 Ray St EC1; mains £4-11.50; ⊖ Farringdon

For our money this is Clerkenwell's best gastropub, which sacrifices none of its old-world pub charm in attracting a well-heeled foodie crowd for its range of great-value dishes (prices in increments of £2). The signature beer-battered cod, chips and mushy peas is well worth its £11.50 price tag.

# SHOREDITCH

### EYRE BROTHERS
Spanish, Portuguese £££

☎ 7613 5346; www.eyrebrothers.co.uk; 70 Leonard St EC2; mains £10-27; ⊘ closed lunch Sat & all day Sun; ⊖ Old St

This sublime, elegant Shoreditch restaurant is well worth travelling to and making reservations for. Its cuisine is Iberian with a touch of African flair, courtesy of the eponymous brothers' upbringing in Mozambique, and it's every bit as exciting as it sounds.

### FIFTEEN
Italian ££

☎ 0871 330 1515, 7251 3909; www.fifteen.net; 15 Westland Pl N1; mains £14-21; ⊖ Old St

It would be easy to dismiss Jamie Oliver's nonprofit training restaurant as a gimmick, but on our latest visit the kitchen was in fine fettle. Here 15 young chefs from disadvantaged backgrounds (indicated by their black, as opposed to white, chef's hats) train with experienced professionals, creating an ambitious and interesting Italian menu. Reservations are usually essential.

### FURNACE
Italian

☎ 7613 0598; www.hoxtonfurnace.com; 1 Ruf■ St N1; mains £6.85-10; ⊘ closed lunch Sat & all day Sun; ⊖ Old St

Furnace serves up the best pizza i Hoxton – what more do you need t know? If this isn't enough, it's got grea staff, a good and affordable wine sele■ tion, a funky, buzzing feel within its bri■ walls and great pasta dishes, too. But g for the pizza – the suckling pig toppin■ is unmissable.

### SONG QUE
Vietnamese

☎ 7613 3222; 134 Kingsland Rd E2; mains £5-7 ⊖ Old St or Liverpool St

With the kind of demand for seats tha most London restaurants can only drear of, this perennial favourite in Hoxton Vietnamese quarter always has a line c people waiting for a table. Service is fre netic and sometimes rude, but the foo is great and good value.

# SPITALFIELDS

### MESÓN LOS BARRILES
Spanish £

☎ 7375 3136; 8a Lamb St E1; mains £10.50- 17.50; ⊘ closed Sat, dinner Sun; ⊖ Liverpool S

Stick to the old school with this long established family restaurant. While th fresh fish here is great, the real draw ■ the excellent selection of tapas (£3.5 to £11.95). Sawdust on the floor and ai■ dried hams overhead add to the rusti market feel of the place.

### BRICK LANE BEIGEL BAKE
Bagels £

☎ 7729 0616; 159 Brick Lane E2; filled bagels 70p-£2.90; ⊘ 24hr; ⊖ Liverpool St

You won't find fresher (or cheaper) bagel anywhere in London than at this baker and delicatessen; just ask any taxi drive (it's their favourite nosherie).

### GREEN & RED — Mexican ££

☎ 7749 9670; www.greenred.co.uk; 51 Bethnal Green Rd E1; mains £10.50-14.50; ☺ closed lunch Sat & Sun; ✆ Liverpool St

On a corner where Banglatown grinds up against Shoreditch, Green & Red stylishly showcases traditional Jaliscan cooking. While it offers up tacos and burritos at lunchtime, come the evening the menu features far more authentic dishes, such as slow-roasted pork belly with avocado salsa and stuffed chayote with cheese, pumpkin and chilli.

# DRINKING

## CLERKENWELL

### FILTHY MACNASTY'S — Pub

☎ 7837 6067; www.filthymacnastys.com; 68 Amwell St EC1; ✆ Angel or Farringdon

The local of 'Amwell Village', tucked between Clerkenwell and Islington, is this stellar Irish music pub and whiskey bar that is every bit as cool as its name suggests. The two-room pub attracts an up-for-it young crowd who come for live bands in the back room, the great whiskey list and – we're assured – the best toilet graffiti In London.

### JERUSALEM TAVERN — Pub

☎ 7490 4281; www.stpetersbrewery.co.uk; 55 Britton St EC1; ☺ closed Sat & Sun; ✆ Farringdon

Starting life as one of the first London coffee houses (it was originally founded in 1703), with the 18th-century decor of occasional tile mosaics still visible, the JT is an absolute stunner, though sadly it's both massively popular and tiny, so come early to get a seat. There's good lunch food and, this being the only London outlet of St Peter's Brewery (based in North Suffolk), it has a brilliant range of drinks: organic bitters; cream stouts; wheat and fruit beers – many of which are dispensed in green apothecary-style bottles.

### YE OLDE MITRE — Pub

☎ 7405 4751; 1 Ely Ct EC1; ☺ closed Sat & Sun; ✆ Chancery Lane or Farringdon

Stocking up on food (p214) at Spitalfields

DOUG MCKINLAY

A delightfully cosy historic pub, tucked away in a backstreet off Hatton Garden, Ye Olde Mitre was built for the servants of Ely Palace. There's still a memento of Elizabeth I – the stump of a cherry tree around which she once danced. There's no music, so the rooms only echo to the sound of amiable chitchat and the clink of glasses.

# SHOREDITCH
## BAR KICK                                          Bar
☎ 7739 8700; 127 Shoreditch High St E1; ⏲ to midnight Thu-Sat; ⊖ Old St or Liverpool St
A much larger sister venue to Clerkenwell's **Café Kick** ( ☎ 7837 8077; 43 Exmouth Market, EC1; ⏲ noon-11pm Mon-Thu, to midnight Fri & Sat; ⊖ Farringdon or Angel), this place has a

slightly edgier Shoreditch vibe. This time too, there's some floor space left ove after four footy tables were installed, s there are leather sofas and simple table and chairs.

## BRICKLAYERS ARMS                               Pu
☎ 7739 5245; 63 Charlotte Rd EC2; ⊖ Old St
A determinedly down-to-earth stalwa of the Hoxton scene, the Bricklayer Arms drinking locale succeeds in attract ing an unpretentious but cool-lookin crowd who spill out into the street i the summer months. This funky old meets-new-style pub has a friendly an unpretentious atmosphere, and there' good Thai food on offer in the restauran upstairs as well.

## DREAMBAGSJAGUARSHOES    DJ Ba
☎ 7729 5830; www.dreambagsjaguarshoes. com; 34-36 Kingsland Rd E2; ⏲ to 1am Tue-Sun to midnight Mon; ⊖ Old St
The intriguingly named bar receive its nomenclature after the two shop whose space it now occupies, and thi nonchalance is a typical example of the we-couldn't-care-less Shoreditch chic The small interior is filled with sofas and formica-topped tables, a DJ plays in the corner, and art exhibitions deck the graffiti-covered walls.

## GEORGE & DRAGON           DJ Bar, Pub
☎ 7012 1100; 2-4 Hackney Rd E2; ⊖ Old St
Once a scuzzy local pub, the George (as ye shall dub it if you value you Shoreditch High St cred) was taken over and decorated with the owner' grandma's antiques (antlers, racoon tails, old clocks), cardboard cut-outs o Cher and fairy lights, turning this one-room pub into what has remained the epicentre of the Hoxton scene for more

St John's Gate (p209)

DOUG MCKINLAY

Outdoor art at White Cube Gallery (p210)

...han a decade. Definitely not a place for a quiet pint.

**MOTHER BAR** DJ Bar
☎ 7739 5949; www.333mother.com; 333 Old St EC1; ⌚ to midnight Sun-Thu, to 2am Fri & Sat; ⊖ Old St
Where can you go dancing til late on a Sunday night, you may wonder? Come to Mother. Still one of the best bars in town, it's above Shoreditch's original hipster club, **333** (p218). Though it's mobbed at weekends, don't be put off – there's a lounge, a dance floor and a fun, up-for-it crowd.

**OLD BLUE LAST** DJ Bar, Pub
☎ 7739 7033; www.oldbluelast.com; 38 Great Eastern Rd, EC2; ⌚ to midnight Mon-Wed, until 2.30am Thu & Sun, to 1.30am Fri & Sat; ⊖ Old St or Liverpool St
You might walk nonchalantly into this East End pub expecting to find old geezers sitting at the bar, but instead you're greeted by a hip teenage-and-up crowd

of Hoxtonites. The seedy look is courtesy of *Vice* magazine, the hipster bible/global that owns the place. It hosts some of the best Shoreditch parties, has a rocking jukebox and does a mean square pie to boot.

**RED LION** DJ Pub
☎ 7729 7920; www.redlionhoxton.com; 41 Hoxton St N1; ⌚ to midnight Mon-Sat, to 11pm Sun; ⊖ Old St
Our favourite spot for pre-club drinks in Hoxton, this denizen of the scene is run by the team behind both the successful **333** (p218) and **Mother Bar** (p217). Despite being situated within spitting distance from Hoxton Sq, it's well enough tucked away down a side street to avoid being overrun by the suburban crowd that now dominates the area at the weekends. Inside it's pure kitsch fun – eclectic DJs spin their stuff downstairs while the friendly crowd spills out onto the street with pints in their hands.

© D HALE-SUTTON/ALAMY

**Fifteen (p214)**

## SPITALFIELDS

### GOLDEN HEART                    Pub
☎ 7247 2158; 110 Commercial St E1;
⊖ Liverpool St

It's an unsurprisingly trendy Hoxton crowd that mixes in the surprisingly un-trendy interior of this brilliant Spitalfields boozer. While it's famous as the watering hole for the cream of London's art crowd, our favourite part about any visit is a chat with Sandra, the landlady-celebrity who talks to all comers and ensures that the bullshit never outstrips the fun.

### TEN BELLS                       Pub
☎ 7366 1721; 84 Commercial St E1;
⊖ Liverpool St

This landmark pub, opposite Spitalfields Market (p212) and next to the area's strik-

ing church, is famous for being one Jack the Ripper's pick-up joints, althoug these days it's about as far from a mu seum piece as you can get. In fact, as most of the young and hip crowd abou the history, and few will have any ide that this beautifully decorated, airy an friendly place has anything sinister abo its Victorian past.

## ENTERTAINMENT & ACTIVITIES

### 93 FEET EAST                     Clubbir
☎ 7247 3293; www.93feeteast.co.uk; 150 Bric Lane E2; ⏱ 5-11pm Mon-Thu, 5pm-1am Fri, noon-1am Sat, noon-10.30pm Sun; ⊖ Liverpoo St or Aldgate East

Brick Lane's hot spot is evident by th long queue outside. This great venue ha a courtyard, three big rooms and an ou door terrace that gets crowded on sunn afternoons, and it's packed with a coo East London crowd.

### 333                              Clubbir
☎ 7739 5949; www.333mother.com; 333 Old St EC1; ⏱ 10pm-5am Fri, 10pm-4am Sat & Sun; ⊖ Old St

Hoxton's true old-timer, 333's stripped down manner doesn't bow to Shoreditch silly cool and just keeps going, despite no being what it once was in terms of pul ing power. The club still hosts great night that are simultaneously scruffy and inno vative and is a key player on the electro glam and indie rave scene.

### CARGO                            Clubbir
☎ 7739 3440; www.cargo-london.com; 83 Riv ington St EC2; ⏱ noon-1am Mon-Thu, noon-3ar Fri, 6pm-3am Sat, noon-midnight Sun; ⊖ Old S or Liverpool St

Cargo is one of London's most eclecti clubs. It has three different spaces dance-floor room, bar and lounge, nd a little diner – under brick railway rches. The music policy is innovative, ith plenty of Latin House, nu-jazz, funk, roove and soul, DJs, global or up-and-oming bands, demos and rare grooves. ome of its nights have included the ark burlesque Torture Gardens annual arty, African music festival, Balkan rass bands and Cuban ska. There's also n excellent bar.

### ATCH                                                    Clubbing
☎ 7729 6097; www.myspace.com/thecatchbar; 2 Kingsland Rd E2; ☾ 6pm-midnight on-Wed, to 2am Thu-Sat, to 1am Sun; ⊖ Old St
doesn't look like much, but Catch is ne of the best nights out in Shoreditch. pstairs, every other Saturday, you can ear Get Rude, hosted by DJ duo Zombie isco Squad, which mixes bass, tropical nd electro music. Downstairs you get a ig house-party vibe with DJs who mix p pretty much anything from '90s Euro isco to chart hits to electro and techno. 's free, open late and great fun.

### AST VILLAGE                                              Clubbing
☎ 7739 5173; www.eastvillageclub.com; 9 Great Eastern St EC2; ☾ 5pm-1am on & Tue, to 3.30am Wed-Sun; ⊖ Old St
he old Medicine Bar's popularity flagged o much that it was only a matter of ime before someone snapped up the ine location and did something worth-vhile with it. Well, finally the space has een transformed into a club that has een house lovers flocking from all over ondon. There's a wide array of quality DJs on the program, though our favourite s the New York-style disco punk night, weatshop.

### FABRIC                                                   Clubbing
☎ 7336 8898, 7490 0444; www.fabriclondon. com; 77a Charterhouse St EC1; ☾ 9.30pm-5am Fri & Sun, 10pm-7am Sat; ⊖ Farringdon
This most impressive of superclubs is still the first stop on the London scene for many international clubbers, as the lengthy queues attest. The crowd is hip and well dressed without overkill, and the music – mainly electro, house, drum and bass, and breakbeat – is as superb as you'd expect from London's top-rated club.

### FAVELA CHIC                                              Clubbing
☎ 7613 5228; www.favelachic.com; 91 Great Eastern St E1; ☾ 6pm-late Tue-Sun; ⊖ Old St
Smaller sister of the original Paris club, this place profits from 'slum chic' just like the producers of Havaiana flip-flops did. It's a one-room bar-club with per-manently long queues on Friday and Saturday and innovative music nights. The decor is very much about the vin-tage, distressed and flea-market pieces, though markedly self-consciously so, but if you can endure the long wait and get past the high 'n' mighty door whores, you'll have a good night.

### LAST DAYS OF DECADENCE                             Clubbing
☎ 7033 0085; www.thelastdaysofdecadence. com; 145 Shoreditch High St E1; ☾ 8pm-2.30am Thu, Fri & Sat, to midnight Sun-Wed; ⊖ Old St
A brand-new club that opened in the height of the recession, this is a place that celebrates the 1930s through its heady, abandon-fuelled parties and through its Great Depression-inspired name. Not that it sticks to 1930s music, however – you'll find regular nights hosting DJs such as the out-there trannie DJ Jodie Harsh on Fridays' Circus, and Last Days of Decadence's eponymous night that mixes up D&B, nu-rave and jungle. On a quieter note, there are free jazz gigs on

333 club (p218)

MICHAEL KEMP/ALA

Tuesdays, and on Monday nights there are life-drawing classes – £10 a go.

### SADLER'S WELLS
Dance

☎ 7863 8000; www.sadlers-wells.com; Rosebery Ave EC1; admission £10-60; ⊖ Angel

The theatre site dates from 1683 but was completely rebuilt in 1998; today it is the most eclectic and modern dance venue in town, with experimental dance shows (anyone for the Mahabharata on the boards?), hip-hop conventions and an annual flamenco festival in March. The **Lilian Baylis Studio** stages smaller productions while the **Peacock Theatre** ( ☎ 7863 8222; www.sadlers-wells.com; Portugal St WC2; ⊖ Holborn) is a kind of West End branch, hosting smaller dance and music performances.

# SHOPPING

This is the area for discovering cool boutiques or wandering market stalls for vintage clothes and up-and-coming designers. There are tonnes of shops

off Brick Lane, especially burgeor ing Cheshire St, Hanwell St and th Old Truman Brewery on Dray Wall Spitalfields Market (p212) should als not be missed at the weekend for its li tle designer stalls and quirky shops.

### MAGMA
Book

☎ 7242 9503; www.magmabooks.com; 117-11 Clerkenwell Rd EC1; ⊖ Farringdon

This much-loved shop sells books, mag azines, T-shirts and almost anything o the design cutting edge. There's a smalle branch in **Covent Garden** (Map p66 ☎ 7240 8498; 8 Earlham St, ⊖ Covent Garden which now includes a design sale shop Great for present shopping.

### ANTONI & ALISON
Fashion & Designe

☎ 7833 2002; www.antoniandalison.co.uk; 43 Rosebery Ave EC1; ⏱ 10.30am-6.30pm Mon-Fri; ⊖ Farringdon

The original independent London fashion house, A&A sells quirky tees, mad flora skirts, gorgeous leather purses and funk cashmere knits among other gorgeous lit

e things in its Rosebery Ave shop. Look
it for its brilliant sales.

## OXTON BOUTIQUE
Fashion & Designer

7684 2083; www.hoxtonboutique.co.uk; 2
oxton St;  10.30am-6.30pm Mon-Fri, 11am-
m Sat;  Old St

you want to look like a true Hoxtonite,
ome here for your (women's) street wear –
here's Isabel Marant, Hussein Chalayan,
epetto shoes and the shop's own brand,
HOBO+. The boutique is meant to re-
emble Studio 54, with a mirror ball, white
alls and neon lights.

## ADEN SHOWROOMS
Fashion & Designer

7247 2431; www.laden.co.uk; 103 Brick
ane E1;  11am-6.30pm Mon-Fri, to 7pm Sat,
.30am-6pm Sun;  Liverpool St or
dgate East

he unofficial flagship for the latest
oxton street wear, Laden was once
.ondon's best-kept secret', though a
ew of celebrity endorsements have
ade the showrooms' reputation soar
nd the 55 independent designers it
tocks much in demand. A perfect one-
:op shop for both womenswear and
nenswear.

## IO-ONE
Fashion & Designer

7613 5314; www.no-one.co.uk; 1 Kingsland
d E2;  11am-7pm Mon-Sat, noon-6pm Sun;
> Old St or Liverpool St

his boutique, brought to you by the
ame people as hip nearby drinkery
reambagsjaguarshoes (p216) can be
ound inside the Old Shoreditch station
ar. It's all ultrahip, with fashion maga-
ines, quirky accessories and shoes, and
tocks Eley Kishimoto, Peter Jensen and
ew labels for women and men.

## START
Fashion & Designer

7739 3636; www.start-london.com; 42-44
Rivington St;  10.30am-6.30pm Mon-Fri,
11am-6pm Sat, 1-5pm Sun;  Liverpool St or
Old St

'Where fashion meets rock n roll' is the
appropriate tagline to this group of three
boutiques brought to you by former Fall
guitarist Brix Smith, a cult rocker who
loves girly clothes. Designer labels such
as Miu Miu and Helmut Lang dominate
and Smith prides herself on her selection
of flattering jeans. A similarly excellent
store, **Start Menswear** (59 Rivington St), is
over the road, and there is a third location, **Start Made to Measure** (40 Rivington
St), showcasing formal wear.

DOUG MCKINLAY

**Old and new architecture at Spitalfields**

NEIL SETCHFI

Taking a break from shopping at Spitalfields Market (p212)

## TATTY DEVINE
Jewellery & Accessories

☎ 7739 9191; www.tattydevine.com; 236 Brick Lane E2; ⊙ 11am-6pm Tue-Sun; ⊖ Liverpool St

Duo Harriet Vine and Rosie Wolfenden make hip and witty jewellery that's become the favourite of many young Londoners. Their original designs featur record earrings and plectrum bracelet (that high-street stores have ripped o since), pea necklaces, knitted stilettos, an key rings that look like crinkle-cut crisp Perspex name necklaces (made to orde £25) are also a treat.

# ↘THE EAST END,
# DOCKLANDS
# & GREENWICH

# THE EAST END, DOCKLANDS & GREENWICH

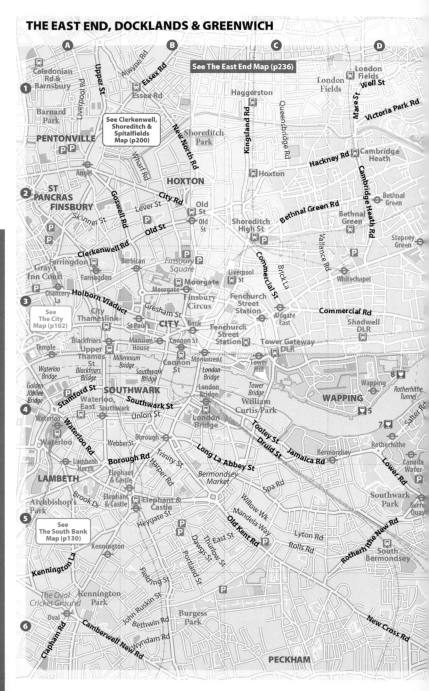

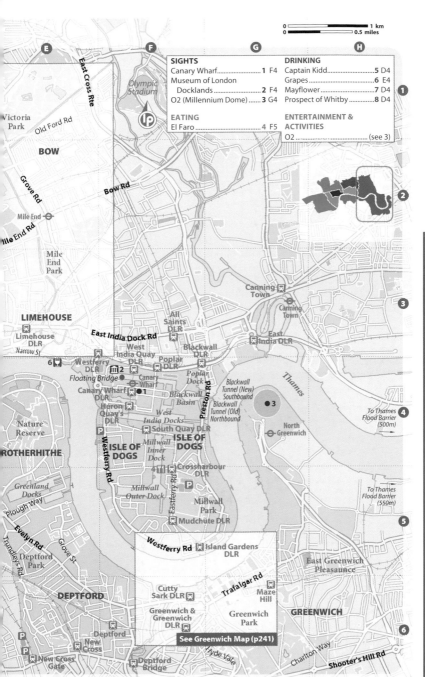

| SIGHTS | | |
|---|---|---|
| Canary Wharf | **1** | F4 |
| Museum of London | | |
| Docklands | **2** | F4 |
| O2 (Millennium Dome) | **3** | G4 |

| EATING | | |
|---|---|---|
| El Faro | 4 | F5 |

| DRINKING | | |
|---|---|---|
| Captain Kidd | **5** | D4 |
| Grapes | **6** | E4 |
| Mayflower | **7** | D4 |
| Prospect of Whitby | **8** | D4 |

**ENTERTAINMENT & ACTIVITIES**

| O2 | (see 3) |
|---|---|

0 _____ 1 km
0 _____ 0.5 miles

# HIGHLIGHTS

## ↘ STAND ON THE MERIDIAN

Time is generally a pretty intangible concept, but it's fair to say that the closest you can get to touching it is by paying a visit to the **Royal Observatory** (p233) in Greenwich, and straddling hemispheres and time zones as you stand on the actual meridian line itself. Get here for 1pm on any day of the week to see the red time ball at the top of the Royal Observatory drop.

## ↘ NATIONAL MARITIME MUSEUM

Though you'd hardly guess from its less-than-thrilling name, the **National Maritime Museum** (p230) is a fantastic place and arguably Greenwich's biggest attraction, detailing the fascinating global maritime expansion of a small island that once had the largest Empire in history. Look out for the bullet that killed Admiral Nelson at Trafalgar, and the uniform coat he was wearing at the fatal moment.

### ↘ SEE THE DOCKLANDS SKYLINE

The Docklands redevelopment has moved into its mature stage and what began as a post-industrial wasteland is now one of the world's top financial centres and has an impressive skyline dominated by **Canary Wharf** (p230). Take a wander around to see how the future of London is shaping up.

### ↘ WHITECHAPEL GALLERY

On one of London's most diverse and culturally vibrant thoroughfares, this fantastic East End modern art **gallery** (p229) is a great place to take the pulse of contemporary art with its ground-breaking exhibits. Looking better than ever after a recent refit, this is one of London's top art attractions.

### ↘ ENJOY GREENWICH PARK

By any standards **Greenwich Park** (p234), designed by Le Nôtre, the man responsible for the gardens at Versailles, is a pretty special place. The London views from the top of the hill are spectacular and the entire place is wonderful for a long walk and a picnic when the weather's good. Don't miss the deer park in the southeast corner.

1 DOUG MCKINLAY; 2 NEIL SETCHFIELD; 3 NEIL SETCHFIELD; 4 EDMUND SUMNER/PHOTOLIBRARY; 5 DOUG MCKINLAY

1 Royal Observatory (p233); 2 National Maritime Museum (p230); 3 Canary Wharf (p230); 4 Whitechapel Gallery (p229); 5 Greenwich Park (p234)

# BEST...

## THINGS FOR FREE

- **Whitechapel Gallery** (p229) East London's most exciting contemporary art museum is free.
- **Royal Observatory** (p233) Seeing the home of world time costs nothing.
- **Queen's House** (p234) Visit the art collection inside this wonderful mansion.
- **Old Royal Naval College** (p232) See the fascinating interior of this Wren masterpiece.

## QUIRKY THINGS

- **Fabrications** (p242) A unique shop of reused materials.
- **Bethnal Green Working Men's Club** (p240) Party the night away with the cool kids in an unchanged East End social club.
- **Bistrotheque** (p238) Madcap cabaret and off-beat shows.
- **Compendia** (p242) Every board game you could want and far more at this Greenwich shop.

## ASIAN CUISINE

- **Tayyabs** (p236) Our favourite Punjabi restaurant.
- **Café Spice Namaste** (p235) Upmarket Indian restaurant on the edge of the City.
- **Mirch Masala** (p236) A great alternative to Tayyabs when it's busy.
- **Namo** (p237) Fantastic modern Vietnamese.

## DRINKING SPOTS BY THE RIVER

- **Grapes** (p238) Grab a pint, pull up a chair and watch the river.
- **Prospect of Whitby** (p239) The oldest riverside pub in London.
- **Mayflower** (p239) A pilgrimage site for many American visitors.
- **Trafalgar Tavern** (p240) Former drinkers here have included Dickens and Gladstone.

LEFT: TRAVIS DREVER; RIGHT: DOUG MCKINI

Left: Old Royal Naval College (p232); Right: Grapes pub (238)

# DISCOVER THE EAST END, DOCKLANDS & GREENWICH

The East End of London is a neighbourhood both deeply traditional and yet constantly in flux, with immigrants arriving and settling here unbroken for several centuries. It's a sprawling, multicultural neighbourhood that is somehow still home to London's best known inhabitant, the cockney. Today it's a great area in which to eat, drink and explore.

To the south of the East End is the Docklands, once the hub of the British Empire and its enormous global trade, but an area that became a post-industrial wasteland after WWII. After a massive program of regeneration over the past three decades it really is a vision of London's future as well as an area rich in history.

Finally, quaint, villagelike Greenwich is home to the Royal Observatory and thus to world time. A trip to this gorgeous borough will be one of the highlights of any visit to London, particularly if you take a boat down the river to the Thames Barrier to get there.

# SIGHTS
## THE EAST END
### WHITECHAPEL GALLERY Map p236
☎ 7522 7888; www.whitechapelgallery.org; 77-82 Whitechapel High St E1; admission free; 11am-6pm Tue-Sun, to 9pm Thu; ⊖ Aldgate East; &

This ground-breaking gallery, which moved into its main art nouveau building in 1899, has now extended into the library next door, bringing its total number of galleries to 10 and doubling its exhibition space. Founded by the Victorian philanthropist Canon Samuel Barnett at the end of the 19th century to bring art to the people of East London, it has made its name by putting on exhibitions by both established and emerging artists, cartoonists and architects, including Jackson Pollock (his first UK show), Gary Hume, Robert Crumb and Mies van der Rohe. Picasso's *Guernica* was first shown here in 1939; and a tapestry of the painting, on loan from

the UN building in New York, went on display in 2009, to mark the reopening. The gallery's ambitiously themed shows change every couple of months – check the program online – and there's also live music, poetry readings, talks and films until late on Thursday and sometimes on Friday. And don't miss the phenomenal 'social sculptures' in various (and ephemeral) spaces throughout. Other features are an excellent bookshop, the **Whitechapel Gallery Dining Room** (p236) and an uberdesigned cafe on the 1st floor.

### WHITECHAPEL ROAD
Map p236

Within a few minutes' walk of Whitechapel tube station you'll find the large **East London Mosque** (46-92 Whitechapel Rd E1) and behind it on Fieldgate St the Great Synagogue built in 1899.

You're now also deep in Jack the Ripper territory. In fact, Mary Ann Nichols, first of the serial killer's five victims, was hacked to death on 31 August 1888 on what is now Durward St, north of (and just behind) Whitechapel tube station.

# DOCKLANDS
## MUSEUM OF LONDON DOCKLANDS Map p224

☎ 7001 9844; www.museumindocklands.org.uk; No 1 Warehouse, West India Quay E14; adult/concession/after 4.30pm £5/3/free; ☽ 10am-6pm; ⊖ Canary Wharf or DLR West India Quay; &

Housed in a converted 200-year-old warehouse once used to store sugar, rum and coffee, this museum offers a comprehensive overview of the entire history of the Thames from the arrival of the Romans in AD 43. But it's at its best when dealing with specifics close by such as the controversial transformation of the decrepit docks into Docklands in the 1980s.

The tour begins on the 3rd floor (take the lift to the top) with the Roman settlement of Londinium – don't miss the delightful Roman blue-glass bowl discovered in pieces at a building site in Prescot St E1 in 2008 – and works its way downwards through the ages. Keep an eye open for the scale mode of the old London Bridge and the *Rhinebeck Panorama* (1805–10), a huge mural of the upper Pool of London. An excellent new gallery called London, Sugar & Slavery examines the capital's role in the transatlantic slave trade.

Kids adore such exhibits as Sailortown (an excellent re-creation of the cobbled streets, bars and lodging houses of a mid-19th-century dockside community and nearby Chinatown) and the hands-on Mudlarks gallery, where five- to 12-year-olds can explore the history of the Thames, tipping the clipper, trying on old-fashioned diving helmets, learning to use winches and even constructing a simple model of Canary Wharf.

## CANARY WHARF Map p224
⊖ Canary Wharf or DLR Canary Wharf

Cesar Pelli's 244m-high **Canary Wha Tower**, which was built in 1991 at Canada Sq and has been described a a 'square prism with a pyramidal top presides over a veritable array of ver ues including a toytown and financi theme park. It's surrounded by more r cent towers housing HSBC and Citigrou and offices for Bank of America, Barclay Morgan Stanley, Credit Suisse and mor It took a long time for the place to com this far. Canary Wharf Tower, still th tallest building in the UK and one c the largest property developments i Europe, had to be saved from bankruptc twice before it reached today's levels c occupancy.

# GREENWICH
## NATIONAL MARITIME MUSEUM Map p241

☎ 8858 4422, recorded information 8312 6565 www.nmm.ac.uk; Romney Rd SE10; admission free; ☽ 10am-5pm; ᕩ Greenwich or DLR Cutty Sark; &

Though it hardly sounds like a crowd pleaser, this museum designed to tell th long and convoluted history of Britain a a seafaring nation is the best attraction i Greenwich. From the moment you ste through the entrance of this magnificen neoclassical building you'll be won ove And it just gets better as you progres through the glass-roofed Neptune Cou into the rest of the three-storey building

The exhibits are arranged by theme focusing on Explorers, Maritime London Art and Sea and so on. Visual highlight include the 19m-long golden state barg built in 1732 for Frederick, Prince of Wales and the huge ship's propeller installe on level 1. The museum also owns th uniform coat that Britain's greatest sea

THE EAST END, DOCKLANDS & GREENWICH

SIGHTS

City Hall

NEIL SETCHFIELD

## ↘ IF YOU LIKE...

If you liked **Canary Wharf** (p230) then don't miss out on some of London's other modern architectural landmarks:

- **Lloyds of London** A stone's throw from the now far-more-famous 'Gherkin' this Richard Rogers structure dates from 1986 and marked a new era in London's architecture with its postmodern features such as exterior glass lifts and futuristic silver casement.
- **Thames Flood Barrier** Head to Charlton in far East London to see this 80s marvel of technology. The flood barrier's nine glittering silver piers are an incredible sight.
- **City Hall** The lopsided 'egg' is the unusual glass headquarters for the London Assembly and mayor, and you'll not be able to miss it if you walk across Tower Bridge. Anybody can go to the 6th-floor's 'London's Living Room' for great views.
- **British Library** The modern home to the British Library (previously housed in the British Museum) on Euston Rd was built in 1998 and has been a success possibly more for its inner rather than outer beauty. Its red brick exterior has gained few plaudits, but its wonderfully bright interior never fails to impress.

aring hero, Horatio Nelson, was wearing when he was fatally shot (including the actual bullet), plus a replica of the lifeboat *James Caird* used by explorer Ernest Shackleton and a handful of his men after the *Endurance* sank on their epic mission in Antarctica. The restored stained glass from the Baltic Exchange, blown up by the IRA in 1992, is now a memorial to the victims of WWI.

The environmentally minded are catered for with the Your Ocean exhibit on level 1, examining the science, history, health and future of the sea. Kids will love firing a cannon in the All Hands exhibit or manoeuvring a tanker into port by using the state-of-the-art Bridge Simulator on level 2. Fashionistas and stylists will be wowed on the ground floor by Rank and Style (uniforms and leisurewear worn at sea) and the Passengers exhibit (classic travel posters and the mock-up of the cocktail bar of a cruise ship).

## OLD ROYAL NAVAL COLLEGE
Map p241

☎ 8269 4799; www.oldroyalnavalcollege.
org; King William Walk SE10; admission free;
🚇 Greenwich or DLR Cutty Sark

When Christopher Wren was commissioned by William and Mary to build a naval hospital here in 1692, he designed it in two separate halves so as not to spoil the view of the river from the **Queen's House** (p234), Inigo Jones' miniature masterpiece to the south. Today it also frames Canary Wharf and the skyscrapers of Docklands to the north.

Built on the site of the Old Palace of Placentia, where Henry VIII was born in 1491, the hospital was initially intended for those wounded in the victory over the French at La Hogue. In 1869 the building was converted to a Naval College. Now even the navy has left and the premises are home to the University of Greenwich and Trinity College of Music.

There are two main rooms in the College which are open to the public. In the King William Building, the **Painted Hall** (🕙 10am-5pm daily) is one of Europe's greatest banquet rooms and is covered in decorative 'allegorical Baroque' murals by artist James Thornhill, who also painted the cupola of St Paul's Cathedral. The mural above the Lower Hall shows William and Mary enthroned amid symbols of the Virtues. Beneath William's feet you can see the defeated French king Louis XIV grovelling with a furled flag in hand. Up a few steps is the Upper Hall

where, on the western wall, George I depicted with his family. In the bottom right-hand corner Thornhill drew himself into the picture, pointing toward his work.

Situated off the Upper Hall of the College is the **Nelson Room**, originally designed by Nicholas Hawksmoor then used as a smoking room and now open to the public. In January 1806 the brandy-soaked (for embalming purposes, of course) body of the great naval hero himself lay in state here before his funeral at St Paul's. Today the room contains a plaster replica of the statue atop Nelson's column in Trafalgar Sq as well as other memorabilia, including lots of hospital silver. Look outside to the courtyard through the window; the cobbles form an outline of the Union Flag (Union Jack).

A 90-minute **guided tour** (☎ 8269 4791 adult/under 16yr £5/free; 🕙 tours 11.30am & 2pm) from the Painted Hall will take you to places not normally open to the public: the Jacobean undercroft of the former Placentia palace and the 140-year-old Victorian Skittle Alley, featuring enormous hand-carved wooden bowling balls and pins.

The **chapel** (🕙 10am-5pm Mon-Sat, 12.30-5pm Sun) in the Queen Mary Building opposite the Painted Hall is decorated in a lighter rococo style. The eastern end of the chapel is dominated by a painting by the 18th-century American artist Benjamin West showing The Preservation of St Paul after Shipwreck at Malta. It's certainly a beautiful room, but is more famous for its organ and acoustics. If possible come on the first Sunday of the month, when there's a free 50-minute **organ recital** at 3pm, or time your visit for sung Eucharist at 11am on Sunday.

DOUG MCKINLAY

Royal Observatory

## ◥ ROYAL OBSERVATORY

Following an ambitious £15-million renovation the Royal Observatory is now divided into two sections.

The northern half deals with time and is contained in the original Observatory that Charles II had built on a hill in the middle of Greenwich Park in 1675, intending that astronomy be used to establish longitude at sea. It contains the Octagon Room, designed by Wren, and the nearby Sextant Room where John Flamsteed (1646–1719), the first astronomer royal, made his observations and calculations.

The globe is divided between east and west at the Royal Observatory, and in the Meridian Courtyard (✪ 10am-5pm Sep-Apr, to 8pm May-Aug) you can place one foot either side of the meridian line and straddle the two hemispheres. Every day at 1pm the red time ball at the top of the Royal Observatory continues to drop as has done regularly since 1833. You can get great views of Greenwich and spy on your fellow tourists at the same time by visiting the unique Camera Obscura.

The southern half of the Royal Observatory is devoted to astronomy and includes the 120-seat state-of-the-art Peter Harrison Planetarium (☎ 8312 8565; www.nmm.ac.uk/astronomy; adult/child/family £6/4/16; ✪ hourly shows 1-4pm Mon-Fri, 11am-5pm Sat & Sun), with a digital laser projector that can show entire heavens on the inside of its bronze-clad roof and is the most advanced planetarium in all of Europe. Galleries here trace the history of astronomy and interactive displays focus on such subjects as meteorites, space missions and the effects of gravity.

**Things you need to know:** Map p241; ☎ 8858 4422, recorded information 8312 6565; www.nmm.ac.uk/places/royal-observatory; Greenwich Park, Blackheath Ave SE10; admission free; ✪ 10am-5pm; ⚐ Greenwich or DLR Cutty Sark; ♿

## QUEEN'S HOUSE
Map p224

☎ 8858 4422, recorded information 8312 6565; www.nmm.ac.uk/places/queens-house; Romney Rd SE10; admission free; ⏲ 10am-5pm; 🚇 Greenwich or DLR Cutty Sark; ♿

The first Palladian building by architect Inigo Jones after he returned from Italy, what was at first called the 'House of Delight', is indeed far more enticing than the art collection it contains, even though it includes some Turners, Holbeins, Hogarths and Gainsboroughs. The house was begun in 1616 for Anne of Denmark, wife of James I, but was not completed until 1638, when it became the home of Charles I and his queen, Henrietta Maria. The **Great Hall** is the principal room – a

lovely cube shape, with an elaborate tiled floor and the helix-shaped **Tuli Staircase** (named for the flowers o the wrought-iron balustrade) leadin to a gallery on level 2, hung with pain ings and portraits with a sea or seafa ing theme from the National Maritim Museum's fine art collection. Don't mis the paintings in the Historic Greenwic gallery on level 1.

## GREENWICH PARK
Map p241

☎ 8858 2608; www.royalparks.gov.uk; ⏲ dawn-dusk, cars from 7am; 🚇 Greenwich or Maze Hill, DLR Cutty Sark

This is one of London's largest and lovel est parks, with a grand avenue, wide-ope spaces, a rose garden, picturesque walk and impressive views across the Rive Thames to Docklands from the top of th hill near the statue of General Wolfe oppo site the Royal Observatory. Covering a fu 73 hectares, it is the oldest enclosed roya park and is partly the work of Le Nôtre who landscaped the palace gardens c Versailles for Louis XIV. It contains severa historic sights, a teahouse near the Roya Observatory, a cafe behind the Nationa Maritime Museum and a deer park in th southeastern corner.

## O2 (FORMER MILLENNIUM DOME
Map p224

☎ 8463 2000, bookings 0844 856 0202; www. theo2.co.uk; Millennium Way SE10; ⊖ North Greenwich

The 380m-wide circular Millenniun Dome (renamed O2) cost £750 millior to build and more than £5 million i year just to keep it erect. It closed at th end of 2000, having failed miserably ir its bid to attract 12 million visitors, anc was until 2007 for the most part unem ployed. Since then it has hosted big act

ELLIOT DANIEL

O2 (former Millennium Dome)

ke Madonna, Prince, Justin Timberlake nd Barbra Streisand in its 23,000-seat **02 .rena** and soul, pop and jazz bands in he 2350-seat **IndigO2**. Massive exhibions (Tutankhamen and the Golden Age f the Pharaohs, The Human Body) and porting events have made their temorary homes here, and there's a slew f bars, clubs and restaurants sheltering nder what was originally derided as 'the atest in tent technology'.

# SLEEPING
## THE EAST END & DOCKLANDS
### 40 WINKS
Map p236 Guesthouse ££

☎ 7790 0259; www.40winks.org; 109 Mile End d E1; s £60-80, d £95-100; ⊖ Stepney Green

hort on space but not on style, this twooom boutique guesthouse in less-thanlesirable Stepney Green oozes charm nd chotchkies. It is housed in an early-8th-century town house owned by a sucessful designer and has been used as a ocation for a number of fashion shoots. he rooms (the single is quite compact) ontain most everything you'll need; eveything else – shops, cinema, the tube – is ive minutes away.

## GREENWICH
### HARBOUR MASTER'S HOUSE
Map p241 Apartment ££

☎ 8293 9597; http://website.lineone.net/~ harourmaster; 20 Ballast Quay SE10; s & d £75-85, r & q £85-95; ® Greenwich, DLR Cutty Sark

This self-contained three-room basement apartment is right on the river in a Grade II Heritage-listed Georgian building dating from 1855. It combines such mod cons as heated towel rails and full kitchen with the charm of vaulted whiteprick ceilings and a vague maritime feel.

As it's quite compact, it's likely to work best for couples.

### NUMBER 16 ST ALFEGE'S
Map p241 B&B £

☎ 8853 4337; www.st-alfeges.co.uk; 16 St Alfege's Passage SE10; s/d £75/90; ® Greenwich, DLR Cutty Sark

Just about the most coveted address in Greenwich ever since it appeared on Channel 5's Hotel Inspector, this gayowned B&B in the heart of Greenwich has two well-appointed doubles and a single, individually decorated in shades of blue, green or yellow and all with bathroom. The owners do their best to make everyone, gay or straight, feel at home, with chats and cups of tea. For such a central location, the immediate neighbourhood is quiet. Turn the corner into Roan St to find the main door.

# EATING
## THE EAST END & DOCKLANDS
### CAFÉ SPICE NAMASTE
Map p236 Indian ££

☎ 7488 9242; www.cafespice.co.uk; 16 Prescot St E1; mains £13.75-19.50, 2-course set lunch £16.95; ⊗ closed lunch Sat & all day Sun; ⊖ Tower Hill

Chef Cyrus Todiwala has taken an old magistrates court just a 10-minute walk from Tower Hill and decorated it in 'carnival' colours; the service and atmosphere are as bright as the walls. The Parsee and Goan menu is famous for its superlative *dhansaak* (lamb stew with rice and lentils; £14.95) but just as good are the spicy chicken *frango piri-piri* and the Goan kingprawn curry. Bonuses: they make their own chutneys here and there's a little garden behind the dining room open in the warmer months.

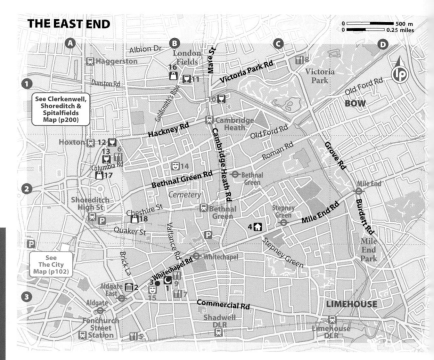

## WHITECHAPEL GALLERY DINING ROOM

Map p236        Modern European ££

☎ 7522 7888; www.whitechapelgallery.org; 77-82 Whitechapel High St E1; mains £13.50-17.75, 2-/3-course lunch £15/20; ✆ closed dinner Sun & all day Mon; ⊖ Aldgate East

The recently reopened **gallery** (p229), at the forefront of art in London with its seminal exhibitions of new work and retrospectives, has also put in place a small but perfectly formed dining room with high-profile chef Maria Elia at the helm. The menu is short but comprehensive with things like roast rabbit, grilled sea bream and inventive vegetarian dishes.

## TAYYABS Map p236      Indian, Pakistani £

☎ 7247 9543; www.tayyabs.co.uk; 83-89 Fieldgate St E1; mains £6.20-13.80; ⊖ Whitechapel

This buzzing (OK, crowded) Punjabi res taurant is in another league to its Bric Lane equivalents. *Seekh* kebabs, *masal* fish and other starters served on sizzling hot plates are delicious, as are accompa niments such as dhal, naan and raita. Bu with Tayyabs now appearing regularly ir guidebooks and the huge London Roya Hospital round the corner, you shoulc expect to wait for a table.

## MIRCH MASALA

Map p236        Indian, Pakistan *£*

☎ 7377 0155; www.mirchmasalarestaurant. co.uk; 111-113 Commercial Rd E1; mains £4.50-10; ⊖ Whitechapel, ᠍ 15 or 115

'Chilli and Spice', part of a small chair based in the epicentre of London sub continental food, Southall, is a less hec tic alternative to Tayyabs and the fooc is almost up the same level. Order the

THE EAST END, DOCKLANDS & GREENWICH

EATING

# THE EAST END

prawn tikka (£8) as a 'warmer' followed by the *masala karella* (£4.50), a currylike dish made from bitter gourd, and a *karahi* meat dish.

## LAXEIRO

Map p236                                    Spanish ££

☎ 7729 1147; www.laxeiro.co.uk; 93 Columbia Rd E2; tapas £3.95-8.95, paella £19.50-23.50; ⊗ closed dinner Sun & all day Monday; ⊖ Bethnal Green, 🚊 Cambridge Heath, 🚌 8 or 55

This homely place dead in the centre of Columbia Rd, the site of London's famous Sunday flower market, serves generous-sized tapas (it prefers to call them *raciones*). Tapas change every two weeks but the *cochinillo* (tender suckling pig) is a constant. The handful of more ambitious dishes includes paella to be shared.

## NAMO Map p236                          Vietnamese £

☎ 8533 0639; www.namo.co.uk; 178 Victoria Park Rd E9; mains £6.50-9; ⊗ lunch Thu-Sun, dinner Tue-Sun; ⊖ Mile End, then 🚌 277

This very bohemian place takes the Vietnamese dishes so characteristic of nearby Dalston and pulls them into the 21st century; expect things like chilli jam with your slow-cooked pork and a new take on *bun hue*, Vietnam's signature beef noodle soup. Seating is cramped, but the array of plants and flowers brings nearby Victoria Park even closer.

## EL FARO Map p224                        Spanish ££

☎ 7987 5511; www.el-faro.co.uk; 3 Turnberry Quay, Pepper St E14; mains £14.50-18.95; ⊗ closed dinner Sun; DLR Crossharbour

An E14 address rarely signifies a destination restaurant but hop on the DLR (a picturesque and worthwhile ride) and travel to the 'Lighthouse' for what are known as the best (and most inventive) tapas (£4.45 to £10.95) and Spanish dishes in town. The location on a basin in the Docklands is restful and within easy walking distance of Canary Wharf.

# GREENWICH

## SE10 RESTAURANT & BAR

Map p241                           Modern European ££

☎ 8858 9764; www.se10restaurant.co.uk; 62 Thames St SE10; mains £13-19.50, 2-/3-course set lunch weekdays £11.75/14.95, weekend £17.95/21.95; ⊗ lunch & dinner Thu-Sun; DLR Cutty Sark

This outwardly scruffy restaurant and wine bar, west of the Cutty Sark DLR station, hides a light, airy and very warm interior of yellow-and-gold hues. There's a good concentration of fish dishes – though you'd hardly even know the Thames was at the back door – and traditional British dishes (though with only one mean vegetarian option). The desserts are pure comfort food, especially the sticky-toffee pudding. Sundays host both breakfast (£5.59 to £7.95) and lunch.

# DRINKING
## THE EAST END
### BISTROTHEQUE
Map p236                                 Bar, Cabaret Bar

☎ 8983 7900; www.bistrotheque.com; 23-27 Wadeston St E2; ◷ 6pm-midnight Tue-Sat, 4-11pm Sun; ⊖ Bethnal Green, ▤ Cambridge Heath, ▥ 55

This place in a converted East End warehouse offers three things: drinking in the Napoleon bar, transvestite lip-synch cabaret in the Cabaret Room (9.30pm Friday and Saturday) on the ground floor and dining in its stylish white restaurant above. The bar is a moody, slightly decadent room with dark walls (the oak panels came from a stately home in Northumberland) and plush seating, the drinks are expertly mixed and the bar staff always friendly.

### JOINERS ARMS Map p236                        Gay
☎ 7739 9854; 116 Hackney Rd E2; ◷ 6pm-2am Fri & Sat; ⊖ Shoreditch or Old St

Determinedly rundown and cheesy, the Joiners is Hoxton's only totally gay pubclub (perhaps reflecting the degree to which such distinctions are blurred around E2). It's a crowded, funky old boozer where hip gay boys and a smattering of celebrities hang out at the bar, dance and watch people play pool all night.

### DOVE FREEHOUSE Map p236                       Pub
☎ 7275 7617; www.belgianbars.com; 24 Broadway Market E8; ◷ noon-11pm Mon-Thu, to midnight Fri & Sat; ▤ London Fields, ▥ 48, 55, 106 or 394

This pub attracts at any time with its rambling series of rooms and wide range –

some 20 on draft – of Belgian Trappis wheat and fruit-flavoured beers. Bu there's something about the dim bac room, with its ethnic bohemian chic an decent gastropub menu, which make this pub a great place to hunker dow against the chill.

### ROYAL OAK Map p236                             Pu
☎ 7729 2220; 73 Columbia Rd E2; ◷ 5-11pm Mon, from noon Tue-Sun; ▤ Cambridge Heath, ▥ 8 or 55

Not to be confused with the similarl named pub south of the river, this tra ditional boozer was recently gentrifie (at long last!) and has a good selectio of bitter and a better-than-average win list. It gets into its stride on Sunday whe London's famous flower market is on jus outside the door.

### CAPTAIN KIDD
Map p224                                          Pu
☎ 7480 5759; 108 Wapping High St E1; ⊖ Liverpool St or Tower Hill, then ▥ 100

With its large windows, fine beer garde and mock scaffold recalling the hang ing nearby of the eponymous pirate i 1701, this is a favourite riverside pu in Wapping that only dates back to th 1980s. There's a restaurant predictabl called the Gallows on the 1st floor.

## DOCKLANDS
### GRAPES Map p224                                Pu
☎ 7987 4396; 76 Narrow St E14; DLR Westferry

One of Limehouse's renowned historic pubs – there's been a drinking house here since 1583, we're told – the Grapes is cosy and as narrow as the name of the street it's on. Actually, it's tiny, especially the riverside terrace, which can only really comfortably fit about a half-dozen close friends. But it continues to radiate olde

orlde charm, the choice of beer is good
nd they love dogs here.

**ROSPECT OF WHITBY** Map p224    Pub
☎ 7481 1095; 57 Wapping Wall E1; ⊖ Tower
II, then 🚌 100
nce known as the Devil's Tavern, the
Vhitby's said to date from 1520, making
the oldest riverside pub in London. It's
rmly on the tourist trail now, but there's
smallish terrace to the front and the
de overlooking the Thames, a decent
staurant upstairs and open fires in win-
er. Check out the wonderful pewter bar –
amuel Pepys once sidled up to it to sup.

# GREENWICH
**UTTY SARK TAVERN** Map p241    Pub
☎ 8858 3146; 4-6 Ballast Quay SE10; DLR Cutty
ark, 🚌 177 or 180
oused in a delightful Georgian building
irectly on the Thames, the Cutty Sark is
ne of the few independent pubs left in
reenwich. There are half a dozen ales on
up and a wonderful sitting-out area along
he river just opposite. Count on about

a 15-minute walk from the DLR station
or hop on a bus along Trafalgar Rd and
walk north.

**GREENWICH UNION** Map p241    Pub
☎ 8692 6258; www.greenwichunion.com; 56
Royal Hill SE10; DLR Cutty Sark
This award-winning pub offers a range
of six or seven beers produced by a local
microbrewery, including raspberry and
wheat varieties. It's a handsome place,
serving good food and attracting locals,
especially families at the weekend.

**MAYFLOWER** Map p224    Pub
☎ 7237 4088; 117 Rotherhithe St SE16;
⊖ Rotherhithe
Northwest of Deptford in Rotherhithe,
this 15th-century pub, originally called
the Shippe but rebuilt and renamed the
Spread Eagle in the 18th century, is now
named after the vessel that took the
pilgrims to America in 1620; US visitors
might want to make their own pilgrimage
here. The ship set sail from Rotherhithe,
and Captain Christopher Jones

Painted Hall, Old Royal Naval College (p232)

supposedly charted out its course here while supping schooners. There's seating on a small back terrace, from which you can view the Thames.

### TRAFALGAR TAVERN Map p241 Pub

☎ 8858 2437; www.trafalgartavern.co.uk; 6 Park Row SE10; ☽ noon-11pm Mon-Thu, to midnight Fri & Sat, to 10.30pm Sun; DLR Cutty Sark
This cavernous pub with big windows looking onto the Thames and the O2 (the erstwhile Millennium Dome) is steeped in history and you can see some of it illustrated in the prints on the walls. Dickens apparently knocked back a few here – and used it as the setting for the wedding breakfast scene in *Our Mutual Friend* – and prime ministers Gladstone and Disraeli used to dine on the pub's celebrated whitebait, when the start of the season was so keenly anticipated that Parliament would suspend sitting for a day.

# ENTERTAINMENT & ACTIVITIES

### BETHNAL GREEN WORKING MEN'S CLUB Map p236 Clubbing

☎ 7739 2727; www.workersplaytime.net; 42-44 Pollard Row E2; ☽ hr vary; ⊖ Bethnal Green
This is a true rags-to-riches story: BGWMC was on the brink of bankruptcy, its working men about to become destitute and pintless, until a clever promoter spread the news of trashy burlesque nights taking place in the club's main hall – sticky carpets, shimmery stage set 'n' all – and (literally) overnight, half of London stormed the venue, making it one of the most successful and popular clubs in the capital. There are regular burlesque bonanzas in addition to tassel-twirling contests, alternative Eurovision nights and many more sweet selections. Check

the website for what's on when you'r around.

### LABAN Map p241 Dan

☎ information 8691 8600, bookings 8469 9500 www.laban.org; Creekside SE8; admission £3-1; ⦿ Deptford Bridge, DLR Greenwich
This is an independent dance trainin school, which also presents studer performances, graduation shows an regular pieces by the resident troup Transitions Dance Company, as well other assorted dance, music and phys cal performances. Its stunning £23 mi lion home was designed by Herzog & d Meuron, the same people who built th Tate Modern (see p140).

### O2 Map p224 Rock & PC

☎ 0871 984 0002; www.theo2.co.uk; Peninsula Sq SE10; ⊖ North Greenwich
Formerly the doomed Millennium Dom this pricey fiasco has now reinvente itself as one of the city's major conce venues, hosting all the biggies – th Rolling Stones, Prince, Elton John, Scisso Sisters and many others, inside the 20,000 capacity stadium. Ticket prices start at £2! This was also the venue where Michae Jackson was meant to appear for his mara thon tour, just before his untimely death

### RHYTHM FACTORY

Map p236 Rock & Po
☎ 7247 9386; www.rhythmfactory.co.uk; 16-18 Whitechapel Rd E1; ☽ to 3am Sun-Thu, to 5am Fri & Sat; ⊖ Aldgate East
Perennially hip and popular, the Rhythm Factory is a relaxed and friendly coffe shop with a Thai lunch and dinner men during the day, but come the evening th large back room is opened up, and tonne of bands and DJs of all genres keep th up-for-it crowd happy until late.

THE EAST END, DOCKLANDS & GREENWICH

SHOPPING

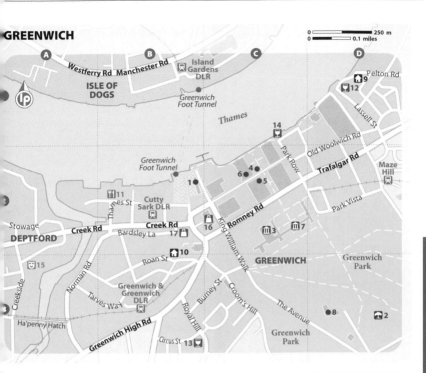

# GREENWICH

# SHOPPING
## THE EAST END &
## DOCKLANDS

Shopping options are limited in the East End but the Burberry and Carhartt connections ensure a steady flow, while the boutiques and galleries lining **Columbia Road E2** (Map p236; www.columbiaroad. info; Cambridge Heath, 8 or 55), which are usually open at the weekend only, and, to a lesser extent, the shops along **Broadway Market** (Map p236; www.broadwaymarket.co.uk; London Fields or Cambridge Heath, 48, 55, 106 or 394) in Hackney are among London's up-and-coming retail scenes. There's a massive underground shopping mall beneath the skyscrapers around Canary Wharf, with upmarket shops, bars and restaurants.

Canary Wharf (p230)

NEIL SETCHFIELD

## FABRICATIONS Map p236 Homewares

☎ 7275 8043; www.fabrications1.co.uk; 7 Broadway Market E8; ⏰ noon-5pm Tue-Fri, 10am-5.30pm Sat; ᴿ London Fields or Cambridge Heath, 🚌 48, 55, 106 or 394

This shop does a lot for the recycling cause, making mostly soft furnishings for the home such as cushions, rugs and mats from unusual and unexpected material, from bicycle tyre tubes to used ribbon.

## LABOUR & WAIT Map p236 Homewares

☎ 7729 6253; www.labourandwait.co.uk; 18 Cheshire St E2; ⏰ 11am-5pm Wed & Fri, 1-5pm Sat, 10am-5pm Sun; ⊖ Liverpool St or Aldgate East

Dedicated to simple and functional yet scrumptiously stylish traditional British homewares, Labour & Wait specialises items by independent manufacturers wh make their products the old-fashione way. There are school tumblers, enam coffee pots, luxurious lambswool bla kets, elegant ostrich-feather dusters ar gardening tools. Note the limited ope ing hours.

## GREENWICH & SOUTHEAST LONDON

Greenwich is paradise for lovers of ret clothes stores and second-hand boo shops, which seem to surface eve few steps. The vintage clothes shop are cheaper than those in the West En and there are some retro househol shops and general gift shops arour DLR Cutty Sark.

### EMPORIUM Map p241 Fashion & Design

☎ 8305 1670; 330-332 Creek Rd SE10; ⏰ 10.30am-6pm Wed-Sun; DLR Cutty Sark

Each piece is individual at this lovely vir tage shop (unisex), where glass cabinet are crammed with costume jewellery, ol perfume bottles and straw hats, whi gorgeous jackets and blazers interming on the clothes racks.

### COMPENDIA Map p241 Gifts & Souveni

☎ 8293 6616; www.compendia.co.uk; 10 Greenwich Market; ⏰ 11am-5.30pm Mon-Fri, from 10am Sat & Sun; DLR Cutty Sark

Compendia's owners are madly enthus astic about games – board or any othe kind – and they'll look for the rarest c things if you ask them to. The shop is e cellent for gifts you can enjoy with you mates – backgammon, chess, Scrabble solitaire and rarities such as Mexican Trai Domino, which claims to be the world fastest game.

# SOUTHWEST LONDON

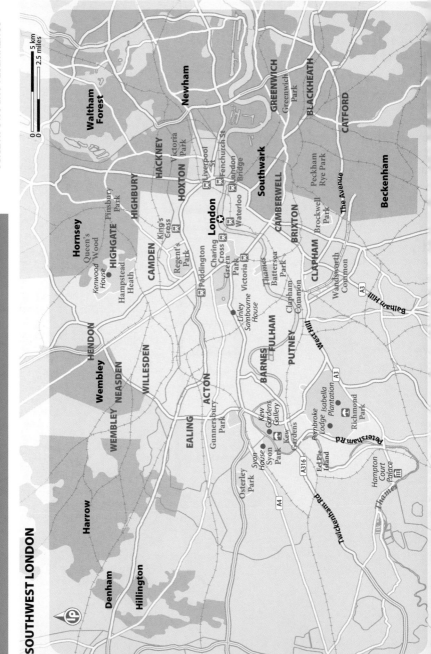

0 ___ 5 km
0 ___ 2.5 miles

Waltham
Forest

Newham

GREENWICH
Greenwich
Park

BLACKHEATH

CATFORD

HACKNEY

HOXTON       Victoria
             Park
             Liverpool
             St
HIGHBURY              Fenchurch St
                     London
                     Bridge
Finsbury
Park
Hornsey        London
             Southwark          Peckham
Queen's                         Rye Park
Wood    HIGHGATE                         CAMBERWELL
              King's        Waterloo            The Avenue    Beckenham
Kenwood       Cross                    BRIXTON
House   CAMDEN                         Brockwell
        Hampstead   Regent's  Charing          Park
        Heath       Park      Cross
                    Paddington  Green
                                Park              Wandsworth
                                      Thames      Common    CLAPHAM
HENDON                         Victoria  Battersea
                                         Park              A3
                                     Clapham           Balham Hill
Wembley                         Linley  Common
NEASDEN                         Sambourne
          WILLESDEN             House
WEMBLEY                    FULHAM
                    BARNES
          ACTON          PUTNEY       West Hill
                  Gunnersbury                      A3
          EALING   Park          Pembroke  Isabella
                         Kew      Lodge     Plantation
                         Gardens
                         Gallery          Richmond
                    Kew              Park
                    Gardens    Petersham Rd
Harrow         Osterley    Syon
               Park     House   Eel Pie
                        Syon    Island
                        Park  A316
                                      Hampton
                        A4            Court
Denham                       Twickenham Rd   Palace
                                      Thames
Hillington

# SOUTHWEST LONDON DAY TRIPS

The well-to-do have been retreating from the city to the palaces and villas of London's delightful riverside boroughs for more than 500 years, and the area's appeal to those wishing to escape the more frenetic pace of life in zones 1 and 2 is still very much apparent. Richmond and Kew in particular offer an expensive slice of village life far removed from the crowds of central London, and offer a range of outstanding and world-famous sights that more than repay the effort of coming out here for a day. It's feasible to see both the magnificent Hampton Court Palace and sublime Kew Gardens in one day – and even to have time for a walk in beautiful Richmond Park and a sniff round the shops of genteel Richmond Hill if you start early enough.

# SIGHTS
## RICHMOND

If anywhere in London could be described as a village, Richmond – with its delightful green and riverside vistas – is it. Centuries of history, some stunning Georgian architecture and the graceful curve of the Thames has made this one of London's swankiest locales, home to ageing rock stars and city high-flyers alike.

### RICHMOND PARK

☎ 8948 3209; www.royalparks.gov.uk; admission free; ⏰ 7am-dusk Mar-Sep, from 7.30am Oct-Feb; ⊖ / 🚉 Richmond, then 🚌 65 or 371

At just over 1000 hectares (the largest urban parkland in Europe), this Park offers everything from formal gardens and ancient oaks to unsurpassed views of central London 12 miles away. It's easy to escape the several roads that cut up the rambling wilderness, making the park an excellent spot for a quiet walk or picnic, even in summer when Richmond's riverside can be heaving. Such is its magic, it somehow comes as no surprise to happen upon herds of more than 600 red and fallow deer basking under the trees. Be advised that the creatures can be less than docile in rutting season (May to July) and

when the does bear young (September and October). It's a great place for bird-watchers too, with a wide range of habitats, from neat gardens to woodland and assorted ponds.

Coming from Richmond, it's easiest to enter via Richmond Gate or from Petersham Rd. Take a map with you and wander around the grounds; flower-lovers should make a special trip to **Isabella Plantation**, a stunning woodland garden created after WWII, in April and May when the rhododendrons and azaleas are in bloom.

**Pembroke Lodge** ( ⏰ 10am-5.30pm summer, to 4.30pm winter), the childhood home of Bertrand Russell, is now a cafe set in a beautiful 13-hectare garden and affording great views of the city from the back terrace.

### HAMPTON COURT PALACE
Off Map p244

☎ 0870 751 5175; www.hrp.org.uk/Hampton CourtPalace; Hampton Court Rd, East Molesey KT8; all-inclusive ticket adult/5-15yr/senior & student/family £13.30/6.65/11.30/37; ⏰ 10am-6pm late March-Oct, to 4.30pm Nov-late Mar; 🚉 Hampton Court; ♿

London's most spectacular Tudor palace is the 16th-century Hampton Court Palace in the city's suburbs, easily reached by train from Waterloo Station. Here history is palpable, from the kitchens where you see food being prepared and the grand living quarters of Henry VIII to the spectacular gardens complete with a 300-year-old maze. This is one of the best days out London has to offer and should not be missed by anyone with any interest in British history. Set aside plenty of time to do it justice, bearing in mind that if you come by boat from central London the trip will have already eaten up half the day.

Like so many royal residences, Hampton Court Palace was not built for the monarchy at all. In 1515 Cardinal Thomas Wolsey, Lord Chancellor of England, built himself a palace in keeping with his sense of self-importance. Unfortunately, even Wolsey couldn't persuade the pope to grant Henry VIII a divorce from Catherine of Aragon and relations between king and chancellor soured. Against that background, you only need to take one look at the palace to understand why Wolsey felt obliged to present it to Henry, a monarch not too fond of anyone trying to muscle

in on his mastery. The hapless Wolsey w. charged with high treason but died befo he could come to trial, in 1530.

As soon as he acquired the palac Henry set to work expanding it, addir the Great Hall, the exquisite Chapel Roy and the sprawling kitchens. By 1540 th was one of the grandest and most s phisticated palaces in Europe, but Hen only spent an average three weeks a ye. here. In the late 17th century, William ar Mary employed Sir Christopher Wren t build extensions. The result is a beautif blend of Tudor and 'restrained baroqu architecture.

Tickets are on sale in the shop to th left as you walk up the path towards th main **Trophy Gate**. Be sure to pick up leaflet listing the daily program, which w help you plan your visit. This is importar as some of the free guided tours requi advance booking.

Passing through the main gate yo arrive first in the **Base Court** and the the **Clock Court**, named after the 16th century astronomical clock that sti

Hampton Court Palace (p245)

GUY MOBE

hows the sun revolving round the earth. he second court is your starting point; om here you can follow any or all of the x sets of rooms in the complex. Here ehind the colonnade you'll also find the seful **Introductory Exhibition**, explaining what's where and how the compound unctions.

The stairs inside Anne Boleyn's ateway lead up to **Henry VIII's State partments**, including the **Great Hall**, he largest single room in the palace, decrated with tapestries and what is considered the country's best hammer-beam oof. The Horn Room, hung with impressive antlers, leads to the Great Watching hamber where guards controlled access o the king. Leading off from the chamer is the smaller Pages' Chamber and the aunted Gallery. Arrested for adultery and etained in the palace in 1542, Henry's ifth wife, Catherine Howard, managed o evade her guards and ran screaming own the corridor in search of the king. Her woeful ghost is said to do the same hing to this day.

Further along the corridor is the beauiful **Chapel Royal**, built in just nine months and still a place of worship after 450 years. The blue-and-gold vaulted eiling was originally intended for Christ Church, Oxford, but was installed here nstead; the 18th-century reredos was arved by Grinling Gibbons.

Also dating from Henry's day are the delightful **Tudor kitchens**, again accessible from Anne Boleyn's Gateway and originally able to rustle up meals for a royal household of some 1200 people. The kitchens have been fitted out to look as they might have done in Tudor days and palace 'servants' turn the spits, stuff the peacocks and frost the marzipan with real gold leaf. Don't miss the Great Wine Cellar, which handled the 300 barrels each

of ale and wine consumed here annually in the mid-16th century.

West of the colonnade in the Clock Court is the entrance to the **Wolsey Rooms** and the **Young Henry VIII Exhibition**. East of the colonnade you'll find the stairs to the **King's Apartments**, completed by Wren for William III in 1702. A tour of the apartments takes you up the grand King's Staircase, painted by Antonio Verrio in about 1700 and flattering the king by comparing him to Alexander the Great. Highlights include the King's Presence Chamber, dominated by a throne backed with scarlet hangings. The King's Great Bedchamber, with a bed topped with ostrich plumes, and the King's Closet (where His Majesty's toilet has a velvet seat) should not be missed.

William's wife, Mary II, had her own **Queen's State Apartments**, accessible up the Queen's Staircase, decorated by William Kent. When Mary died in 1694, work on these was incomplete; they were finished during the reign of George II. The rooms are shown as they might have been when Queen Caroline used them for entertaining between 1716 and 1737. Compared with the King's Apartments, those for the queen seem austere, although the Queen's Audience Chamber has a throne as imposing as that of the king.

Beyond the Cartoon Gallery are the **Queen's Private Apartments**: her drawing room and bedchamber, where she and the king would sleep if they wanted to be alone. Particularly interesting are the Queen's Bathroom, with its tub set on a floor cloth to soak up any spillage, and the Oratory, an attractive room with its exquisite 16th-century Persian carpet.

Once you're finished with the palace interior there are still the gardens to appreciate. Carriage rides for up to five people around the gardens cost £10 and last 20 minutes. Look out for the **Real Tennis Court**, dating from the 1620s and designed for real tennis, a rather different version of the game from that played today. In the restored 24-hectare Riverside Gardens, you'll find the **Great Vine**. Planted in 1768, it's still producing just under 320kg of grapes per year; it's an old vine, no doubt about it, but not the world's oldest, as they say it is here (that one is in Slovenia). The **Lower Orangery** in the gardens houses Andrea Mantegna's nine *Triumphs of Caesar* paintings, bought by Charles I in 1629; the Banqueting House was designed for William III and painted by Antonio Verrio. Look out for the iron screens designed by Jean Tijou.

No-one should leave Hampton Court without losing themselves in the famous 800m-long **maze**, made of hornbeam and yew and planted in 1690. The average visitor takes 20 minutes to reach the centre. The maze is included in entry, although those not visiting the palace can enter for £3.50 (£2.50/10 for children/families). Last admission is 5.15pm in summer and 3.45pm in winter.

There are trains every half-hour from Waterloo direct to Hampton Court station (30 minutes); it's a three-minute walk to the palace entrance. The palace can also be reached from Westminster Pier in central London twice daily on riverboats operated by **Westminster Passenger Services Association** (p249) from April to October. This is a great trip if the weather is good, but it takes three hours.

# KEW

## KEW GARDENS

☎ 8332 5655; www.kew.org; Kew Rd TW9; adult/under 17yr/senior & student £13/free/11; ☉ gardens 9.30am-6.30pm Mon-Fri, to 7.30pm Sat & Sun Apr-Aug, to 6pm Sep & Oct, 9.30am-

4.15pm Nov-Feb, glasshouses 9.30am-5.30pm April-Oct, 9.30am-3.45pm Nov-Feb; ⊖ / ⍟ Kew Gardens; ♿

Royal Botanic Gardens at Kew is one of the most popular attractions in London, which means it can get very crowded during summer, especially at weekends. Spring is probably the best time to visit but at any time of year this 120-hectare expanse of lawns, formal gardens and greenhouses has delights to offer. As well as being a public garden, Kew is an important research centre, and it maintains its reputation as the most exhaustive botanical collection in the world.

Its wonderful plants and trees aside, Kew has several specific sights within its borders. Assuming you come by tube and enter via Victoria Gate, you'll come almost immediately to a large pond overlooked by the enormous **Palm House**, hothouse of metal and curved sheets of glass dating from 1848 and housing all sorts of exotic tropical greenery; the aerial walkway offers a birds'-eye view of the lush vegetation. Just northwest of the Palm House is the tiny but irresistible **Water Lily House** (☉ Mar-Dec), dating from 1852 and the hottest glasshouse at Kew.

Further north is the stunning **Princess of Wales Conservatory**, opened in 1987 and housing plants in 10 different climatic zones – everything from a desert to a mangrove swamp. In the tropical zone you'll find the most famous of Kew's 38,000-odd plant species, the 3m-tall *titan arum,* or 'corpse flower', which is overpoweringly obnoxious-smelling when it blooms in April. Just beyond the conservatory is **Kew Gardens Gallery** bordering Kew Green, which houses exhibitions of paintings and photos mostly of a horticultural theme.

You can get to Kew Gardens by tube or train. Come out of the station and

DOUG MCKINLAY

Butterfly in the Princess of Wales Conservatory, Kew Gardens (p248)

walk straight (west) along Station Ave, cross Kew Gardens Rd and then continue straight along Lichfield Rd. This will bring you to Victoria Gate. Alternatively, from April to October, boats run by the **Westminster Passenger Services Association** ( ☎ 7930 2062; www.wpsa.co.uk) sail from Westminster Pier to Kew Gardens up to four times a day (see p249).

There is now a Rhizotron and Xstrata Treetop Walkway which takes you underground and then 18 metres up in the air, for an alternative and new view of tree anatomy.

# ARCHITECTURE

30 St Mary Axe, or 'the Gherkin' (p118)

RICHARD I'ANS

**Some cities have a unifying architectural style, but London is a glorious architectural mongrel, with a heritage forged over 2000 years of conflict, expansion and reinvention. If there was such a thing as a distinctive London building, it would have to be the tall Georgian town house, seen all over the West End and throughout West London. These handsome homes are a monument to a city on the up-and-up, when even residential housing was given that extra flourish.**

Considering that more than one million bombs fell on London during WWII, it's re markable that any ancient architecture survived, but London is awash with historica treasures. Traces of medieval London are hard to find thanks to the Great Fire of 1666 but several works by the celebrated Inigo Jones (1573–1652) have endured through the centuries, including Covent Garden Piazza (p68) and the gorgeous Queen's House at Greenwich (p234).

There are a few even older treasures – the Tower of London (p121) partly dates back to the 11th century, while Westminster Abbey (p91) and Temple Church (p117 are 12th- to 13th-century creations, and the gatehouse to St Bartholomew-the-Great church (p116) dates from 1595.

## AFTER THE GREAT FIRE

After the fire, renowned architect Sir Christopher Wren was commissioned to oversee reconstruction, but his grand scheme for a new city layout of broad, symmetrical av enues never made it past the planners. His legacy lives on, however, in the stunning

## ⬎ THE THRICE OLYMPIC CITY

Of course the 2012 Olympics has seen a huge redevelopment program for East London, by far London's poorest area and one that has been desperately in need of investment for decades. Even in the shadow of the global economic turndown, London's third games has retained its £9 billion budget and is throwing up some big must-see new structures. Head to the Olympics site in Stratford to see behemoths such as the 80,000-capacity Olympic Stadium, the Aquatics Centre and the London Velopark rising up from the horizon.

t Paul's Cathedral (p113), the maritime precincts at Greenwich (p230) and the many hurches dotted around the City.

Wren-protégé Nicholas Hawksmoor joined contemporary James Gibb in creatng a new style known as English Baroque, which found its greatest expression in pitalfields' Christ Church and St Martin-in-the-Fields on Trafalgar Sq (p64). However, emnants of Inigo Jones' classicism endured, morphing into neo-Palladianism in the ieorgian era.

Like Wren before him, Georgian architect John Nash aimed to impose some symnetry on unruly London, and was slightly more successful in achieving this through rand creations like Trafalgar Sq and the curving arcade of Regent St. Built in similar tyle, the surrounding squares of St James's are still some of the finest public spaces ı London – little wonder then that Queen Victoria decided to move into the recently acated Buckingham Palace (p94) in 1837.

## TOWARDS MODERNITY

ragmatism replaced grand vision with the arrival of the Victorians, who wanted ornate ivic buildings that reflected the glory of empire but were open to the masses, not just he privileged few. The turrets, towers and arches of the Victorian neo-Gothic style ire best exemplified by the Kensington Museums (see Sights, p185) and St Pancras Chambers. The Victorians were also responsible for creating huge slums of cheap teraced houses that are now worth around £400,000 to £900,000 each.

A flirtation with Art Deco before WWII was followed by a functional, even brutal, nodernism afterward, as the city rushed to build new housing to replace the terraces ost in the Blitz. The next big wave of development came in the derelict wasteland of he former London docks (p230), which were razed of their working-class terraces and varehouses and rebuilt as towering skyscrapers and 'loft' apartments for Thatcher's ruppies.

## CONTEMPORARY ARCHITECTURE

There was then a lull in new construction until 2000, when a glut of big millennial projects brought some new structures to the centre of London and rejuvenated othrs: the London Eye (p139), Tate Modern (p140) and the Millennium Bridge (p141) all nlivened the South Bank, while Norman Foster's wonderful 30 St Mary Axe (p118), petter known as the 'Gherkin' marked the start of a new wave of skyscraper construction.

LONDON IN FOCUS

ARCHITECTURE

## ↘ THE BEST

CELEBRATE 10 YEARS OF TATE MODERN

DOUG MCKINLAY

Tate Modern (p140)

## LONDON ARCHITECTURAL SIGHTS

- **Palace of Westminster** (p93)
- **Queen's House** (p234)
- **Barbican** (p119)
- **Docklands** (p230)
- **Tate Modern** (p140)
- **30 St Mary Axe** (p118)

The enthusiasm for new developmen has caused nervous jitters among custo dians of London's architectural heritag including the UN World Heritage commi tee, though the world economic crisis ha slowed the pace of London's race for th sky.

# CLUBBING

NEIL SETCHFIELD

Clubbing in London

**London is one of Europe's clubbing capitals, not just for the number of venues booming basslines out into the night, but for the sheer, dazzling variety of musical forms on offer. You'll find everything from vintage disco and soul to old-school house, indie, funk, punk, R&B, drum and bass, hip hop, electro, techno and everything in between. Hell, there are even a few classic Russian pop nights in town.**

The West End has the highest concentration of clubs and bars and there's always something going on in and around Soho, the hedonistic village at the heart of the capital. However, here you'll need to take local advice in order to avoid ending up in tourist traps with overpriced drinks and undertalented DJs. Other less-than-pleasant consequences of the West End's popularity are the binge-drinking and a lack of public toilets in such a crowded area. Indeed, the situation at the weekends got so bad at one point that Westminster Council resorted to setting up open-air public urinals throughout on Friday and Saturday nights, something that it's now impossible to imagine the West End without, so successful have they been!

## OUTSIDE THE WEST END

To avoid the crowds of the West End, do what most Londoners do and head away from the city centre to the bars and clubs of Clerkenwell and Shoreditch, where the very best clubs are, from the so-called 'super club' Fabric (p219) to lesser known delights such Old St old-timer 333 (p218), Brick Lane hipster hang out 93 Feet East (p218) and the excellent and sadly now very widely known Bethnal Green Working Men's Club (p240).

LONDON IN FOCUS

CLUBBING

Elsewhere in the city, indie kids and rock fans will usually want to head for Camden, famously the home of Britpop and more recently everyone's favourite self-destructive diva Amy Winehouse. Here venues host cool DJ nights as well as live indie bands. Fans of the urban dance scene will want to head to the East End where cutting-edge grime and krunk clubs keep the punters happy with their multicultural melange throughout the night.

## CLUB ETIQUETTE

There is almost never a formal dress code at London clubs – it's almost unheard of for a place to have a 'no trainers' rule, as in many other parts of the UK, for example. But in the cooler places when it's busy and the door whores are feeling picky, it's usually a lack of style they'll penalise. If you're worried then dress up, arrive early and don't get shirty if you have to wait fo a while to get in.

Nearly all London clubs have a coat check (£1) and while many clubs have toile attendants who will fuss around you and attempt to turn on the taps for you whe you wash your hands, it's totally unnecessary to tip them – no Londoner does. Club generally start early in London – arrival between 11pm and midnight is normal, an only very big clubs stay open past 3 or 4am, meaning that you'll often find yourself ou on the street before the underground is running.

For events listings there is a huge amount available online: check out www.dontstayir com or the weekly listings magazine *Time Out* (£2.99).

↘ **THE BEST**

Fabric (p219)

KATHY DEWITT/ALA

### LONDON CLUBS

- **Fabric** (p219)
- **93 Feet East** (p218)
- **Madame Jo Jo's** (p79)
- **Last Days of Decadence** (p219)
- **Heaven** (p77)
- **Bethnal Green Working Men's Club** (p240)

# FAMILY TRAVEL

DOUG MCKINLAY

atural History Museum (p187)

he idea that children should be seen and not heard went out with he Victorians. London is becoming more child-friendly every year, vith new activities and special events for kids adding interest at nuseums and monuments. Remember, however, that children are asily exhausted by the crowds and long walks involved in a day ut in London – don't plan too much and build in some rest time in ondon's public parks.

n excellent activity for children is a sleepover at the Science Museum (p187) or Natural istory Museum (p187), though you'll need to book months ahead. The Museum of ondon (p115) and Museum of London Docklands (p230) have great activities during chool holidays, and the Natural History Museum offers fantastic free explorer back-acks for under sevens. Most attractions offer family tickets and discounted entry for ids under 15 or 16 years (children under five are usually free).

All kids will love London Zoo (p170), the London Eye (p139), the London Dungeon )143), Madame Tussauds (p163) and HMS Belfast (p144).

Other slightly less obvious ideas include the exciting climbs up St Paul's Cathedral )113), the Monument (p119), feeding the ducks in St James's Park (p96) and watching he performers at Covent Garden Piazza (p68).

## EATING & DRINKING WITH KIDS

estaurants in London are generally very accommodating to young children. High hairs are usually available, but it's always good to call ahead and ask if they're avail-ble. One particularly child-friendly chain of restaurants is Giraffe (www.giraffe.net),

LONDON IN FOCUS

FAMILY TRAVEL

## ⤵ THE NITTY GRITTY

- **Changing facilities** Sometimes available in bars and restaurants
- **Cots** Available in most hotels, but always request them in advance
- **Health** Generally excellent health-care standards
- **Highchairs** Most restaurants have these available
- **Nappies (diapers)** Available everywhere
- **Transport** Trains and buses are fine for strollers

which can rather resemble a kinderga ten at lunchtime in some branches, b is one of those places you won't hav to feel self-conscious when the kids a shrieking.

You may feel rather less welcon bringing younger children out to smart restaurants in the evenings, howeve Babysitting services are widely availab! ask at your hotel if it offesr any babys ting services, or try Top Notch Nanni (www.topnotchnannies.com) or Sitte (www.sitters.co.uk).

The one place that isn't traditional very child-friendly is the pub. By law m nors aren't allowed into the main bar a pub (though walking through is absolutely fine), but many pubs have areas whe children are welcome, usually a garden or outdoor space.

## GETTING AROUND WITH KIDS

When it comes to getting around, buses are much more child-friendly than th tube, which is often very crowded and can be extremely hot in the summer month (though air conditioning is finally being introduced on new rolling stock on som lines). As well as being big, red and iconic, buses in London are usually the famou 'double decker' type and kids love to sit on the top deck and get great views of th city as you travel.

An even better option is the open-topped bus tours that are always fun for fam lies. Children aged five to 10 years travel free on public transport if accompanied b an adult, and children aged 11 to 15 years travel free on the buses with an Oyste photocard (follow the Oyster link at www.tfl.gov.uk). Child discounts also apply o London's riverboats.

# FOOD & DRINK

DOUG MCKINLAY

ating out in London

DESTINATION IN FOCUS

FOOD & DRINK

recent years food in London has changed beyond all recognition, nd the British capital is now one of the best places to eat in the orld. Whether you're looking for *haute cuisine* or a good takeaway, ou won't come away disappointed. Don't believe what people may ave told you about London's terrible restaurants in the past – ow your only problem will be paying for the pleasure of eating ut here.

ne culinary revolution began in the mid-1990s with the advent of the so-called 'gastro-ub' – a smattering of savvy central London pubs that replaced their stodgy microwave eals with freshly prepared contemporary cuisine, bringing little-known ingredients to ne plates of many locals for the first time. The gastropub has rather had its day now, nough you'll still find them across the city, signposting an area's 'up-and-coming' sta-us and providing meeting places for the young urban professionals slowly colonising ondon's poorer boroughs.

## WORLD-CLASS DINING

ondon has 48 Michelin starred restaurants, including two three-star restaurants, the nost famous of which is Gordon Ramsay (p194) in Chelsea. The picks in the city today re therefore nothing short of sublime if you want to have a memorable meal (and specially if you don't mind splashing out – as with almost everything in London, you'll et what you pay for). For top tables, you'll always need to reserve in advance, and for ne very best you'll need to book several months ahead.

Some dining experiences we heartily recommend you not to miss are Yauatcha (p73), St John (p213), Nobu (p99), Hakkasan (p172), Bocca di Lupo (p73) and Locanda Locatelli (p173).

But it's not all about Michelin stars and three-month waiting lists for reservations. Some of London's most glorious treats are both easily accessible without a long-standing booking and not too expensive either. A few current favourites of ours include Clerkenwell's Modern Pantry (p213), the South Bank's Anchor & Hope (p148), Fitzrovia's Fino (p173), Marylebone's temple of fusion Providores & Tapa Room (p174) and Moorish Moro (p213) at Exmouth Market.

## FOOD FROM EVERYWHERE

One of the huge advantages London has as a culinary destination is the sheer range of migrant communities living across i vast swathe. While you can find multi-ethnic restaurants and takeaways pretty muc anywhere, your best bet for a good range of choices and an authentic, quality meal to head for the areas where a particular type of restaurant is most common.

So, if you want top-notch Anatolian food, you should head to Islington or Hackne which also boasts London's best Vietnamese food. Fans of Korean barbecues will fir the best in town in the backstreets of Soho and Holborn. Chinese restaurants domina Gerrard and Lisle Sts in Chinatown (p61), but also Queensway in Bayswater.

The best Indian – or, more accurately, Bangladeshi and Pakistani – food is fou out east around Commercial and Whitechapel Rds. Edgware Rd in West London is th undisputed Lebanese food capital of London, while South Kensington is a tradition place for Polish food. You'll find lots of other cuisines – from Eritrean to Burmes elsewhere in the capital, and part of the joy of London is trying dishes you've neve had before.

## ↘ THE BEST

JOHNNY GREIG UK/A1

Brick Lane Beigel Bake (p214)

### LONDON CHEAP EATS

- **Tayyabs** (p236)
- **Busaba Eathai** (p173)
- **Golden Hind** (p174)
- **Brick Lane Beigel Bake** (p214)
- **Song Que** (p214)
- **Mirch Masala** (p236)

# GAY & LESBIAN

GUY MOBERLY

exual Freedom parade

**he pink pound certainly flexes its muscle in London. The legalisation f gay sex may only have happened in 1967, but you wouldn't now that it had ever been proscribed from the plentiful gay venues otted around the city. A world capital of gaydom on par with New ork and San Francisco, London is home to enormous gay and esbian communities that fan out throughout the city.**

he long-established gay village of Soho, once so central to any gay experience of London, as lost its pre-eminence in a city where redevelopment and high rents have pushed people ut to cheaper neighbourhoods. Soho retains the largest number of gay bars and pubs, hough: walk down Old Compton St at any time and you'll notice omnipresent gay and sbian life – but many of the city's better clubs and venues are now to be found elsewhere.

The alternative two focuses of the city's gay life are in Vauxhall, south of the river, nd Shoreditch, in London's east. Vauxhall, once a bleak concrete jungle, is now home London's mainstream muscle boys, who party from Thursday to Tuesday without reak. Fashionable Shoreditch is home to London's more alternative gay scene, often ery well mixed in with local straight people; here you'll find arty parties and the hip- er bars and clubs, where the muscle boys fear to tread. In general, however, London's ultitude of gay communities are very well integrated into wider society and don't enerally ghettoise themselves these days.

## ESBIAN LONDON

he lesbian scene in London is far less visible than the flamboyant gay one, though here are still a couple of excellent lesbian bars in Soho and plenty going on elsewhere around the city. Certain areas of the capital are well known to have thriving lesbian communities and are worth a visit in their own right – particularly Stoke Newington and Hackney in northeast London. Check out the excellent lesbian London website www.gingerbeer.co.uk for the full lowdown on events, club nights and bars.

## QUEER LIFE

The situation in the UK has improved immeasurably in the past decade for gay and lesbian rights and recognition: protection from discrimination is now enshrined in law, and civil partnerships now allow gay couples the same rights as straight couples, even with respect to adoption. That's not to say homophobia doesn't exist – outside the bubble of Soho, abuse on the street at public displays of affection is still not unusual and sad it's always best to assess the area you're in before walking hand in hand togethe down the street.

Lists of gay-run and gay-friendly accommodation and services are available from Vis London (www.visitlondon.com) and you can make your visit to London as gay as yo choose – there are gay restaurants, hotels, taxi companies, wedding planners, shop

**↘THE BEST**

DOSFOTOS/LEBRECHT MUSIC & ARTS/A

Clubbing in Heaven (p77)

### GAY VENUES

- **Heaven** (p77)
- **Friendly Society** (p77)
- **Barcode** (p77)
- **Candy Bar** (p77)
- **Joiners Arms** (p238)
- **George & Dragon** (p216)

GIANNI MURATORE/ALA

Gay Pride parade (p48)

nd even sports groups throughout the city. Don't miss the annual Gay Pride festival, ne of the world's biggest, held annually in late July (see p48).

You can also keep up to date with events on the scene with the following free publi-ations: Boyz (www.boyz.co.uk) and Pink Paper (www.pinkpaper.com) – available from ny gay bar or club. Weekly listings magazine *Time Out* also publishes comprehensive ay listings.

LONDON IN FOCUS

GAY & LESBIAN

# HISTORY

St Paul's Cathedral (p113)

**The Romans are the real fathers of London, despite there having been a settlement on the same site for several thousand years before their arrival. Amazingly, the Roman wall built around the settlement of Londinium still more or less demarcates the City of London from neighbouring London boroughs today.**

The Romans colonised Britain in AD 43, establishing the port of Londinium. They built wooden bridge across the Thames (near the site of today's London Bridge) and create a thriving colonial outpost before abandoning Britain for good in 410.

## SAXON & NORMAN LONDON

Saxon settlers who colonised the southeast of England from the 5th century onward established themselves in Londinium. Saxon London grew into a prosperous and wel organised town divided into 20 wards, each with its own alderman, and resident colonie of German merchants and French vintners. But Viking raids finally broke the weaken g Saxon leadership, which was forced to accept the Danish leader Canute as king o

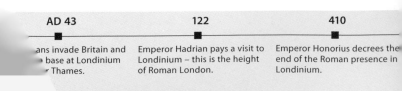

| AD 43 | 122 | 410 |
|---|---|---|
| ans invade Britain and base at Londinium Thames. | Emperor Hadrian pays a visit to Londinium – this is the height of Roman London. | Emperor Honorius decrees the end of the Roman presence in Londinium. |

ngland in 1016. With the death of anute's son Harthacanute in 1042, the hrone passed to the Saxon Edward the onfessor.

When Edward died in 1066, he nointed Harold Godwinson, the Earl f Wessex, his successor on his death-ed, but this enraged William, the Duke f Normandy, who believed Edward ad promised him the throne. William nounted a massive invasion of England rom France and on 14 October defeated Harold at the Battle of Hastings, before narching on London to claim his prize. William the Conqueror was crowned king f England in Westminster Abbey on 25 December 1066, ensuring the Norman onquest was complete.

## MEDIEVAL & TUDOR LONDON

uccessive medieval kings were happy o let the City of London keep its inde-pendence as long as its merchants con-inued to finance their wars and building projects. Later London became one of the

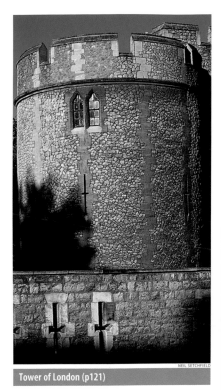

NEIL SETCHFIELD

Tower of London (p121)

LONDON IN FOCUS

HISTORY

argest and most important cities in Europe during the reign of the Tudors, which co-ncided with the discovery of the Americas and thriving world trade.

Henry VIII reigned from 1509 to 1547, built palaces at Whitehall and St James's, and bullied his lord chancellor, Cardinal Thomas Wolsey, into gifting him Hampton Court. His most significant contribution, however, was the split with the Catholic Church in 1534 after the Pope refused to annul his marriage to the non-heir-producing Catherine of Aragon.

The 45-year reign (1558–1603) of his daughter Elizabeth I is still looked upon as one of the most extraordinary periods in English history. During these four decades English literature reached new and still unbeaten heights, and religious tolerance gradually became accepted doctrine. England became a naval superpower, having defeated the Spanish Armada in 1588, and the city established itself as the premier world trade market with the opening of the Royal Exchange in 1566.

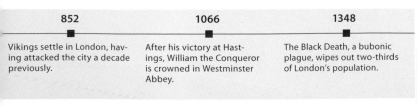

| 852 | 1066 | 1348 |
|---|---|---|
| Vikings settle in London, having attacked the city a decade previously. | After his victory at Hastings, William the Conqueror is crowned in Westminster Abbey. | The Black Death, a bubonic plague, wipes out two-thirds of London's population. |

Natural History Museum (p187)

## CIVIL WAR, PLAGUE & FIRE

The English Civil Wars culminated in the execution of Charles I on 30 January 1649 and saw Oliver Cromwell rule the country as a republic for the next 11 years. During the Commonwealth of England, as the English republic was known, Cromwell banned theatre, dancing, Christmas and just about anything remotely fun. After Cromwell' death, parliament restored the exiled Charles II to the throne in 1660.

Charles II's reign saw great tragedy in the city: in 1665 the Great Plague decimated the population, and then the following year the Great Fire of London occurred (see p267).

One positive aspect of the inferno was that it cleared the way for master architect Christopher Wren to build his magnificent churches. The crowning glory of the 'Great Rebuilding', Wren's St Paul's Cathedral, was completed in 1710 – one of the largest cathedrals in Europe, it remains one of the city's most prominent and visible landmarks

## VICTORIAN LONDON

While the growth and achievements of the previous century were impressive, they paled in comparison with the Victorian era, which began when Queen Victoria was crowned in 1838. During the Industrial Revolution London became the nerve centre of the largest and richest empire the world has ever known, one that covered a quarter

| 1599 | 1666 | 1807 |
|---|---|---|
| ■ | ■ | ■ |
| The Globe Theatre opens in Southwark and *Macbeth*, *King Lear* and *Hamlet* all premiere here. | The Great Fire of London burns for five days, leaving the city of Shakespeare in ruins. | Parliament finally abolishes the slave trade, after a long campaign led by William Wilberforce. |

LONDON IN FOCUS

HISTORY

f the earth's surface area and ruled more than 500 million people.

Queen Victoria lived to celebrate her Diamond Jubilee in 1897, but died four years later aged 81 and was laid to rest in Windsor. Her reign is seen as the climax of Britain's world supremacy, when London was the de facto capital of the world.

## THE WORLD WARS

What became known as the Great War (WWI) broke out in August 1914, and the first German bombs fell from zeppelins near the Guildhall a year later, killing 39 people. Planes were soon dropping bombs on the capital, killing in all some 650 Londoners (half the national total of civilian casualties).

After the war the population of London continued to rise, reaching nearly 7.5 million in 1921. Prime Minister Neville Chamberlain's policy of appeasing Adolf Hitler during the 1930s eventually proved misguided as Germany's expansion could not be sated. When Germany invaded Poland on 1 September 1939, Britain declared war, having signed a mutual-assistance pact with the Poles a few days beforehand. WWII (1939–45), Europe's darkest hour, had begun.

Winston Churchill, prime minister from 1940, orchestrated much of the nation's war strategy from the Cabinet War Rooms deep below Whitehall, and it was from here that he made his stirring wartime speeches. By the time Nazi Germany capitulated in May 1945, up to a third of the East End and the City had been flattened, 32,000 Londoners had been killed and a further 50,000 had been seriously wounded.

## POSTWAR LONDON

Once the celebrations of Victory in Europe (VE) day had died down, the nation faced the huge toll that the war had taken. The years of austerity had begun, with much rationing of essential items and high-rise residences being built on bombsites. Rationing of most goods ended in 1953, the year the current queen, Elizabeth II, was crowned following

> ### GREAT FIRE OF LONDON
>
> The Great Fire of London broke out in a bakery in Pudding Lane on the evening of 2 September 1666. Initially dismissed by the mayor as 'something a woman might pisse out,' the fire spread uncontrollably and destroyed 89 churches and more than 13,000 houses as it raged for days.
>
> The fire changed London forever. Many Londoners left for the countryside or to seek their fortunes in the New World, while the city itself rebuilt its medieval heart with grand buildings such as Wren's St Paul's Cathedral (see p113). Wren's magnificent Monument (see p119) stands as a memorial to the fire and its victims.

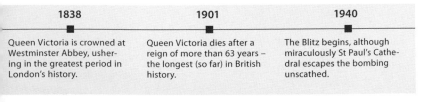

| 1838 | 1901 | 1940 |
|---|---|---|
| Queen Victoria is crowned at Westminster Abbey, ushering in the greatest period in London's history. | Queen Victoria dies after a reign of more than 63 years – the longest (so far) in British history. | The Blitz begins, although miraculously St Paul's Cathedral escapes the bombing unscathed. |

## ↘ THE BEST

Statues at Westminster Abbey (p91)

JULIET COOMBE

### LONDON HISTORICAL TREASURES

- **Tower of London** (p121)
- **British Museum** (p161)
- **Westminster Abbey** (p91)
- **St Paul's Cathedral** (p113)
- **Hampton Court Palace** (p245)

the death of her much-loved father Kin
George VI the year before.

Immigrants from around the world
particularly the former British colonies
flocked to postwar London, where a dwir
dling population had led to labour shor
ages, and the city's character change
forever. London was the place to be du
ing the 1960s, when it became the ep
centre of cool in fashion and music, an
the streets were awash with colour an
vitality. In the 1970s, however, came pun
economic depression and the election c
the country's first female Prime Ministe
in 1979.

Ruling for the whole of the 1980s an
embarking on an unprecedented progran
of privatisation, Margaret Thatcher is easil
the most significant of Britain's postwa
leaders and opinions about her remain po
larised in Britain today. While poorer Londoners suffered under Thatcher's significan
trimming back of the welfare state, things had rarely looked better for the wealthy a
London underwent explosive economic growth.

In 1992, to the amazement of most Londoners, the Conservatives were elected fo
a fourth successive term in government, despite Mrs Thatcher being jettisoned by he
party shortly beforehand. By 1995 the writing was on the wall for the Conservatives
as the Labour Party, apparently unelectable for a decade, came back with a new face

## TODAY'S BRITAIN

Invigorated by its sheer desperation to return to power, the Labour Party elected the
thoroughly telegenic Tony Blair to lead it, who in turn managed to ditch some of the
more socialist-sounding clauses in its party credo and, in a stroke of genius, reinven
the brand as New Labour, finally leading to a huge landslide win in the May 1997
general election. The Conservatives were atomised throughout the country, and the
Blair era had begun.

Most importantly for London, Labour recognised the legitimate demand the city
had for local government, and created the London Assembly and the post of mayor. Ir
Ken Livingstone London elected a mayor who would make big differences to the city

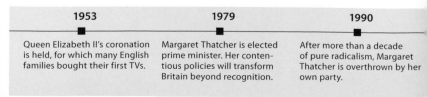

| 1953 | 1979 | 1990 |
|---|---|---|
| Queen Elizabeth II's coronation is held, for which many English families bought their first TVs. | Margaret Thatcher is elected prime minister. Her contentious policies will transform Britain beyond recognition. | After more than a decade of pure radicalism, Margaret Thatcher is overthrown by her own party. |

## THE BLITZ

The Blitz (from the German *'blitzkrieg'* or 'lightning war') lasted for 57 nights, and then continued intermittently until May 1941. The Underground was turned into a giant bomb shelter, although this was not always safe – one bomb rolled down the escalator at Bank station and exploded on the platform, killing more than 100 people. Londoners responded with legendary resilience and stoicism.

The Royal Family – still immensely popular and enormously respected at the time – were also to play their role, refusing to leave London during the bombing, even after Buckingham Palace was hit. The Queen at the time (the current monarch's late mother) famously said that the bombing of her home meant that 'now we can look the East End in the face.'

ivingstone introduced a very successful congestion charge and began tackling the mammoth task of bringing London's chronically backward public transport network nto the 21st century. In 2008 he was defeated by Boris Johnson, a Conservative, who emains Mayor of London today. In 2010, after a general election in which no party eceived an overall parliamentary majority, the leader of the Conservative Party, David Cameron, became Prime Minister with support from the Liberal Democrats, the third argest party, which allowed the formation of a coalition government.

| 1997 | 2005 | 2012 |
|---|---|---|
| Tony Blair rides into office with one of the biggest electoral landslides in British history. | 52 people are killed by suicide bombers attacking the London transport network on 7 July. | London hosts its third Olym Games, the first city in hist to do so three times. |

# MUSIC

Jamming in Brick Lane (p213)

DOUG MCKIN

**London is in many ways the home of modern music. From the Beatles to the Rolling Stones and onward through the Sex Pistols, The Clash, The Jam, Queen, Culture Club, Duran Duran, the Pet Shop Boys, Blur and Suede to present-day sensations such as MIA, Lily Allen and Amy Winehouse, London has produced much of the soundtrack to modern life.**

While all these famous names leap to mind when talking about the London musi scene, the city has been producing cutting-edge music for centuries – George Frideri Handel wrote some of his most famous oratorios from his home in Mayfair betweer 1723 and 1759.

Probably the most famous event in the modern-day classical calendar is the annua Proms (p197), which has expanded its repertoire in recent years to appeal to a broade audience – the 2008 concerts featured a *Doctor Who* show at the Royal Albert Hall complete with Daleks. The Royal Festival Hall also turned a few heads by choosing Motorhead for its grand reopening concert in 2007.

If there's one music genre that rocks London's world, it's guitar music. Famous ven ues in the West End, Shoreditch and Camden are still providing a forum for teen: ith guitars and dreams of world domination. Then also a thriving London jazz scene l happily tootling away in clubs like Ronnie Scott's (p80). To take the pulse of the temporary London music scene, check out the gig listings in weekly listings mag *Out* and select any one of dozens of gigs in a wide range of genres playing each across the capital.

# SHOPPING

Shoppers peruse a colourful shopping strip

Many people visit London just to shop, lured here by the tremendous range of things on sale, rather than bargain prices. While big chain stores are everywhere, London is most notable for its fantastic department stores and its small independent shops. Indeed, even world-famous designers like Stella McCartney and Matthew Williamson have one-off boutiques where ordinary mortals can browse the latest in high fashion away from the snobbery of the big couture houses.

Fashion is probably London's biggest retail commodity. The city has been setting trends ever since Mary Quant dreamt up miniskirts, and big designers' ideas are translated into high-street fashion faster than you can say Yves Saint Laurent. While Mayfair mainly caters to the high end of the market, low priced high street outlets such as Primark and Topshop offer catwalk style on a shoestring.

For street fashion and the cutting-edge for which London is so rightly famed, head to Shoreditch in East London, where you'll see lots of magazine-ready looks before you even get out of Old St tube station. Wander the boutiques of Spitalfields, Brick Lane, Rivington St and the surrounding area to find the looks that will soon be spreading globally.

## HIGH FASHION

High fashion is squarely located between Oxford Circus and Knightsbridge, with the two big designer streets being Bond St in Mayfair and Sloane St in Knightsbridge. Here you'll find nothing but big international names and prices to match.

An alternative place to shop for top brands is in one of London's world-famous depar
ment stores. Harrods (p198), Harvey Nichols (p198), Selfridges (p175) and Liberty (p8.
are the top four to prioritise. If you're planning a splurge, time your visit to coincid
with the sales in June and July or January.

## MARKETS & OTHER TREATS

London has plenty more than high fashion and street fashion to offer its visitors. Th
West End offers plenty of nonsartorial choice, from the great furniture and electron
shopping of Tottenham Court Rd to the small independent bookshops of Charin
Cross Rd. For exotic flavours head to Ridley Rd in Hackeny or Whitechapel High St i
the East End, while for antiques and art Mayfair and St James's are your best bet. Don
miss Regent St's Apple Store (p82) for all your Mac goodies, super traditional Fortnu
& Mason (p82) on Piccadilly for all your anglophile paraphernalia and, if you're wit
kids, Hamleys (p84), London's most famous toy store.

Markets are also a highlight of the capital. No weekend here is complete without
mooch around one of the flea markets (see p211). Our personal favourites are Portobell
Market (p211)and Spitalfields Market (p212).

## FOOD HALLS & FARMERS' MARKETS

London has shaken off its reputation as a foodie desert with some excellent foo
markets – Borough Market (p145), in particular – and dozens of smaller local farm
ers' markets and delis stocked with fine cheeses, charcuterie and artisan ingredient:
Farmers' markets tend to be small and local and take part on Saturday or Sunda
mornings. Ones particularly worth visiting include those at Islington, Marylebon
and Notting Hill.

A taste of the mediterranean at Spitalfields Market (p212)

# THE BEST

oots at Brick Lane market (p220)

## SHOPPING STRIPS

- **Oxford Street** (p81)
- **Brick Lane** (p220)
- **Knightsbridge** (p198)
- **Spitalfields Market** (p212)
- **Regent Street** (p63)

To really taste how the other half live though, head for the fabulous displays and mouth-watering delicacies on display at the famous food halls of Harrods, Harvey Nichols and Selfridges.

LONDON IN FOCUS

SHOPPING

# ⇘ THEATRE

Royal Albert Hall (p190)

ELLIOT DA

Along with Broadway in New York, London's West End is the most important stage in the English-speaking world for drama and musical theatre. Some visitors plan a trip to London for the sole purpose of taking in a musical or a big name show. Performances range from the sublime – Michael Bourne's all-male *Swan Lake* – to the rousing – *Les Misérables*, now the longest-running London musical of all time – and if nothing appeals, you can always go and see *The Mousetrap*, which has been running nonstop since the early 1950s and is now the longest running play in the world.

Despite the high profile of musical theatre, more exciting things are happening i the fields of dance and drama. Kevin Spacey's role as the artistic director  of th revitalised Old Vic finally seems to have paid off and Nicholas Hytner and Davi Lan have attracted some sterling new talent to the National Theatre and Young V respectively. Meanwhile, Sadler's Wells in Clerkenwell continues to lead the way i the field of dance, providing a forum for rare foreign art forms like Japanese *kabuk* among other offerings.

Shakespeare's legacy is generously attended to on the city's stages, most notabl at the Globe Theatre. Since it opened in 1997 Shakespeare's Globe has enjoye considerable success as a working theatre (as opposed to a mere curiosity). Artisti director Dominic Dromgoole, having taken over the reins at the start of 2006, ha ensured that Shakespeare's plays remain at the core of the theatre's program bu at the same time has produced a wider range of European and British classics, a

ell as originating new material, something of which the Bard himself would no
oubt approve.

## WEST END DRAMA

he West End continues to see big name Hollywood stars slumming it with actors
n Equity minimum (the standard basic wage for all actors in the UK) and seems
o have created something of a name for itself as a place for Hollywood A-listers to
einvigorate their credentials with a little theatre work, treading the London thea-
e boards. Big names seen here in the past few years include Christian Slater, Jeff
oldblum, Daniel Radcliffe and Kathleen Turner. Add to this the great British stars of
he theatre who themselves are no strangers in Hollywood such as Dame Judi Dench,
r Ian McKellen and Michael Gambon, and you have a potent pool of internationally
cclaimed acting talent.

Check ahead of your visit for what theatre works are due to be on during your stay –
's easy to book theatre tickets online and you can also read reviews online too to
now what's best to see, helping you make an informed choice. It's always a good
lea to check what's coming up at the National Theatre (p140).

## MUSICAL MUSTS

he big name musical theatre establishments in London have taken a few risks of
te – critics are still gushing with praise for Damon Albarn and Jamie Hewlett's recent
orillaz-style pop opera *Monkey: Journey to the West* at the Royal Opera House. But
ll the old favourites remain – *The Phantom of the Opera* continues to pack them in at
er Majesty's Theatre, and *The Lion King* at the Lyceum Theatre, *Mamma Mia* at the
rince of Wales Theatre and *Billy Elliot* at the Victoria Palace Theatre are all booking
or months and months ahead.

CHARLOTTE HINDLE

**Shakespeare's Globe (p142)**

### THE BEST

National Theatre (p140)

## LONDON STAGES

- Old Vic (p152)
- National Theatre (p140)
- Shakespeare's Globe (p142)
- Royal Court Theatre (p197)
- Young Vic (p152)
- Barbican (p119)

Recent new hits worth looking out fo include *Oliver!* at the Drury Lane Theatr *Sister Act* at the London Palladium ar *Legally Blond, The Musical* at the Savc Theatre.

For comprehensive listings, visit www officiallondontheatre.co.uk.

# ↘ DIRECTORY & TRANSPORT

# DIRECTORY

## CLIMATE

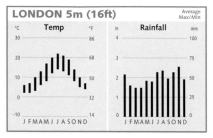

## CUSTOMS REGULATIONS

Like other nations belonging to the European Union (EU), the UK has a two-tier customs system: one for goods bought duty-free and one for goods bought in another EU country where taxes and duties have already been paid.

For goods purchased at airports or on ferries outside the EU, you are allowed to import 200 cigarettes, 50 cigars or 250g of tobacco; 4L of still wine plus 1L of spirits over 22% or 2L of wine (sparkling or otherwise); 60ml of perfume; and other duty-free goods to the value of £300. Although you can no longer bring in duty-free goods from another EU country, you can bring in duty-paid goods that cost less than you'd pay for the same items in your destination country.

## EMBASSIES

The following is a list of selected foreign representative offices in London.

**Australia** (Map p66; ☎ 7379 4334; www.australia.org.uk; Australia House, The Strand WC2; ⊖ Holborn or Temple)

**Canada** Embassy (Map p66; ☎ 7258 6476; www.canada.org.uk; Canada House, Trafalgar Sq SW1; ⊖ Charing Cross); Consulate (Map p86; ☎ 7258 6600; 1 Grosvenor Square, W1; ⊖ Bond St)

**Ireland** (Map p178; ☎ 7235 2171; www embassyofireland.co.uk; 17 Grosvenor Pl SW ⊖ Hyde Park Corner)

**New Zealand** (Map p70; ☎ 7930 842 www.nzembassy.com; New Zealand House, 8 Haymarket SW1; ⊖ Piccadilly Circus)

**South Africa** (Map p66; ☎ 7451 729 www.southafricahouse.com; South Africa Hous Trafalgar Sq WC2; ⊖ Charing Cross)

**USA** (Map p86; ☎ 7499 9000; www. embassy.org.uk; 5 Upper Grosvenor St W ⊖ Bond St)

## HOLIDAYS

With typically four to five weeks' annu leave, Britons get fewer holidays tha their European compatriots, but mo than their American friends.

### PUBLIC HOLIDAYS

Most attractions and businesses clos for a couple of days over Christma and those places that normally shut o Sunday will probably also do so on ban holiday Mondays.

**New Year's Day** 1 January
**Good Friday/Easter Monday** Lat March/April
**May Day Holiday** First Monday in Ma
**Spring Bank Holiday** Last Monday i May
**Summer Bank Holiday** Last Monda in August
**Christmas Day** 25 December
**Boxing Day** 26 December

## INTERNET ACCESS

The most readily available internet caf chain in London is **easyInternetcafe** (www easyinternetcafe.com), with branches through out the city. Prices vary depending on th time of day, but start at £1 per hour.

Wireless access is improving. The City of London is one big wi-fi zone (see www thecloud.net), which is free for the firs

DIRECTORY

month you use it and then you have to
ay; Islington's Upper St is a 'technology
mile' of free wi-fi access, and Leicester Sq
as free wi-fi access. For more info on wi-fi
pots, go to www.wi-fihotspotlist.com.

## MAPS

The *London A-Z* series produces a range of
xcellent maps and hand-held street atlases.
ll areas of London mapped on this system
an be accessed at www.streetmap.co.uk,
ne of London's most useful websites.

## MEDICAL SERVICES

eciprocal arrangements with the UK allow
ustralian residents, New Zealand nation-
ls, and residents and nationals of several
ther countries to receive free emergency
medical treatment and subsidised dental
are through the **National Health Service
NHS; ☎ 0845 4647; www.nhsdirect.nhs.uk)**. They
an use hospital emergency departments,
GPs and dentists (check the Yellow Pages).
isitors staying 12 months or longer, with
he proper documentation, will receive care
under the NHS by registering with a practice
ear their residence. EU nationals can ob-
ain free emergency treatment on presenta-
ion of a European Health Insurance card.

## MONEY

Despite being a member of the EU, the
UK has not signed up to the euro and has
etained the pound sterling (£) as its unit
of currency. One pound sterling is made
up of 100 pence (called 'pee', colloquially).
Notes come in denominations of £5, £10,
£20 and £50, while coins are 1p, 2p, 5p,
10p, 20p, 50p, £1 and £2.

## TAXES & REFUNDS

t's sometimes possible for visitors to
claim a refund of VAT paid on goods, resulting in considerable savings. You're
eligible if you have spent fewer than 365

### BOOK YOUR STAY ONLINE

For more accommodation reviews and recommendations by Lonely Planet authors, check out the on-line booking service at www.lonelyplanet.com. You'll find the true, insider lowdown on the best places to stay. Reviews are thorough and independent. Best of all, you can book online.

MAPS

days out of the two years prior to making the purchase living in the UK, and if
you're leaving the EU within three months
of making the purchase.

Not all shops participate in the VAT
refund scheme, called the Retail Export
Scheme or Tax-Free Shopping, and different shops will have different minimum
purchase conditions (normally around
£75 in any one shop). On request, partici-
pating shops will give you a special form
(VAT 407). This must be presented with
the goods and receipts to customs when
you depart the country.

## TELEPHONE

London's area code is ☎ 020, followed by
an eight-digit number beginning with 7
(central London) or 8 (Greater London). You
only need to dial the ☎ 020 when you are
calling London from elsewhere in the UK.

To call London from abroad, dial your
country's international access code, then 44
(the UK's country code), then 20 (dropping
the initial 0), followed by the eight-digit
phone number.

### MOBILE PHONES

If you have a GSM phone, check with
your service provider about using it in
the UK, and beware of calls being routed

internationally. It's usually most convenient to buy a local SIM card from any mobile phone shop, though in order to do that you must ensure your handset is unlocked before you leave home – contact your home cell provider before you travel.

## TIME

Wherever you are in the world, the time on your watch is measured in relation to the time at Greenwich in London – Greenwich Mean Time (GMT). British Summer Time, the UK's form of daylight-saving time, muddies the water so that even London is ahead of GMT from late March to late October.

## TOURIST INFORMATION

**Visit London** (☎ 7234 5800, 0870 156 6366; www.visitlondon.com), formerly the London Tourist Board, can fill you in on everything from tourist attractions and events (such as the Changing of the Guard) to river trips and tours, accommodation, eating, theatre, shopping, children's London, and gay and lesbian venues.

London's main tourist office is the **Britain Visitor Centre** (Map p71; 1 Regent St SW1; ☼ 9.30am-6pm Mon, 9am-6.30pm Tue-Fri, 10am-4pm Sat & Sun, to 5pm Sat Jun-Sep; ↔ Piccadilly Circus).

## TRAVELLERS WITH DISABILITIES

For disabled travellers London is an odd mix of user-friendliness and downright disinterest. New hotels and modern tourist attractions are legally required to be accessible to people in wheelchairs, but many B&Bs and guesthouses are in older buildings, which are hard (if not impossible) to adapt. This means that travellers who have mobility problems may end up paying more for accommodation.

Transport for London's **Access Mobility for Disabled Passenge** (☎ 7222 1234, textphone 7918 3015; Winds House, 42/50 Victoria St, London SW1 9TN) ca give you detailed advice and it publishe *Access to the Underground,* which indicate which tube stations have ramps and lif (all DLR stations do).

## VISAS

Citizens of Australia, Canada, Nev Zealand, South Africa and the USA ar given, at their point of arrival, 'leave t enter' the UK for up to six months but ar prohibited from working without a wor permit. If you're a citizen of the EU, yo don't need a visa to enter the country an may live and work here freely for as lon as you like.

Visa regulations are always subject t change, so check at www.ukvisas.gov.u or with your local British embassy befor leaving home.

# TRANSPORT
## GETTING THERE & AWAY
### AIR

London is served by five major airports Heathrow, which is the largest, to the wes Gatwick to the south; Stansted to the east Luton to the north; and London City.

### HEATHROW AIRPORT

Some 15 miles west of central London **Heathrow** (LHR; ☎ 0844 335 1801; www.heath rowairport.com) is the world's busiest in ternational airport and now counts five terminals.

Here are options for getting to/from Heathrow Airport:
**Heathrow Connect** (☎ 0845 678 6975 www.heathrowconnect.com) Travelling be tween Heathrow and Paddington station, this modern passenger train service (one way £7.40, 25 minutes

# ⬥ CLIMATE CHANGE & TRAVEL

Every form of transport that relies on carbon-based fuel generates $CO_2$, the main cause of human-induced climate change. Modern travel is dependent on aeroplanes, which might use less fuel per kilometre per person than most cars but travel much greater distances. The altitude at which aircraft emit gases (including $CO_2$) and particles also contributes to their climate change impact. Many websites offer 'carbon calculators' that allow people to estimate the carbon emissions generated by their journey and, for those who wish to do so, to offset the impact of the greenhouse gases emitted with contributions to portfolios of climate-friendly initiatives throughout the world. Lonely Planet offsets the carbon footprint of all staff and author travel.

very 30 minutes) makes five stops en route at places like Southall and Ealing Broadway.

**Heathrow Express** (☎ 0845 600 1515; www.heathrowexpress.com) This ultramodern train (one way/return £16.50/32, 5 minutes, every 15 minutes) whisks passengers from Heathrow Central station (serving Terminals 1, 2 and 3) and Terminal 5 to Paddington. Terminal 4 passengers will need to take the free shuttle train available to Heathrow Central and board the Heathrow Express there.

**National Express** (☎ 0871 781 8181; www. nationalexpress.com) Coaches (one way/return from £5/9, tickets valid three months, 45 minutes to 90 minutes, every 30 minutes to one hour) link the new Heathrow Central Bus Station with **Victoria coach station** (164 Buckingham Palace Rd SW1; ⊖ Victoria) about 45 times per day.

**Underground** (☎ 7222 1234; www.tfl.gov. uk) The tube (one way £4, from central London one hour, every five to nine minutes) is the cheapest way of getting to Heathrow. It runs from just after 5/5.45am from/to the airport (5.50/7am Sunday) to 11.45/12.30am (11.30pm Sunday in both directions).

## GATWICK AIRPORT

Located some 30 miles south of central London, **Gatwick** (LGW; ☎ 0844 335 1802; www.gatwickairport.com) is smaller and better organised than Heathrow. The North and South Terminals are linked by an efficient rail service, with the journey time about three minutes.

Here are options for getting to/from Gatwick Airport:

**easyBus** (☎ 0870 141 7217; www.easybus. co.uk) This budget outfit runs 19-seater minibuses (one way £10, from £2 online, 70 minutes, every 20 minutes) from Fulham Broadway tube station on the District line to the North terminal from 6.40am to 11pm daily.

**First Capital Connect** (☎ 0845 748 4950; www.firstcapitalconnect.co.uk) This rail service (one way/return £9.80/12.70, one hour to 70 minutes) runs through East Croydon, London Bridge, Blackfriars and St Pancras International.

**Gatwick Express** (☎ 0845 850 1530; www. gatwickexpress.com) Trains (one way/return £16.90/28.80, 30 minutes, every 15 minutes) link the station near the South Terminal with Victoria station.

**National Express** (☎ 0871 781 8181; www. nationalexpress.com) Coaches (one way/return £7.30/15.10, tickets valid three months, 65 minutes to 90 minutes) run from Gatwick to Victoria coach station about 18 times per day.

**Southern Trains** (☎ 0845 748 4950; www. southernrailway.com) This rail service (one way/return from £9.80/12.70, 30 to 50 minutes, every 15 to 30 minutes, every hour from midnight to 4am) runs from Victoria station to both terminals.

## STANSTED AIRPORT

London's third-busiest international gateway, **Stansted** (STN; ☎ 0844 335 1803; www.stanstedairport.com) is 35 miles north-east of central London, heading towards Cambridge.

Options for getting to/from Stansted Airport:

**easyBus** (☎ 0870 141 7217; www.easybus. co.uk) Minibuses (one way £10, from £2 online, 90 minutes, every 20 to 30 minutes) from Victoria coach station to Stansted via Gloucester Pl W1 at the Baker St tube station go from 3am to 10.20pm daily.

**National Express** (☎ 0871 781 8181; www. nationalexpress.com) Coaches run around the clock, offering some 120 services per day. The A6 runs to Victoria coach station (one way/return £10.50/18, 85 to 110 minutes, every 10 to 20 minutes) via North London. The A9 runs to Strat-ford (£8.50/16, 45 minutes to one hour, every 30 minutes), from where you can catch a Jubilee line tube (20 minutes) into central London.

**Stansted Express** (☎ 0845 850 0150; www. standstedexpress.com) This rail service (one way/return £19/28.80, £18/26.80 online, 45 minutes, every 15 to 30 minutes) links the airport and Liverpool St station. From the airport the first train leaves at 5.30am, the last just before midnight. Trains depart Liverpool St station from 4.10am to just before 11.30pm.

## LONDON CITY AIRPORT

**London City Airport** (LCY; ☎ 7646 000, www.londoncityairport.com) is predom nantly a gateway airport for busines travellers.

**Docklands Light Railway** (DLR; ☎ 736 9700; www.tfl.gov.uk/dlr) The Docklands Ligh Railway stops at the London City Airpor station (one way £4, with an Oyster car £2.20-2.70). The journey to Bank statio takes just over 20 minutes, and trains g every eight to 15 minutes from 5.30am t 12.30am Monday to Saturday, and 7am t 11.30pm Sunday.

## LUTON AIRPORT

A smallish airport 32 miles north o London, **Luton** (LTN; ☎ 01582-405100; www london-luton.co.uk) caters mainly for cheap charter flights.

Here are options for getting to/from Luton Airport:

**easyBus** (☎ 0870 141 7217; www.easybus co.uk) Minibuses (one way £10, from £2 online, 80 minutes, every 30 minutes depart from Victoria coach station to Luton via Marble Arch, Baker St and Finchley Rd tube stations every half hour round the clock, with the same frequencies coming from the airport.

**Green Line bus 757** (☎ 0844 801 7261 www.greenline.co.uk) Buses to Luton (one way/return £13/14.15, tickets valid three months, one hour) run from Buck ingham Palace Rd just south of Victoria station, leaving approximately every half-hour round the clock.

**First Capital Connect** (☎ 0845 748 4950 www.first capitalconnect.co.uk) Trains (off-peak one way/return £11.90/21.40, 30 to 40 minutes, every six to 15 minutes 7am to 10pm) run from London Bridge, Blackfriars and St Pancras International stations to Luton Airport Parkway sta-tion, from where an airport shuttle bus

...ill take you to the airport in eight
...inutes.

# GETTING AROUND

## BICYCLE

...ycling along London's canals or along
...he South Bank is delightful, but head-
...ng through the heavy traffic, with its ag-
...ressive drivers and noxious fumes, can
...e pretty grim.

### HIRE

**London Bicycle Tour Company** (Map
...130; ☎ 7928 6838; www.londonbicycle.
...om; 1a Gabriel's Wharf, 56 Upper Ground SE1;
⊖ Waterloo or Blackfriars) Rentals cost £4
...er hour or £19 for the first day, £9
...or days two and three, £6 for days
...our and five, £49 for the first week
...nd £10 for second week. It also offers
...½-hour bike tours of London daily at
...0.30am for £15.95 and at noon and
...2.30pm (£18.95 each) on weekends.
...or an extra £5 you get to keep the
...ike for 24 hours after the tour. Routes
...re on its website. You will need to
...rovide credit card details as a deposit
...nd must show ID.

**On Your Bike** (Map p130; ☎ 7378 6669;
www.onyourbike.com; 52-54 Tooley St SE1;
⊙ 7.30am-7.30pm Mon-Fri, 10am-6pm Sat,
11am-5pm Sun; ⊖ London Bridge) Rent-
...als cost £12.50 for the first day, £8 for
...ubsequent days, £35 per week. Prices
...nclude hire of a helmet. A deposit of
£150 (via credit card) is necessary and
...you will be required to show ID.

## BUS

...Getting on today's modern double-deckers,
...you see more of the city than while below
...ground on the tube. Just beware that the
...going can be slow, thanks to traffic jams
...and the more than four million commut-
...ers that get on and off the buses every day.

### FARES

Any single-journey adult bus ticket within
London costs £2 (or £1 with an Oyster
card; see p284). Children under 11 travel
free; those aged 11 to 18 years do as
well but require an Oyster photocard.
Travelcards (p285) are valid on all buses,
including night buses. Be advised that at
some central London bus stops (where
signs have a yellow background), drivers no longer sell tickets and you must
buy before you board from the machines
provided.

## CAR & MOTORCYCLE

London was the world's first major city
to introduce a congestion charge to re-
duce the flow of traffic into its centre from
Monday to Friday. While the traffic entering the 'congestion zone' has fallen as a
result, driving in London can still be very
slow work.

As you enter the zone, you will see a
large letter 'C' in a red circle. If you enter
the zone between 7am and 6pm Monday
to Friday (excluding public holidays), you
must pay the £8 charge on the same day
(or £10 on the first charging day after
travel) to avoid receiving a £120 fine. For
full details log on to www.tfl.gov.uk/road
users/congestioncharging.

## TAXI
### BLACK CABS

The London **black cab** (www.londonblack
cabs.co.uk) is as much a feature of the cityscape as the red bus double-decker bus.
Cabs are available for hire when the yellow sign above the windscreen is lit; just
stick your arm out to signal one. Fares
are metered, with the flag-fall charge of
£2.20 (covering the first 336m during a
weekday), rising by increments of 20p for
each subsequent 168m. Fares are more
expensive in the evenings and overnight.

# ⇘ OYSTER CARD

The credit-card style Oyster card is the London commuter's best friend, and tannoy/loud speaker reminders to 'touch in and touch out' have become as common as the warning to 'mind the gap' at stations. You pay a £3 refundable deposit for the card, which soon pays for itself.

The Oyster card is a smart card on which you can store either credit towards so-called 'prepay' fares, a Travelcard or both. When entering the tube or boarding a bus, you need to touch your card on a reader (which has a yellow circle with the image of an Oyster card on them) at the tube gates or near the driver to register your journey. The system will then deduct the appropriate amount of credit from your card as necessary. The benefit lies in the fact that fares for Oyster-users are lower than the normal ones. If you are making many journeys during the day, you will never pay more than the appropriate Travelcard (peak or off peak) once the daily 'price cap' has been reached.

When leaving tube stations, you must also touch the card on a reader, so the system knows your journey was only, say, a zone 1 and 2 journey. Regular commuters can also store weekly or monthly Travelcards on their Oyster cards.

You can tip taxi drivers up to 10% but few Londoners do, simply rounding up to the nearest pound.

## MINICABS

Minicabs, which are now licensed, are (usually) cheaper freelance competitors of black cabs. However, minicab drivers are often untrained and far less sure of the way than black-cab drivers; it's not unusual for Londoners to have to direct the driver. Minicabs cannot legally be hailed on the street; they must be hired by phone or directly from one of the minicab offices (every high street has at least one). Minicabs don't have meters, so it's essential to fix a price before you start. Most don't bargain – there's usually a fare set by the dispatcher – but it never hurts to try. It's not usual to tip minicab drivers.

Ask a local for the name of a reputable minicab company in the neighbourhood (every Londoner has a regular he or she uses) or phone a large 24-hour operator such as **Addison Lee** (☎ 7387 8888) or **GLH**

Express (☎ 7272 3322). Women travelling alone at night can choose **Lady Cab** (☎ 7272 3800), which has women drivers.

## TRAIN

### DOCKLANDS LIGHT RAILWAY

The driverless **Docklands Light Railway** (DLR; ☎ 7363 9700; www.tfl.gov.uk/dlr) is basically an adjunct to the Underground. It links the City at Bank and Tower Hill Gateway stations with Beckton and Stratford to the east and northeast, the Docklands (as far as Island Gardens at the southern end of the Isle of Dogs), Greenwich and Lewisham and to the south and Woolwich via London City Airport to the southeast. The DLR runs from 5.30am to 12.30am Monday to Saturday and from 7am to 11.30pm Sunday.

### INTERNATIONAL CONNECTIONS

The high-speed passenger rail service **Eurostar** (☎ 0870 518 6186; www.eurostar.com) links St Pancras International station with are du Nord in Paris, making the journey just two hours and 15 minutes with up two dozen daily departures. (The trip o Brussels, on any of a dozen daily trains, ow takes just one hour and 50 minutes.) ares vary enormously. To Paris/Brussels, or example, costs run between £59 for cheap midweek return (with an overnight required) to £309 for a fully flexible eturn.

For other European train enquiries contact **Rail Europe** ( ☎ **0844 848 5848; www.raileurope.co.uk**).

## UNDERGROUND

he London Underground, or 'the tube', s overall the quickest and easiest way of getting around the city.

### FARES

The Underground divides London into six concentric zones. Fares for the more central zones are more expensive than for those zones further out. If you're caught on the Underground without a valid ticket (and that includes crossing into a zone that your ticket doesn't cover) you're liable for an on-the-spot fine of £50.

### TRAVEL PASSES & DISCOUNT FARES

The three-day Travelcard for zones 1 and 2 (£18.40) is valid all day; the one for zones 1 to 6 is available for use anytime (£42.40) or off-peak hours (£21.20). Off-peak travel is permitted only after 9.30am Monday to Friday and at any time on Saturday and Sunday.

# ⬐ BEHIND THE SCENES

## THE AUTHORS
### TOM MASTERS
**Coordinating author**

Having grown up just a short train journey from London, Tom knew the city well by the time he moved to Bloomsbury aged 18. He spent the following decade and a half studying and working in the big smoke before finally being lured away to Berlin where he currently lives. Returning to London every few months is always a pleasure. You can see more of Tom's work at www.tommasters.net.

**Author thanks** Many thanks to the team at Lonely Planet: Cliff Wilkinson, Sasha Baskett, Herman So, Jeanette Wall and the many others who worked so hard in production. In London thanks as ever to those who make the city so special: Mike Christie, Matt Lucas, Gray Jordan, Zeeba Sadiq, Etienne Gilfillan, Stephen Billington, Malcolm Mackenzie, Adrian Simpson and Frank Max.

### JOE BINDLOSS

Joe Bindloss lived briefly on London's Caledonian Rd as a child and he headed back here as soon as he was old enough to work out the tube map. He's lived in north London ever since, in between stints working overseas. Joe has written for more than 30 Lonely Planet guidebooks, from India and Nepal to Lonely Planet's *Gap Year* book. When not travelling for Lonely Planet, he writes about travel, restaurants and life in London for the *Independent,* the *Guardian, Wanderlust* and other publications. For more information, see www.bindloss.co.uk.

### STEVE FALLON

After almost a decade of living in the centre of the known universe – East London – Steve rhymes in his sleep, eats jellied eel for brekkie, drinks lager by the bucketful and dances round the occasional handbag. As always, while researching London he did

---

## LONELY PLANET AUTHORS

Why is our travel information the best in the world? It's simple: our authors are passionate, dedicated travellers. They don't take freebies in exchange for positive coverage so you can be sure the advice you're given is impartial. They travel widely to all the popular spots, and off the beaten track. They don't research using just the internet or phone. They discover new places not included in any other guidebook. They personally visit thousands of hotels, restaurants, palaces, trails, galleries, temples and more. They speak with dozens of locals every day to make sure you get the kind of insider knowledge only a local could tell you. They take pride in getting all the details right, and in telling it how it is. Think you can do it? Find out how at **lonelyplanet.com**.

everything the hard (read: fun) way: walking the walks, seeing the sights, taking (some) advice from friends, colleagues and the odd taxi driver and digesting everything in sight.

## VESNA MARIC

I'm a passionate Londoner and even after 12 years in this incredible city, my love for it grows every season – in fact I've come to the conclusion that the longer you spend here, the more you'll love it. London's parks are one of the best things about the place, though the museums, galleries, restaurants and nightlife are equally irresistible.

## CONTRIBUTING AUTHOR

The British Museum and the Tower of London highlights were written by **Oliver Berry**. A born and bred Brit, Oliver lives and works in Cornwall as a writer and photographer. His travels for Lonely Planet have carried him from the mountains of Corsica to the beaches of the Cook Islands, but he never manages to stay away from the old home country for long.

## THE PHOTOGRAPHER

Doug McKinlay has been a photographer for over 20 years, having started out as a stringer in exotic war-zone locales from Cambodia to El Salvador. His travel and news images have appeared in publications such as the *Times,* the *Independent,* the *Guardian,* the *Mail, Conde Nast Traveller, Maxim,* the *Observer, High Life, CNN Traveller* and Lonely Planet guidebooks.

# THIS BOOK

This 1st edition of *Discover London* was written by Tom Masters. The content was researched and written by Tom along with Vesna Maric, Steve Fallon and Joe Bindloss. The British Museum and the Tower of London highlights were written by Oliver Berry. It was commissioned in Lonely Planet's London office, and produced by the following:

**Commissioning Editor** Clifton Wilkinson
**Coordinating Editor** Jeanette Wall
**Coordinating Cartographer** Peter Shields
**Coordinating Layout Designer** Kerrianne Southway

BEHIND THE SCENES

**Managing Editors** Sasha Baskett, Brigitte Ellemor
**Managing Cartographers** David Connolly, Herman So
**Managing Layout Designers** Indra Kilfoyle, Celia Wood
**Assisting Editor** Elizabeth Swan
**Assisting Cartographer** Brendan Streager
**Cover Research** Naomi Parker
**Internal Image Research** Jane Hart

**Thanks to** Glenn Beanland, Joshua Geoghegan, Chris Girdler, Michelle Glynn, Bric
Gosnell, Indra Kilfoyle, Alison Lyall, Wayne Murphy, Darren O'Connell, Averil Robertson
Dianne Schallmeiner, Rebecca Skinner, Juan Winata

**Internal photographs** p4 Changing of the Guard, Juliet Coombe; p10 Shaftesbury Av
Ann Cecil; p12 London Eye & Palace of Westminster, Richard I'Anson; p31 London Ey
& County Hall, Richard I'Anson; p39 Tower Bridge, Richard Nebesky; p3, p51 BKB Ba
Old Compton St, Soho, Neil Setchfield; p3, p85 Changing of Guards at Buckinghar
Palace, Judy Bellah; p3, p101 Cityscape from Bar Vertigo in Tower 42, Doug McKinlay
p3, p129 London Eye, Orien Harvey; p3, p153 British Museum, Rick Gerharter; p3, p17
Hyde Park, Doug McKinlay; p3, p199 Verde & Co, Spitalfields, Doug McKinlay; p3, p22
Painted Hall at Greenwich Old Royal Naval College, Travis Drever; p243 Davies Alpin
House, Kew Gardens, Doug McKinlay; p250 Lloyd's of London, Richard I'Anson; p27
Transport Museum, Doug McKinlay

## ACKNOWLEDGMENTS
**Many thanks to the following for the use of their content:**
London Underground Map © Transport for London 2010.
The Central London Bus Map and Tourist Attractions Map © Transport for London 2009

NOTES

NOTES

# ↘ INDEX

## DRINKING

INDEX

DRINKING

INDEX

SIGHTS

INDEX

SLEEPING

## MAP LEGEND

### ROUTES

| | |
|---|---|
| **Tollway** | One-Way Street |
| **Freeway** | Mall/Steps |
| **Primary** | Tunnel |
| Secondary | Pedestrian Overpass |
| Tertiary | Walking Tour |
| Lane | Walking Tour Detour |
| Under Construction | Walking Path |
| Unsealed Road | Track |

### TRANSPORT

| | |
|---|---|
| Ferry | Rail/Underground |
| Metro | Tram |
| Monorail | Cable Car, Funicular |

### HYDROGRAPHY

| | |
|---|---|
| River, Creek | Canal |
| Intermittent River | Water |
| Swamp/Mangrove | Dry Lake/Salt Lake |
| Reef | Glacier |

### BOUNDARIES

| | |
|---|---|
| International | Regional, Suburb |
| State, Provincial | Marine Park |
| Disputed | Cliff/Ancient Wall |

### AREA FEATURES

| | |
|---|---|
| Area of Interest | Forest |
| Beach, Desert | Mall/Market |
| Building/Urban Area | Park |
| Cemetery, Christian | Restricted Area |
| Cemetery, Other | Sports |

### POPULATION

| | |
|---|---|
| **CAPITAL (NATIONAL)** | **CAPITAL (STATE)** |
| **LARGE CITY** | **Medium City** |
| **Small City** | Town, Village |

### SYMBOLS

**Sights/Activities**

- Buddhist
- Canoeing, Kayaking
- Castle, Fortress
- Christian
- Confucian
- Diving
- Hindu
- Islamic
- Jain
- Jewish
- Monument
- Museum, Gallery
- Point of Interest
- Pool
- Ruin
- Sento (Public Hot Baths)
- Shinto
- Sikh
- Skiing
- Surfing, Surf Beach
- Taoist
- Trail Head
- Winery, Vineyard
- Zoo, Bird Sanctuary

**Information**

- Bank, ATM
- Embassy/Consulate
- Hospital, Medical
- Information
- Internet Facilities
- Police Station
- Post Office, GPO
- Telephone
- Toilets
- Wheelchair Access

**Eating**

- Eating

**Drinking**

- Cafe
- Drinking

**Entertainment**

- Entertainment

**Shopping**

- Shopping

**Sleeping**

- Camping
- Sleeping

**Transport**

- Airport, Airfield
- Border Crossing
- Bus Station
- Bicycle Path/Cycling
- FFCC (Barcelona)
- Metro (Barcelona)
- Parking Area
- Petrol Station
- S-Bahn
- Taxi Rank
- Tube Station
- U-Bahn

**Geographic**

- Beach
- Lighthouse
- Lookout
- Mountain, Volcano
- National Park
- Pass, Canyon
- Picnic Area
- River Flow
- Shelter, Hut
- Waterfall

## LONELY PLANET OFFICES

### Australia
Head Office
Locked Bag 1, Footscray, Victoria 3011
☎ 03 8379 8000, fax 03 8379 8111

### USA
150 Linden St, Oakland, CA 94607
☎ 510 250 6400, toll free 800 275 8555,
fax 510 893 8572

### UK
2nd fl, 186 City Rd,
London EC1V 2NT
☎ 020 7106 2100, fax 020 7106 2101

### Contact
talk2us@lonelyplanet.com
lonelyplanet.com/contact

**Published by Lonely Planet Publications Pty Ltd**
ABN 36 005 607 983

Printed by Hang Tai Printing Company, Hong Kong
Printed in China

MIX
Paper from
responsible sources
FSC
www.fsc.org
FSC™ C021741